Adrian Bloom

Summer Garden Glory

ADRIAN BLOOM

SUMMER GARDEN GLORY

How to Make the Most of your Garden from
Spring through to Autumn

To Chris   July '96 Boston.
With many thanks and appreciation
for being a great "Chaperone" on my
travels in winter and summer in the U.S.
A Bloom.

HarperCollinsPublishers·

This book is dedicated to my brother Rob, who died tragically in a car accident in September 1995 and who will always be remembered.

ACKNOWLEDGEMENTS

No book of this nature is the author's alone. I would like to thank the team at HarperCollins and, in particular, Carole McGlynn who as editor showed patience and professionalism throughout, Ruth Prentice for sterling design work as in *Winter Garden Glory* and Richard Bonson for his true-to-life interpretation of my plant associations. I would also like to thank my father, Alan Bloom, for the original groundwork he did on the perennial and alpine plant directories for *Blooms of Bressingham Garden Plants*. Last, but far from least, thanks to my wife Rosemary who, despite the long hours and the weekends when I should have been gardening, supported my efforts in getting *Summer Garden Glory* to publication and who – with the steadfast Michel Boutet – continued to keep Foggy Bottom in top order for the many visitors to our garden.

First published in 1996 by
HarperCollins Publishers

© Text and photographs Adrian Bloom 1996

Adrian Bloom asserts the moral right to be identified as the author of this work.

A catalogue record for this book is available from the British Library

ISBN 0 00 412744 7

Editor: Carole McGlynn
Art Editor: Ruth Prentice
Photographs: Adrian Bloom
Colour illustrations: Richard Bonson
Index: Indexing Specialists

For HarperCollins:
Commissioning Editor: Polly Powell
Production: Bridget Scanlon

Colour origination by Colourscan, Singapore
Printed and bound in Italy by Lego SpA

Introduction 6

THE "BUSY" SEASONS 8

Some Thoughts on Gardening 10
Late Spring/Early Summer 14
Mid-Summer 26
Late Summer 44

SUMMER IN THE SMALLER GARDEN 58

Summer Colour in the Smaller Garden 60
Through the Seasons in the Acer Bed 64
Summer Colour in Containers 66
Mixed Planting for Year-round Colour 68
A Garden Without a Lawn 70
Planting Associations for Summer Colour 72

DIRECTORY OF PLANTS 78

Zones and Planting 88
Trees Directory 89
Shrubs Directory 92
Conifers 108
Perennials Directory 110
Ferns Directory 135
Grasses Directory 136
Alpines Directory 139

Index 142

AUTHOR'S INTRODUCTION

As a garden enthusiast, I often get asked which is my favourite season in the garden. The answer is invariably spring, summer, autumn and winter – which is telling the truth, but avoiding the question! Every season is to be enjoyed in the garden and every season should be planned for interest and pleasure. With the amazing range of plants now available to choose from, this can be achieved in even the smallest garden. And yet, despite the obvious appeal of the garden in high summer, it is perhaps easier to find reasons to consider winter a favourite season, since the garden and our activities are then much quieter, more reflective of simple pleasures, and the interest of the fewer flowering plants, foliage, stems, bark and twigs more treasured. Time seems more plentiful and one can appreciate the changing light and the frost on foliage transforming the appearance of plants and the whole garden scene.

Undoubtedly therefore it was easier to create a strong theme and a more direct message when writing my last book, *Winter Garden Glory*. Having spent the last twenty-five years creating a six-acre garden with year-round interest at Foggy Bottom, I had some reason to encourage other gardeners to give more thought to planning for winter interest. But summer garden glory? Doesn't everyone plant their garden for summer colour? What can I have to say that will be any different from hundreds of other books on the subject? This was certainly a question I asked myself when I sat down to write this book.

While the title is not intended to be totally misleading, *Summer Garden Glory* covers a broader spectrum than its title might imply. Indeed, it starts from where *Winter Garden Glory* finishes, so while the seasons of autumn, winter and early spring are covered by the first title, they are followed by late spring, early, mid- and late summer in the second. And since it is set in the same garden, Foggy Bottom at Bressingham in Norfolk, by using the two books together you can follow in words and photographs some of the changes and moods of the garden through a complete year.

Foggy Bottom is one of the few gardens whose main structure is provided by conifers, among which are interplanted hundreds of other plants, including trees, shrubs, perennials, ornamental grasses, bulbs, alpines and ferns. The conifers provide colour in both winter and summer and have a different effect on the plants around them. All too often, garden writers dismiss conifers and claim that if used anywhere they should be used on their own but I believe they can be assimilated and used to great effect with a wide variety of plants. The conifers themselves of course may change colour from summer to winter and the background colour they provide offers many

THE ACER BED in late spring. A 30-year old specimen Japanese maple, Acer shirasawanum aureum *creates leafy shade for a wide variety of bulbs and perennials. Golden-leaved hostas highlight (centre foreground)* Phlox divaricata *'Blue Dreams',* × Heucherella *'Bridget Bloom' and to the right* Dicentra *'Pearl Drops' (left)*

A VIEW FROM the patio at the rear of the house frames the distant acer bed. On the right, standing on the driveway, is a large ten-year-old container-grown Wisteria sinensis *in full flower at the end of spring (right)*

opportunities for striking plant associations. For instance, a witchhazel, such as *Hamamelis mollis* 'Pallida' will hardly be noticeable against the shaded side of a dark blue conifer in summer, but when the leaves have dropped in winter and the golden, strap-like flowers emerge, the contrast is dramatic. Some stunning combinations can be created by planting a bright blue agapanthus against the background of a golden-leaved conifer, or the shimmering scarlet of *Crocosmia* 'Lucifer' against a steel-blue juniper, at its brightest in mid- to late summer.

As in *Winter Garden Glory,* I have tried in the photographs to capture the feel of the garden, as well as the beauty of its plants, though these have surprisingly been more difficult to portray in the better light available in the "busy seasons".

THE "BUSY" SEASONS

Some Thoughts on Gardening

In *Winter Garden Glory*, my previous book on the seasons at Foggy Bottom, I described autumn, winter and early spring as the "quiet" seasons, compared to the time of the year from late spring to late summer which, by contrast, comprise the "busy" or "noisy" seasons in the garden. As gardeners we all know there is some truth in this for, with the warmth of the later spring sunshine and the mowing of the first new grass, we know we are in for a roller-coaster ride of activity, which will be unlikely to finish until early autumn. Gardening is enjoyment and we should not complain once the warmer weather arrives at last and our garden plants burst into frenetic activity to create the display we have planned for. Now, in the busy seasons, we can expect to plant and to prune, to weed and to trim, to water and feed – and to mow the grass. We appear to be driven by events happening too fast to catch up with, and it seems as though the garden is in control, rather than its owner – a feeling most gardeners are familiar with.

The quiet seasons, on the other hand, with little or no growth taking place, give us the chance to catch up and prepare for the following year, to see in what ways we may be able to plan new features and prepare the ground for planting, perhaps move other plants around to create better associations, or just to give prized specimens more room. Autumn is the time when I usually go round making notes of all the projects that we would like to get done, knowing full well that at best only half will be achieved. A garden is of course a series of living organisms brought together to create an artistic effect, and there is every reason, without pretension, why one should consider creating a garden or a plant association an art

form. Yet what you create in year one will, as plants grow, have changed in years two, three and four and, without constant adjustment, may well not be what was planned for by year ten.

The time scale

Planning a garden can be done on paper, with the correct spacings and positionings carefully worked out, and of course that is the guidance you would expect from a professional garden designer. But at what stage in its life cycle is it planned for perfection? Five years after planting, or ten? Some plants do not change form and size as dramatically as others. My

LATE SUMMER IN a corner of Foggy Bottom: the yellow black-eyed Susan, Rudbeckia *'Goldsturm', is backed by the waving wands of* Stipa gigantea *and the almost luminous lilac flowers of* Phlox *'Franz Schubert' (above)*

father Alan Bloom, who created his famous perennial island beds in the six-acre Dell Garden at Bressingham, can still see today much the same perennial plants and associations as when he planted them nearly forty years ago. Perennials, though in need of replanting and rejuvenating at regular intervals, will mostly reach their ultimate height, with little variation, within two years' growth.

A BRIEF HISTORY OF FOGGY BOTTOM

Rosemary Bloom canoeing across a flooded garden in late summer 1987, when an acre of the garden was under water for ten days.

My wife Rosemary and I gave the name Foggy Bottom to our garden when our ranch-style house was built in 1966. The name had caught my imagination when I came across it while working in the United States and it seemed appropriate to the low-lying treeless meadow below our house, often wreathed in mist and fog, which was eventually to comprise the six acres of our garden. Initially the garden reflected my considerable interest in conifers and heathers and soon the area round the house became carpeted with year-round colour in foliage and flower. By 1973 this quarter-acre or so was full and I started to extend into larger beds and plantings with a backbone structure of conifers, trees and shrubs. I still adhered to the theme of year-round colour, though the range of plants expanded to include more perennials and ornamental grasses. It is not often that one gets an opportunity to see a garden develop and to learn about the changing role of plants and the microclimates they produce over thirty or more years, but Foggy Bottom has created – and continues to create – that opportunity and challenge.

Foggy Bottom has of course changed dramatically over nearly thirty years, and were it not that I have photographs to prove it, it would now seem unbelievable that it was originally just a flat meadow. It has in fact developed, I believe, as a modern garden, one that does not follow any particular fashion, but which uses plants in their own right, not only as ingredients to create an effect. I have been lucky enough over many years to collect plants from all over the world on behalf of our company Blooms of Bressingham, and to test them out in my garden – and gardening on acid to neutral soil has given the opportunity to use a very wide range of plants indeed I have probably used as many as five thousand different species and varieties. Of course, over so many years, I have made mistakes and lost plants, particularly through frost and floods. Having started planting on an open meadow with all plants initially in full sun, there is now shade and shelter and particular microclimates, so many plants and groupings have changed, new plants are now being enjoyed while others have been discarded as being either in the wrong place or of little garden value. Though I spend all the time I can in the garden, with business and other commitments it has been difficult to find the time the garden needs to continue the development, and were it not for Michel Boutet, grandly called Head Gardener, and my wife Rosemary, the garden would soon revert to a forest of conifers and weeds! But success does not come easily or automatically in gardening. The creation of dramatic or pleasing plant associations, vistas and views remains my main driving force, coupled with an intrinsic interest in the plants that go to make them up.

Gardening is exciting and never more so than when trying out some new plant or a new planting, watching them develop and at times tinkering about, adding or taking away ingredients. This book will show, in photographs and words, the rapidly changing seasons from late spring through to late summer at Foggy Bottom, and suggest plants and ideas for giving a changing display in any garden or on any patio. It will show how year-round colour can be achieved in even the most modest plot. There are plant association ideas, and a list of recommended plants. While it cannot be comprehensive, my selection of good-value plants, will, I hope, be applicable to a wide range of conditions and climates, some to suit every gardener.

Trees, shrubs and conifers are somewhat different. When I started planting the slightly sloping meadow in what was to become Foggy Bottom, I put in few plants that were higher than 1.5-1.8m/5-6ft. Nearly thirty years later, some have reached over 18m/60ft, while others have made a considerable spread. With six acres that may not seem much of a problem, but plants and specimens will spoil as they become overgrown or overcrowded in a large garden as well as a smaller one. In some ways, I see the development of Foggy Bottom as a microcosm of the experience many gardeners have, either with their brand new garden on an open site, or dealing with an existing garden with reasonably well established trees.

Garden styles

Each type of garden is a challenge and can be an adventure, with size a determining factor in the plants you might select, but not necessarily a restriction when it comes to what imagination and application might achieve. But we often approach our gardening from different perspectives. Starting with an open meadow around a new house would suggest to me an informal, natural garden because I like vistas and distant views, but someone else may wish to create "rooms" surrounded by hedges. When the well-known gardener and writer Christopher Lloyd visited Foggy Bottom for the first time, when the garden was about twenty years old, having previously been rather damning about conifers and heathers as garden plants, he walked round the garden with me, eventually saying politely, "I can see we have quite different approaches to garden styles." As I wondered what was coming next, he graciously added, "There is room for both."

A LATE SUMMER'S EVENING shows conifers and heathers in the foreground, with flowers still left on Buddleja davidii *'Pink Delight' (above)*

CONIFERS, SHRUBS, PERENNIALS and ferns create an early summer picture. The white-flowered shrub is Viburnum plicatum *'Cascade';* Geranium sylvaticum *'Mayflower' and* Pulmonaria longifolia *the other flowers (left)*

Although I knew of his own garden at Great Dixter, my first visit was not made until the following summer and I could see immediately what he meant. There was not a heather in sight and although he had conifers, they were old yew hedges. The ancient house at Great Dixter already had an established garden and any development called for something in keeping with the traditions of the place; this is what Christopher was carrying on, while at the same time making his own individual mark on the garden. Even if you are bound by certain restrictions, established trees, walls or hedges, it is still possible to make your own unique contribution to the style of a garden.

And what of garden fashions? Well, there are some people who are led by what others create or suggest, but while it is fun to obtain the latest plants to be introduced, it is quite something else to create a whole garden as a fashion. Cottage gardens, formal gardens, single-colour-theme gardens or borders, conifer and heather gardens, even mediterranean gardens – all have their merits, but once planted they are not so easy to change. More modern gardens make much of hard landscaping and tend to be designed without really considering the plants, beyond their use in creating the correct form and colour. I would perhaps go to the other extreme and suggest that such is the diversity of plants that you can create almost any effect you want with them alone. This does not necessarily rule out structures such as walls, fences or pergolas, which are used to support and display plants, but plants can offer so much potential pleasure throughout the year that it seems a pity not to use every possible area of the garden to achieve this.

LATE SPRING/EARLY SUMMER

Spring is always an exciting time in the garden, from the early spring when flowers such as snowdrops and aconites create natural dashes of colour, to the later, more bold-looking daffodils and tulips. But bulbs are not the only flowers of early spring – shrubs, perennials and trees all have their role to play.

Towards the end of April would be called late spring in most of the British Isles because spring is so drawn out, snowdrops having appeared as early as January. We can go through the whole of the month of January in fact without a frost, and then receive some stinging spring frosts in May when plants, now in full soft growth, are least prepared for them. In parts of Canada and the northern, eastern and central United States, winter never seems to end. And when it does, it often changes to summer within a few weeks, so that the spring season can be even more frantic, and there is seldom time for this lovely period to be enjoyed to the full. Having spent two springs in Maryland, I can vouch for the fluctuations that can be experienced there, with temperatures of 75°F/24°C following on from frosty weather, then plunging back to snow or frost again, but late spring frosts are less of a danger. If spring frosts seem like a recurrent theme in my narrative, I suppose it is because, having waited all year for a favourite plant to flower or come into leaf in Foggy Bottom, one night's frost can spoil it all.

A VIEW BETWEEN two upright conifers just coming into new growth highlights bright contrasts between flower and foliage. In the centre one of the most striking hostas, H. fluctuans 'Variegated' is flanked by the scarlet flowers of Rhododendron 'Morgenrote' in the foreground and Acer palmatum 'Garnet' behind.

VALUABLE SPRING PERENNIALS

Some spring plants seem more or less impervious to frost while in flower. Take those two excellent herbaceous perennials, epimediums and pulmonarias. Some of the latter, commonly known as lungworts, start into flower in late winter and continue to flower until the late spring. They are low growing and very accommodating as to soil and situation, flourishing either in full sun or shade where it is not too dry – and when the flowers are finished, many selections have attractively silvered or spotted leaves. They are excellent subjects to plant among shrubs or roses, providing early flowers then attractive ground cover foliage. Like certain groups of plants, they have become better appreciated in recent years, particularly since some excellent new selections have been introduced. Fifteen years ago you would have been lucky to find more than twenty varieties of lungworts being offered, even by a specialist. Now it is more like seventy, so the advice is as always to select the best, ideally those which offer both distinctive flowers in the spring and attractive foliage all summer. Once the flowers are finished, the new leaves start to grow, so it is best to cut off the old flowerheads, unless you want to allow seed to drop, which may produce some interesting progeny.

Epimediums are also becoming more widely appreciated. New introductions from China seem certain to lead to some important new developments in these generally tough perennials which not only have striking flowers, particularly in close up, but stunning leaves, in terms of their delicate patterns and markings, thereafter performing an admirable ground covering role in sun or shade where it is not too dry.

SOME PLANTS FOR FOLIAGE EFFECT

Epimedium × perralchicum *'Frohnleiten' in mid-spring*

Hosta *'Francee' in late spring*

As gardeners we are fortunate to have such a wide range of plant material at our disposal, allowing us to create almost any effect we want. Plants of course need to be selected to suit the soil type, aspect, hardiness and general climatic conditions where we garden and we should bear in mind that foliage, as well as flowers, has an important role to play in our gardening schemes – and our enjoyment of the garden.

Rodgersia podophylla *in late spring*

Whether the foliage is evergreen or deciduous, attractive leaves can be a feature of any plant, from bulbs, alpines, perennials and ferns to shrubs, conifers and trees. Indeed, whole gardens or plant associations can be made from plants with interesting or handsome leaves and many plants, such as some hostas and pulmonarias, have attractive foliage as well as flowers. The foliage of a plant can be used to contrast with that of other plants or to accentuate the flowers, or it can become a focal point in its own right, particularly on those plants with purple, gold, silver or variegated leaves; it can be equally effective seen in close-up or from a distance.

CORYDALIS FLEXUOSA 'China Blue' is a choice but generally easy spring-flowering perennial (above)

DICENTRA SPECTABILIS 'Alba', a white "bleeding heart", looks cool against the ostrich fern, Matteucia struthiopteris (above right)

POLEMONIUM CAERULEUM 'Brise D'Anjou', a Jacob's ladder with brightly variegated leaves, extends the interest well beyond its early summer flowering period. Behind is Phlox divaricata 'Blue Dreams' (right)

Using a camera as much as I do makes one appreciate the close-up detail of both foliage and flower, and in both respects the epimediums can be quite exquisite, though flowers are often hidden.

Generally known as bleeding hearts, the dicentras are indispensible spring perennials. *Dicentra spectabilis* from Japan (also known as lady-in-the bath) has soft, delicate foliage which, however, can be singed by a spring frost, though it is otherwise totally hardy. The species has dangling lockets of pink and white, and there is a pure white form too. Of equal or even better garden value are the North American species and selected cultivars, *D. formosa* from the west coast and *D. eximea* from the east. These make spreading clumps of finely cut foliage above which emerge a succession of pretty, pendulous flowers which continue for weeks, on younger plants, for months. Thriving in most soils which are not too dry, they may require dividing every few years. Three of my favourites forms are *D.* 'Luxuriant', with rich green foliage and bright crimson flowers, *D.* 'Pearl Drops', a selection my father made many years ago, whose glaucous foliage makes an attractive carpet set off by white flowers, and the lighter-green leaved and free flowering *D.* 'Snowflakes'. My father also named a red-flowered variety which he called 'Adrian Bloom' – and I see mentioned in one nursery list a *D.* 'Adrian Bloom Variegated', which sounds sickly to me!

Early spring offers a medley of choice bulbs and perennials. Usually choice looking plants are exactly what they seem, and remain choice and rare because they are difficult or slow to propagate. It was thought when it was first introduced from Western Sichuan in China that *Corydalis flexuosa* would for this reason take years to become available to the average gardener. But here was a plant for light shade whose bright electric blue flowers would make keen gardeners crawl over hot coals to get one, which in peaty soils seemed to romp away, making mats of foliage which by autumn could easily be divided and propagated. To date, four clones or selections have been introduced and are now easily found, which have given pleasure to a great many gardeners.

Not all choice plants are difficult to grow, by any means. Take the trilliums or blood lilies, for instance. Most are native to North America, although there are Asian species too. They are bulbous plants whose leaves unfurl in spring, followed by intriguing and striking flowers. They, like the related erythroniums, ideally need cool shade and a humus-rich soil, but they will survive with less than the ideal. With care, these conditions can usually be found or provided for in most gardens. Perhaps not the most natural, but one of the most sought-after forms is the large-flowered, spectacular *Trillium grandiflorum* 'Flore Pleno', a plant with perfect, fully double pure white flowers, which usually times its flowering for mid-spring and holds on for a prized position in our Chelsea Flower Show exhibit.

The Chelsea Flower Show at the end of May each year is where many new plants are launched – and at Bressingham we have always tried to find something new which would appeal at that time of year. One recent introduction seemed to fit the criteria for the perfect plant *and* be out just at the right time for Chelsea, but time will eventually tell how adaptable it is. This is a Jacob's

THOUGH THE FLOWERS ARE SMALL, the North American native Trillium erectum, *makes a striking woodland or shade-loving plant* (right)

LATE SPRING at Foggy Bottom shows the morning sun shining on new leaves of maple and birch, a rhododendron and, to the right, Prunus *'Amanogowa' in full bloom* (above)

THE DWARF BROOM Cytisus ardoinii *makes a perfect contrast to the fresh green shoots on* Picea glauca *'Laurin' on the right of the picture* (left)

ladder with variegated leaves, named *Polemonium caeruleum* 'Brise D'Anjou' – French because it originated in France and the translation 'Breeze of Anjou' sounds as refreshing as the plant itself. Best in half shade where it is not too dry, this plant creates excellent foliage to which the spikes of blue flowers seem almost an almost unnecessary accessory. It looks good in a container too.

SPRING-FLOWERING SHRUBS

With a garden of six acres there can always be surprises (including sometimes a patch of weeds that has been overlooked!) and certain plants which one has hardly noticed for a whole year since they were last in flower, suddenly shout for attention as they burst into full bloom. Such plants include the brooms – the cytisus and genistas – for instance, both easily grown on a wide range of well drained soils, including alkaline. Their narrow evergreen stems carry flower buds which in spring erupt into colour, mostly yellows but also red, pink and white and some in between. In hot weather they are gone within two or three weeks, but in late spring they are well worth their space in the garden. After flowering, cut back cytisus to half their length with a sharp knife rather than with secateurs. These are plants which are usually bought in flower from garden centres when they have little flowering period left, whereas it is much better to plant them in early spring, buying them with the promise of the colour offered in the description or photograph on the label. Again, position them in the garden where they will brighten up a dull spot during this part of the year.

There is little doubt that we are in the era of the impulse purchase – perhaps we always have been if the item is

IN MID-SPRING the scarlet new shoots of Pieris japonica *'Flaming Silver' erupt into growth* (top), *gradually toning down to pink, cream and white* (above) *before finally becoming variegated, like the rest of the foliage.*

tempting enough – but it is certainly true of plants now that buying from garden centres is rather like shopping at the supermarket. Such plants as the acid-loving pieris, a group of shrubs from Asia, many of which have bright crimson new shoots in late spring, can so tempt the customer that he or she must have it, no matter that the label may say "unsuitable for alkaline soils". It used to be the green-leaved *Pieris* 'Forest Flame' which drew the gardener's eye as fresh scarlet shoots emerged in spring; now, more selections are available and if you have acid soil or a container to put in ericaceous compost, *Pieris* 'Flaming Silver' offers year-round interest, with white-margined leaves and bright red shoots which fade to pink.

Plants with such pulling power are of course favourites with the public, the garden centre and the grower alike. As with any new product, nurserymen these days scour the world looking for new plants which the consumer will want to purchase. This is a necessary business and good economics too, and it makes the world of gardening and horticulture an exciting one to be in, but for the keen gardener it is only the icing on the cake. Some of these plants have not been tried and tested sufficiently and may not enter the hall of fame until after ten years or so of trial by the discerning gardener. But, although the commercial promotion of new plants may be looked upon askance by certain plantspeople, in reality the public is generally getting good new garden plants. If the nurseryman is reacting to public demand, he will be looking for a plant which is ideally compact in habit, free flowering, fragrant, which has a long period of interest and is easy to grow on most soils! Now, isn't that just what most gardeners want?

RHODODENDRONS AND AZALEAS

Gardening on acid soil has led me into the temptation of growing quite a selection of hardy rhododendrons and azaleas, subjects vulnerable to spring frost damage but, when untouched, as bright and spectacular as you could wish. They can be difficult to position among other plants, but I have placed some singly and others in groups where, as they come into flower, they make a relatively brief but bright contribution to spring but where, surrounding them or nearby, are other plants to continue the interest. Combinations using the strongly coloured rhododendrons may not be remembered for their subtle colour tonings, but they certainly create an impact that can make you draw breath. One such is a hardy hybrid, *Rhododendron* 'Amethyst' which in late spring vies for attention beside the striking golden-needled dwarf fir *Abies nordmanniana* 'Golden Spreader'. I believe the person who called this conifer by such a descriptive name was rather premature in doing so, for although it is initially flat and spreading in growth, within ten years or less its desire to become a tree overcomes it and its growth becomes increasingly upward.

The foliage on many rhododendrons is attractive, particularly the new growth, but I think that the deciduous azaleas fit in better with most other garden plants, and among my favourites are the late spring- and early summer-flowering Knaphill hybrids. Attractive in bud, they burst into wonderful brash colours, but subtle pastel shades are among them, and the flowers are seldom caught by late frosts. If you garden on acid soil they are a challenge, not so much to grow but to find plants with which to associate them. *Geranium*

VIBURNUM PLICATUM 'MARIESII' has flowers on branches resembling the icing on a wedding cake (top left)

THE FOGGY BOTTOM cat surveys the scree bed on an early summer morning (top right)

AVOIDING A SPRING FROST on the west side of tall conifers, Rhododendron *'Amethyst' and* Abies nordmanniana *'Golden Spreader' form a strong focal point in the spring garden* (above)

THE PINK TINGES ON the flowers of Rhododendron 'Loders White' is quite typical of this old variety, so far enjoying a frost-free spring (left)

sylvaticum 'Mayflower', a deep blue flowered woodland geranium, is a good choice since its flowering is timed to make a striking contrast to bright orange or yellow. In Foggy Bottom the rhododendrons and azaleas follow on nicely as the winter-flowering heathers finally run out of flower in mid-spring – though the erigena varieties carry on into late spring – and before other flowering shrubs and perennials start coming out in numbers.

ALPINES

Late spring and early summer is the peak flowering time for alpines. The term "alpine" is really a misnomer, as is the American term "rock plants", for almost the same subject. True alpine plants come from high alpine regions and true rock plants, one assumes, from rocky alpine sites. In Britain the term alpine covers dwarf perennials such as armerias, many campanulas, plants like erysimums or perennial wallflowers, ajugas and dwarf astilbes besides many others. The term also covers some dwarf shrubs like helianthemums (the rock roses) and shrubby thymes.

For many years at Foggy Bottom there was no situation or feature that could accommodate alpine plants in the garden, the soil in the top part of the garden being too wet and heavy and the lower part subject to flooding. Such a feature would also have been somewhat incongruous among larger conifers, shrubs and perennials.

Eventually, in 1989, we created an alpine or scree bed in front of the house, which had previously contained conifers and heathers. Additional drainage was put in and gravel mixed with the soil. I then planted a few dwarf shrubs and conifers for a mature effect, interplanted them with alpines, and covered it all

with sharp grit. This scree garden has been a joy, yet also frustrating and much work. We put in too little grit initially and the clay soil and grit made a pretty stiff mix, though every new alpine now goes in with handfuls of grit and a good gravel mulch. Many will know from experience what I mean when I say that some plants – and weeds – have tried to take over, and it is a constant battle to keep everything in balance. When you purchase plants from a specialist nursery or garden centre you need to be absolutely sure it has no perennial or annual weed in it; some of the oxalis are particularly rampant. Undoubtedly, as Rosemary and I know to our cost, this area requires the most intensive attention of any part of the garden.

But, despite the hard work, this garden in miniature has great rewards, with the bulbs, alpines, shrubs and conifers

SYMPHYTUM GRANDIFLORUM 'Hidcote Blue',
although, like some other comfreys, it can be
invasive, makes ideal ground cover beneath
a cherry tree (above)

THE SCREE GARDEN – seen in early summer
with dwarf shrubs, alpines and bulbs in flower,
and the sun flooding its light over the distant
trees (above left)

AN OLD SPECIMEN OF Abies koreana 'Aurea',
the golden-leaved Korean fir, makes a
magnificent display of cones held above the
branches (below left)

providing some startling displays in spring and summer particularly. Once again, the challenge should be to make such a garden furnish more year-round interest, but this involves careful selection of the plants to make it work – while making sure you are the one in control!

At the peak of the alpine season we know for sure that we are into the busy season and the "mid-summer surge" is upon us. The warmer nights and longer days create a burst of activity and growth – in ornamental plants, lawns as well as weeds. There is so much happening in the garden now: all the trees and shrubs still have fresh growth, giving pure colour contrasts, the conifers are breaking their winter buds into bright new foliage, and perennials such as hostas are making the greatest impact with their fresh leaves, a wonderful foil

for others flowers. And how can anyone say that conifers are dull, as new shoots and needles are produced, giving a contrast between new and old, and candles of new growth appear on the pines? Everything is changing so rapidly, you can almost hear the plants growing, but while you do not want to miss anything that happens, you are also very busy catching up on late planting, keeping up with the weeds and cutting the grass, a task now necessary twice a week.

MAKING THE BEST CHOICE

Nowadays, with the advent of smaller specialist nurseries and national collections, the choice of plants is impossible to keep up with. Twenty years or so ago, a garden collection of thirty hardy geraniums would have been impressive. Now that these plants are in high fashion, new varieties and hybrids are being introduced at an alarming rate. In 1989 *The Plant Finder*, that indispensable gardeners' guide to what is in cultivation, listed 189 species and cultivars of geranium. Five years later there were 350. As a nurseryman, you can only hope to keep up by being a specialist.

For the gardener, what is important of course is to consider garden worthiness, colour, leaf, habit, rate of growth and length of flowering. The latter is particularly important and there are varieties like *G. riversleanum* 'Russell Prichard' and 'Mavis Simpson' which flower from early summer until the frosts, as does the popular spreading and climbing hybrid between *G. procurrens* and *G. psilostemon* called 'Ann Folkard'. This has golden-tinged leaves and purple-magenta flowers, which is quite a combination, but for summer-long colour it also takes some beating.

There are geraniums for sun and shade, for moist soils as well as dry. The ground-covering *G. macrorrhizum* and its cultivars and hybrids are indispensible plants for sun or quite deep shade and although some people dislike its pungent fragrance, to me that is the essence of summer itself, its aroma quite pervasive as you walk by on a summer's evening. Geraniums come in some good blues as well as the more obvious pinks and reds, none more popular than 'Johnson's Blue' of which thousands are sold each year. It is perhaps a truer blue than that of *G. himalayense* but no better plant. Could it just be the name – though few gardeners will relate it back to the original Mr. A.T. Johnson after whom is was named around 1950.

I have extended the range of perennials used in Foggy Bottom in recent years partly because I have always had a liking for plants I grew up with, but also because perennials are so truly adaptable to the modern garden and to mixed planting. The structure established at Foggy Bottom with trees, conifers and shrubs and my experimentation with heathers, has somewhat run its course, and though I will always find room for some, the garden needed the colour, the foliage and the changing interest that perennials can give. The more you get involved with plants and gardening, the more you want to experiment and to change. I believe that, all things being equal and space available, most gardeners would probably prefer to have a selection of woody plants, bulbs and perennials rather than be restricted to a single group. The challenge to me is to continue to change and adapt, to create pleasing plant associations, knowing that what is planted today will need readjusting to some extent within a year or two.

I am lucky enough, too, to travel and find new plants from all over the world,

GERANIUM HIMALAYENSE is a reliable blue-flowered hardy geranium for sun or shade (above)

A DECIDUOUS KNAPHILL azalea times its bloom perfectly to contrast with Geranium sylvaticum 'Mayflower' (left)

DODECATHEON PULCHELLUM 'Red Wings' lives up to its name "shooting star", an eye-catcher in a moist spot in semi-shade (left)

EQUALLY EYE-CATCHING AND also a shade lover is the aptly named Omphalodes cappadocica *'Starry Eyes'* (below left)

as well as keeping an eye open for what is new in the U.K. New plants have to be tested and what better place (so my argument goes) than at Foggy Bottom? . But it can sometimes be difficult to reconcile being a collector with attempting to create dramatic effects. To make large drifts of colour, be it heathers, ornamental grasses or perennials, means using fewer varieties, therefore there is less space for "testing". I know this will be a recurring problem, but it is not one I am too anxious about, except that the number of plants I collect which stand waiting in pots or containers "in the wings", waiting to be planted, never seems to diminish.

I believe I have inherited my father's suspicion and certainly initial dislike of roses. In the days of hybrid teas and floribundas, roses of course did not seem to fit in too well with conifers and heathers. In recent years, however, there has been a resurgence of interest in species and hybrid shrub roses as well as ground cover types. Rose breeders have done a marvellous job in creating whole new ranges of plants that are repeat-blooming and relatively trouble-free. Roses are now generally accepted, as they should be, as flowering shrubs which can fit into mixed plantings, rather than necessarily being a feature on their own. And I have certainly come round to the idea that ground cover roses like 'Surrey' and 'Kent', to name but two varieties, do in fact fit in very well with conifer and heather plantings.

But roses and perennials make pretty good bedfellows too. Most roses look dreadful in winter and spring, but underplanting them with various perennials, such as the pulmonarias, gives early spring flowers and summer foliage at the base of the rose, turning a loss into a gain with "companion planting".

MID-SUMMER

The period from late spring to mid-summer is undoubtedly that of the greatest change in the garden, and for most gardeners the most active and exciting time. This is the period of peak activity for garden centres and nurseries which, over the years, have encouraged gardeners to continue planting well into summer by growing and offering nearly all plants as container-grown. But though it is perfectly safe to plant right through the summer – and many shrubs or perennials will give an immediate flowering performance – great care should be taken to ensure their establishment in hot or dry conditions. Soak the plants well before planting, prepare the ground thoroughly and then water in and mulch with well-rotted compost, composted bark, or other inert or weed-free material after planting.

I continue to plant at Foggy Bottom throughout the summer, but in a six-acre garden it is difficult always to remember exactly which plants need specific spot watering, so I generally concentrate on only one or two areas so that these get more attention than longer established plants. Sometimes these summer plantings, particularly if I have only a single specimen, are only temporarily domiciled and will, as they grow, provide more young plants which can be replanted the following spring.

THIS IS ALMOST THE MOST EXCITING point of the year in the garden at Foggy Bottom– the June surge of plant growth brings fresh, clean colours and vitality. A background of shrubs, including the white Viburnum plicatum *'Cascade', shows off the varying textures of hostas, ferns and grasses. The flowering perennial is* Geranium sylvaticum *'Mayflower'.*

FLOWERING SHRUBS

During the late spring and early summer there have been some marvellous displays of flowering shrubs in the garden. Apart from those mentioned individually below, the acid-loving pieris and rhododendrons, magnolias, berberis, camellias, cherries and crab apples as well as lesser-known plants like exochorda and kalmia, add superb early splendour. By mid-summer, the range becomes more limited, but nonetheless there are a great many excellent flowering or foliage shrubs which should be better known and more widely used. Over the years I have been an avid collector of shrubs both large and small, at times being unable to resist trying out some that were probably quite unsuitable for our soil and the frost pocket of our garden.

If you look at almost any garden planted thirty or more years ago, whether in town or country, you will often see very mature shrubs and, depending upon location, in a fairly limited range. Shrubs were looked upon as the mainstay of the garden and as spring turned to summer the progression of flowering would generally be forsythia, *Ribes sanguineum*, the flowering currants, viburnums perhaps and lilac, then in early to mid-summer, weigela, deutzia and philadelphus. On acid soils, rhododendrons would fill in the gaps. But many of these more traditional summer-flowering shrubs have such a short period of flower that any modern gardener, particularly with a smaller plot, would be right in questioning whether they deserve garden space.

There are of course smaller-growing selections and shrubs with coloured or variegated foliage which have a longer appeal. But there is also a range of other good flowering or foliage shrubs now available at most garden centres, which were simply not available thirty years ago. The public has in a way demanded innovation by flocking to buy the more dwarf shrubs with a long period of interest into which category I would put berberis, *Potentilla fruticosa*, hebes, perovskias and spiraeas, as well as the grey- and silver-leaved shrubs such as santolina, lavender and senecio. Among these groups – as with shrubs such as the escallonias and fuchsias, not forgetting roses – there are some to give a continual succession of flower, but it is at this time of year that foliage is increasingly important, and it becomes more so as the summer draws on. Selecting shrubs for several seasons of interest is good sense, particularly if you garden in a small space.

Garden worthiness is a subject one can come back to time and again, and I believe each plant has to earn its place in the garden, for there are so many good plants to choose from. When you get to mid-summer, it is time to start evaluating your garden's performance. If we could choose our weather in summer, most would go for warm, perhaps hot days and cool nights, with occasional evening rains, which would help to keep our plants looking happy – but of course it seldom works out that way. In Britain and in northern Europe we can expect no real extremes, but sometimes we will have a wet summer, sometimes a dry one and this will vary considerably from east to west and north to south. In North America and in southern Europe, hot summers are the rule, as are droughts, and this will dictate what plants can be grown successfully. The fact that the term "shade tree" hardly exists in Britain says much about our climate.

When choosing plants which will become permanent for many years in

LAVANDULA 'BLUE CUSHION' is aptly named for its rounded dwarf habit and flowers as close to blue as any lavender. Like all lavenders, it is both fragrant and a friend to bees (above)

DEUTZIA × HYBRIDA 'PINK POMPON' seemed aptly descriptive of this showy summer-flowering shrub, but after many years under this name it now seems it must be called Deutzia × hybrida *'Rosea Plena'* (right)

your garden – the trees, shrubs and the larger growing conifers – look for potential garden worthiness in terms of your climate and your soil. It is easy to be tempted by pictures in books or even plants at a garden centre by something which is not suitable and will therefore never thrive.

LARGER SHRUBS AND TREES

Trees, shrubs and conifers provide the structure in any garden and are essential on the flat piece of ground now called Foggy Bottom. But, like many people, I

IT IS OFTEN SAID that conifers look the same all year round but in fact some of them can change as dramatically as any flowering shrub when new growth begins in early summer. In the right foreground is a 30-year-old specimen of Thuja orientalis *'Aurea Nana', and in the centre the beautiful blue of* Picea pungens *'Globosa', which both show up against the purple-leaved* Acer palmatum *'Garnet' and* Acer shirasawanum *'Aureum' (above)*

did not always make the best choice when selecting the initial range of trees, nor did I always plant them in the most suitable position. But trees chosen for flower, foliage, fruit or autumn colour can have considerable impact at their particular moment – the Japanese cherries in spring, silver-leaved willows, purple or variegated foliaged maples, golden poplars in summer, sorbus, cotoneaster and thorn trees (*Crataegus* species) in autumn, along with colour from the maples, sweetgums, silver birch and many others.

THIS FIVE-YEAR-OLD Acer negundo 'Flamingo' sits quite happily in a container, given food, water and some annual pruning. Campanula *'Stella' contrasts with the colourful leaves* (top)

A MIXED PLANTING of mostly low-growing shrubs and conifers accentuate the taller blue spruce, Picea pungens *'Globosa' in the background* (above)

Trees do need space, but there are trees which can be pruned as shrubs or grown in containers. *Acer negundo* and its coloured foliage forms is one of those and, whether grown in a container on the patio or as a plant in the open garden, it makes a superb small tree with summer-long colour provided it is pruned back in the early spring, then the new soft growth pinched out during the summer. The best selection is the aptly named *Acer negundo* 'Flamingo' with pink, green and cream shoots, but *A. n.* 'Elegans' is another quite bright cultivar with golden variegated leaves. The Japanese maples make excellent container subjects too.

Conifers provide the real backbone to the structure in Foggy Bottom which becomes truly noticeable only in winter, when all the leaves have fallen from deciduous shrubs and trees. But during the summer the intensity of the East Anglian light creates dazzling reflections from the bright silver-blue of the blue spruce *Picea pungens*, and the golden foliage of many of the lawsons, the *Chamaecyparis lawsoniana* varieties. Among these I have placed either deciduous trees or other conifers of contrasting colours, the pines being a real favourite of mine. When we have to move or remove some of the larger conifers it is amazing how dry the soil is beneath them, and following dry summers some larger lawsons visibly suffer. Originating the northwest of North America, where rainfall is at least twice the British average, this is perhaps not surprising.

In assessing a maturing garden, deciding what to remove is as important a decision as choosing what to plant. And removing a large conifer or tree is no easy task and may, for the average gardener, call for expert help from either

Clematis *'Dr Ruppel'*

Tropaeolum speciosum

THE VERSATILE CLIMBERS

Climbing and scrambling plants have become increasingly popular in recent years as gardeners come to realize that they have a wider use than covering walls and pergolas. One can add to the background tapestry of conifers, trees and taller shrubs, each with its own moment of glory, by planting climbers or scramblers such as honeysuckles, roses, clematis or vines. Sometimes planting too close to the base of a conifer or tree will prevent climbers from getting established, so always plant as much as 1m/3ft or more away and train it in the right direction. Though it may take time to establish, Tropaeolum speciosum, *with its bright scarlet flowers, makes a spectacular summer show scrambling among and over spent rhododendrons and conifers.*

For clothing boundary walls, not only can such freestanding shrubs as pyracantha, chaenomeles and Carpenteria californica *be used, but also a wide range of natural climbers, like vines, ivy and* Euonymus fortunei. *There are some herbaceous climbers which die back to the ground in winter, for example the climbing dicentras and tropaeolums as well as one or two geraniums. Here are some suggestions worth considering:*

Clematis The clematis family cover such a wide range of colour as well as flowering periods that they are indispensable. Whether scrambling over heathers, up conifers or trees, they can add colour and contrast at times of the year when it is most needed, from the early-flowering species – *C. alpina, C. macropetala* and *C. montana* – then the larger-flowered hybrids which can also be used as ground cover over low-growing shrubs or heathers, to, later in the season, *C. viticella, C. orientalis* and *C. tangutica.* I have a quite spectacular show from *C. orientalis* 'Bill Mackenzie' which I planted beneath a purple-leaved silver birch, *Betula pendula* 'Purple Splendour'.

Campsis The trumpet vines, which need a warm climate to perform.

Dicentra scandens and **D. macrocapnos** With glaucous green leaves and yellow lockets in summer, these perennials can make nearly 3m (10ft) of growth in a single year.

Euonymus fortunei The variegated forms more usually grown as shrubs make good climbers on walls, through other shrubs or up tree trunks.

Fremontodendron Though not a true climber and not very hardy, this is an excellent wall shrub which, with sun and good drainage, has a long flowering season.

Geranium procurrens and **G. 'Ann Folkard'** Ideal for use in front of spring-flowering shrubs, these geraniums will climb into them, flowering later in the summer.

Hedera Ivy is as useful on walls as it is as ground cover; there is a wide choice of small-leaved *H. helix helix* varieties and the large-leaved *H. colchica* is also attractive, doing well in shade.

Hydrangea petiolaris The climbing hydrangea is useful for walls, trees or as a freestanding shrub.

Jasminum Several species and cultivars ideal for walls and fences provide evergreen looking foliage and mostly fragrant flowers.

Lonicera The climbing, usually fragrant, honeysuckles are indispensable.

Parthenocissus These ornamental vines with good autumn colour are excellent for clothing walls.

Roses A wide range of climbers and ramblers with an equally wide usage; training and pruning are important.

Vitis Some ornamental selections of note include *V. vinifera* 'Purpurea', with purple leaves, and *V. coignetiae*, with large leaves and good autumn colour.

Tropaeolum There are several species, some tender, but *T. speciosum* is reliable and looks striking grown through conifers and over contrasting foliage.

Wisteria Several selections can be grown, either as a climber or a small tree.

Geranium *'Ann Folkard'*

landscapers or tree surgeons. If a tree, shrub or conifer has given twenty or thirty good years and simply outgrown its welcome, it is perhaps time to say goodbye. And the space it creates will leave you with all sorts of exciting possibilities. This will increasingly become necessary at Foggy Bottom but fortunately, "head gardener" Michel Boutet, who does most of this clearing work, loves such challenges, leaving me the opportunity to create another plant association, or to try out new plants.

PERENNIALS

From mid-summer onwards, perennials and ornamental grasses come into their own and provide the colour, movement and variety which most woody shrubs cannot offer at this time of year. The growing popularity of hardy perennials and ornamental grasses in Britain, Europe and North America appears to be unstoppable. From being the Cinderellas of the garden plant world,

A SLIGHTLY MISTY mid-summer morning is lightened by the sun's rays slanting onto Acer shirasawanum *'Aureum', and the "kitchen beds", seen here from the roof of the house* (right)

THE STILL FRESH green leaves of Alchemilla mollis, *lady's mantle, are enhanced by the droplets from a recent summer shower and make a good companion for* Euphorbia griffithii *'Fireglow'* (below*)*

despite the efforts of my father Alan Bloom back in the 1960s, they have, from a slow start, become exceedingly fashionable. It was thought when the perennial craze started to hit the United States in the early 1980s that within ten years, like many other fads, perennials would be back where they started. Not a bit of it: in fact I would say that the interest there has only just begun. Why then is there such an abiding interest in this group of plants? The answer lies in their versatility. But to that quality should be added those of adaptability and diversity, with flower and foliage in an amazing range.

Because of their low-lying habit and because they were originally found in the wild, the majority of perennials were in the past often viewed by gardeners as weeds – and indeed some still are! Even within my memory, they were still considered so by a great number of gardeners fed on a diet of "trouble free" woody trees and shrubs and by others on the more highly cultivated annuals. But such times are past and perennials are now at their peak of popularity. And in reality aren't perennials the ultimate group of plants that every gardener has been looking for? Perennials can be found in every size and scale, from ground-hugging ajugas to eupatoriums and helianthus 2m/6ft or more high; they can be found with narrow leaves and broad leaves, with cream; and variegated, green or red foliage, there are plants for moist shade as well as for dry sun. With this selection and the amazing variety of colour, shape and form of perennials from all over the world, it is hardly surprising that there is always a perennial to fit every garden, however inhospitable it may seem.

Because my father's nearby Dell Garden had over 5000 species and varieties of perennial flourishing in it before I even started our garden at Foggy Bottom, I felt I should try woody plants first. But as the trees, conifers and shrubs began to grow, the conditions in the garden changed to such an extent that, fifteen years on, there was shade and tree roots where there had been sun, and south-, west- and east-facing beds where once they had all been south-facing. The garden was in a state of constant change and trial. First, great blocks of heathers began to deteriorate in the shade and the ground-cover plantings of junipers had their stems ringed by field mice in winter. So it was time for a change, and it has continued thus ever since, giving the opportunity to introduce new plants, new schemes and new ideas. So perennials and grasses have now become the underplanting and the interplanting between the conifers, trees and shrubs, creating the scope for pattern, movement and more rapid seasonal change, as well as greater variety.

DAYLILIES AND OTHER PLANTS

Perennials and grasses combine to produce textures and colours which create visual diversity. What brighter surprise could be created than by using the vibrant scarlet *Crocosmia* 'Lucifer', whose bright nodding flowers are even attractive when holding green, then brown, seeds in their beak-like heads? When in full flower, 'Lucifer' shows up vividly against the steely blue foliage of *Juniperus chinensis* 'Blue Alps' and other contrasting perennials at its base.

Softer in tone for a more moist spot is a "purple loosestrife", except that this plant is not purple. I came across *Lythrum salicaria* 'Blush' in Canada, where the nurseryman who gave it to me explained that it was now forbidden in his country to grow these mostly Asian

and European imports because they seeded too freely, escaping the captivity of gardens to roam freely in the wild. His loss was our gain, and I have a high regard for these long-flowering perennials which, until this variety was discovered, had been mostly in colours of rose-red to purple. 'Blush' is the softest, most delicate pink you could wish for.

But if lythrums as introduced plants in North America are environmentally suspect, perhaps the hemerocallis, or "daylilies" should also be considered so,

ORNAMENTAL GRASSES ARE becoming ever more popular as are variegated leaved plants. The two features are combined in Miscanthus sinensis *'Variegatus' whose softer tones and vertical habit provide a contrasting background for the short spiked orange flowers of* Crocosmia *'Spitfire' (above)*

at least in certain conditions, though in some quarters it would be heresy to suggest it. The species – small flowered and often fragrant – are all native to Asia, mostly Japan and China, but these lowly subjects have largely become "Americanized" in recent years and, through breeding, transformed beyond recognition. Their flowers have become larger and more varied in colour, shape and form. The breeding programme has developed multitudes of varieties, not all of which turn out to be good garden plants. But they are adaptable to both heat and drought, from Minnesota to Louisiana, and while many look out of place among other perennials, some do earn their place in any garden. Of the 150 or so American-raised varieties we imported at Bressingham some years ago, some did not adapt to the cooler British summers, but others, such as 'Stella d'Oro', the first dwarf yellow long-flowering selection, has added immeasurably to their value.

The intensity of breeding work will undoubtedly continue because of the demand, and more long-flowering types are continually being produced following the commercial success of 'Stella d' Oro', whose sales must now run into several millions of plants. Though the popularity of the daylilies is assured in the United States, where I am told that at least several hundred varieties are introduced each year, the term "daylily" bemuses many British gardeners who are not quite sure how many days the flowers will last! The answer is of course that although each flower lasts but one day, flowering on most varieties will continue for four to six weeks, while 'Stella d' Oro' and other repeat-bloomers will flower from early summer into the autumn with a few rests in between. That represents very good value in the

LYTHRUM SALICARIA 'BLUSH', an import from Canada, is far removed in colour from the original purple loosestrife but it has struck a chord with many gardeners (left)

HEMEROCALLIS 'WHICHFORD' is a classic daylily, with rich green, grassy foliage and fragrant yellow flowers (below left)

PLANTS WITH SUMMER FRAGRANCE

Fragrance is a real bonus in the winter and there are some shrubs which stand out for their sweet fragrance – such as the mahonias, viburnums, hamamelis, sarcococcas, skimmias and many daphnes. In the summer, fragrance adds immeasurably to the enjoyment of gardening and being close to plants when sitting out in the garden. When considering plants for the summer garden, therefore, scent should be considered along with other attrributes. Fragrance can be a subjective matter, however: while most of us would agree on the enjoyment of scented roses or lilacs, other plants, such as the scented leaf geranium, Geranium macrorrhizum, *are far too pungent for some.*

Syringa vulgaris *'Sensation' in early summer*

Clematis heracleifolia var. davidiana *'Wyevale'*

Shrubs and climbers
Aesculus parviflora
Buddleja davidii
Carpenteria californica
Choisya ternata
Clethra alnifolia
Cytisus battendieri
Daphne (many)
Erila arborea
Fothergilla
Jasminum (some)
Lonicera (some)
Philadelphus (many)
Rhododendron, (many)

Perennials, alpines and bulbs
Clematis heracleifolia
Cosmos atrosanguinea
Dianthus (many)
Dictamnus albus
Hemerocallis (some)
Hosta (some)
Iris (some)
Lavandula (most)
Origanum (many)
Paeonia (many)
Phlox paniculata

Iris germanica *'Patterdale'*

PENSTEMON DIGITALIS 'HUSKER'S RED' is an easy plant, as attractive for its purple foliage as for its summer flowers (above)

garden, though the plants will need splitting every couple of years to keep them young and performing well.

AMERICAN INTRODUCTIONS

Plants from North America are of course part of the British gardening heritage. While American collectors may have been introducing hostas and hemerocallis and many other plants from Japan, we British were combing parts of North America for new and interesting species to introduce to Britain – and not only trees, shrubs and conifers, but also standard American wildflowers like *Phlox paniculata* as well as many asters and solidagos (the goldenrods). We too have hybridized species and varieties and introduced new selections for British gardeners. It used to be said by some American gardeners that a plant had to come to Britain or Europe to become "civilized" before being sent back to the United States, when it would immediately become accepted! Now there is much more awareness of the value of the North American flora and the richness that still exists there, as well as the potential for commercial opportunities. Nonetheless it is nice to record that two of my father's selections of *Phlox paniculata*, 'Eva Cullum' and 'Franz Schubert', have recently been well received by American gardeners.

One recent brash introduction which we were delighted to trial and to introduce into Britain was a hardy verbena called 'Homestead Purple'. The story of its discovery is an interesting one. Two good friends of mine, both professors of horticulture at the University of Athens, Georgia, Michael Dirr and Allan Armitage, were driving along a back road in the state of Georgia, when they suddenly spotted a patch of bright purple in an old homestead garden. On closer investigation it proved to be a verbena, which in time turned out to be hardy enough to withstand temperatures of -10°C/14°F, perhaps even lower. They called it 'Homestead Purple' and it made its debut appearance at the 1994 Royal Horticultural Society's prestigious Chelsea Flower Show, where it was acclaimed by British gardeners. Its bright purple flowers will hit you between the eyes from early summer until the frosts. For sheer summer colour this perennial has a well-deserved place in the garden at Foggy Bottom. We have also used it in a hanging basket and a window box where it looks most attractive.

SUCH VIBRANT COLOUR MAY BE too much for some, but Verbena *'Homestead Purple' flowers all summer and makes a strong focal point in garden or window box. It has come through three winters with temperatures as low as -10°C/14°F in the author's garden* (above)

PLANTS ENJOYED BY BEES

In collecting nectar to make honey, the bees are doing all gardeners an enormous favour. Not only do they provide enjoyment for us as they go about their business, but some of the best garden plants have arisen from the accidental hybridizing created by bees as they carry pollen from one plant to another. This can certainly lead to new seedlings being distinctly different from either parent plant – though it is sometimes difficult to be sure which both parents were. Some plants will be almost certain to come true from seed, while other vary tremendously. Plants such as the spring-flowering pulmonaria and many of the foxgloves and aquilegias are notorious for their promiscuity. But if you plant the beautiful white foxglove Digitalis purpurea *'Alba' near the species or seedlings of the pink- or red-flowered foxglove, you will almost certainly find within a few years that the resulting crosses of these indispensable biennials are almost all red or pink. To prevent this degeneration, at Foggy Bottom we pull up most of the pink-flowered seedlings as soon as the first flowers open.*

All the plants shown opposite are herbaceous perennials, but there are many other plants enjoyed by bees and butterflies too.
Main picture: Delphinium belladonna 'Peace' (syn. 'Volkerfrieden')
Top left: *Both butterflies and bees are attracted to* Allium senescens 'Glaucum'
Top centre: Digitalis purpurea albiflora
Top right: Heuchera 'Rosemary Bloom'
Centre left: Erigeron 'Vanity'
Centre centre: Eryngium 'Jos Eijking'
Centre right: Eryngium alpinum 'Superbum'
Bottom left: Centaurea macrocephala
Bottom centre: Gaillardia 'Goblin'
Bottom right: Helenium 'Waltraud'

THE FREE FLOWERING penstemons provide a summer-long show with a wide range of colours. Penstemon 'Blackbird' (foreground) is backed by Mother of Pearl' and 'Hidcote Pink' (above)

VARIED ORIGINS

Plants for summer colour will seldom be found among British natives, so for summer-colour plants we generally need to turn to more exotic locations. That said, the callunas or lings and other heathers, where they will grow, can create sheets of colour when seen from a distance. And members of the mallow family, particularly *Lavatera olbia* and *L. thuringiaca*, which are European natives, have become exceedingly popular since new colours and strains have been introduced. The lavateras come in pink, white and burgundy colours and most of them bloom from mid-summer onwards, depending on their location, and produce countless flowers for

LAVATERA 'PINK FRILLS' is a dwarf shrubby mallow whose flower petals are pretilly frilled (above left)

CAMPANULA PERSICIFOLIA 'Chettle Charm' flowers on tall spikes, its subtle colouring silhouetted against a purple beech in the background (above right)

months on end. Some, like *Lavatera* 'Barnsley', can grow very tall, and with its soft, semi-woody stems can blow over or break unless it is in a sheltered spot, but the unceasing show of white, pink-centred flowers is worthy of garden space if it can be found. Even though they may not survive severe climates, the lavateras are valuable enough to be considered or used as annuals.

The same might also be said of the

diascias, a group of perennials introduced from South Africa many years
ago, but which have recently become
extremely popular. Though many
species are annual, several others are
perennial, these mostly originating from
the Drakensberg Mountains and generally hardy to -10°C/14°F, sometimes
lower. As always when a group of plants
becomed popular, new varieties will be
almost certain to follow, and some of
the new diascias are very good in terms
of summer-long flowering on soils that
are not too dry. Small- and large-flowered, with heights from 10cm/4in to
40cm/1ft 3in, and in colours from light
pink to rose-pink and lilac, all will give a
flowering performance over many
weeks, if not months.

One of my current favourites is
'Blackthorn Apricot' which makes a carpet of colour among which I have
spread seed of the biennial *Eryngium
giganteum*, the notorious 'Miss Willmott's Ghost'. This group has been
planted in what we call our mediterranean bed, a sunny, south-facing area
backed by tall conifers. I am gradually
planting in it a selection of perennials
and shrubs which will happily grow and
survive the rather dry but heavy soil.
The conifers have provided shelter for a
Melianthus major, another South African
plant of great merit for its foliage. I
would not have even tried it a few years
ago, before I had sufficient shelter, for it
is unlikely to take more than -10°C/14°F
in winter, and even then would need

*MISS WILLMOTT'S GHOST, Eryngium
giganteum, always seems to have a ghost-like
quality. It is planted here between an olearia
and in the foreground the soft-toned Diascia
'Blackthorn Apricot' (left)*

*GERANIUM CINEREUM 'Laurence Flatman'
nestles on a low Norfolk flint wall, determinedly
making a summer-long show even if it is
squeezed by the yew behind* (above)

A GOLDEN LAWSON'S CYPRESS, Chamaecyparis
lawsoniana *'Stewartii', provides the
background to the contrasting lilac,* Syringa
vulgaris *'Sensation',* Euphorbia characias *ssp.*
wulfenii *and* Veronica armena *in early
summer* (far left)

*THE SUN FILTERS through the glowing carmine
flowers of* Rosa moyesii *'Geranium' on a mid-
summer morning* (left)

some protection. But even if the foliage dies back each year, or you have to keep it in a container as a patio plant, its blue-grey, deeply cut overlapping leaves provide a dramatic foliage effect in summer. It grows to 3m/10ft or more in its native Southern Cape Province, but only to 1.2-1.5m/3-4ft in a season in Britain.

This mediterranean bed also contains olearias, *Euphorbia characias* ssp. *wulfenii, Eucalyptus niphophila, Spartium junceum,* rosemary and ceanothus – plants which come from Mediterranean climates in Europe, California, New Zealand and Australia – with a Chilean native, an azara, thrown in. I'm no purist when it comes to using plants, although those that fit best together visually often do prefer similar conditions, even though they may come from different continents. This example underlines just how international our gardening palette has become, and how much we owe to both old and new plant hunters for their endeavours over the years.

BALANCED COMBINATIONS

Foggy Bottom is quite an open garden and has developed along natural, meandering lines – or at least that has been the intention – against structural backbones around which beds and borders have been created. As you walk round, you will see some interesting cameos or plant associations which might fit into a smaller garden, but you will also hopefully look up to enjoy the broader view and the vistas, since there is always something in the distance to draw the eye. Colour combinations can start from the ground and work upwards, but they might also work in reverse, starting from the top with a cone-laden blue spruce, for example, or a purple-leaved silver birch. As the eye runs along, the colours and contrasts will appear too bright for some, particularly on a sunny day – the blues with golds and purples. Thank goodness for green, you might say!

As tastes change and adapt, so will our gardens but, above all else, the theme running through should be to create year-round colour for our climate. In the English climate, the sun can be a relatively rare commodity, especially in winter. There are some beds in Foggy Bottom which are considerably brighter in winter than summer, and I have been making a concentrated effort to provide more summer colour in recent years, which means bright foliage and long-flowering plants if one is to be achieved without sacrificing the other. I have made good use of such plants as *Cornus alba* 'Sibirica Variegata' or *Cornus alba* 'Aurea', the dogwoods which have summer-long foliage contrast and winter stems, as well as the long-flowering shrubby potentillas, ground-cover roses and *Polygonum affine* 'Dimity' (now called *Persicaria*) which makes leafy ground cover from which arise a succession of bottlebrush spikes, white, pink and deepening to red as summer progresses to autumn.

So when does mid-summer end and late summer begin? Though some topics and plants have been included in the period from mid-summer to late summer, a great many more have been left out altogether. What, no iris, paeonias and poppies, you may well ask? The answer is that while some of the plants I recommend can be found in the Directory (see page 78), this trundle through the summer seasons is inevitably selective, as one must be in an individual garden, and this allows me to be more discursive. But do not think, as we come to the late summer period, that all is over in the garden, for some of the best is yet to come.

LATE SUMMER

More than one gardening journalist I have read has made the point that August should be written off as a gardening month. I suppose that if you take a full month's holiday at this time and go away to a summer retreat, that is perhaps an understandable point of view. In climates where summers become unbearable in August, this would be understandable too. But for those that wish for it, the garden in August can be as colourful and interesting as any time of the year. Apart from the range of plants that exist among the perennials and ornamental grasses to give late summer colour and interest, also to be considered are the elements of water and the use of containers. These will adorn the terrace, patio or other favourite spots, when you can sit in the shade sipping iced tea or lemon and enjoy the rewards of your earlier labours.

THE VALUE OF WATER

Water can of course be a crucial element in any garden in more ways than one. It is vital to the survival of your plants although most, if well planted and mulched, will survive without additional watering provided they are given conditions approximating to their requirements – which is not as much gobbledegook as it sounds. You will choose sun lovers for a sunny position – but take advice or read to see how much moisture is required; you will select shade lovers for shade, but is it dry shade or moist shade those plants want? Plantings in their first year will require more attention than those which are more established, and new plants, particularly the more valuable trees or shrubs, may require a large hole prepared and filled with quantities of thoroughly mixed in, well-composted humus in the form of farmyard manure,

BLACK CLOUDS highlight the background to this view of Foggy Bottom on a late Summer's afternoon, the dipping sun casting light and long shadows from west to east. Buddleja davidii *'Pink Delight' is in the left foreground, rising above a patchwork of heathers and conifers*

SUMMER SPECTACULAR

The perennials and alpines in these photographs (alpines mostly being dwarf perennials) show the brilliance and diversity that can be obtained from early to late summer.

Top row, from left to right: Dendranthema weyrichii, *a dwarf early flowering chrysanthemum.*

Geranium subcaulescens 'Splendens', *an undeniably striking dwarf hardy geranium. Early summer.*

Lupinus *'Russell Hybrids', universally popular perennials. Mid-summer.*

Phlox paniculata 'Flamingo', *a "border phlox" with fragrance and colour for late summer.*

Second row, from left to right: Geranium × oxonianum 'Bressingham's Delight' *an easily grown free-flowering hardy geranium. Mid-summer.*

Hemerocallis *'Holiday Mood': summer colours on this brightly coloured daylily. Mid-summer.*

Campanula cochleariifolia, *an alpine miniature campanula ideal for rock or scree gardens. Mid-summer.*

Achillea *'Anthea', the second flowering on this compact grey-leaved yarrow. Late summer.*

Bottom row, from left to right: Helenium *'Coppelia', a first rate sneezeweed for late summer colour.*

Phlox divaricata *'Blue Dreams', a late spring and early summer flowering garden-worthy phlox. Early summer.*

Mimulus *'Puck': striking bicolor effect for many weeks with this "monkey musk". Early summer.*

Rudbeckia fulgida var. deamii: *few perennials are more valuable for late summer than this black-eyed susan.*

TWO EARLY MORNING VIEWS highlighting the pond at Foggy Bottom in late summer. Early morning sun lightens the Rudbeckia fulgida *var.* sullivantii *'Goldsturm', happy at the water's edge (*left*). A slight mystery surrounds the shadows close to the pond as the first rays of light filter onto plants in the distance (*below*).*

leafmould, or even straw which will hold moisture. When Rosemary and I visited that great garden, La Vasterival in Normandy, created and run by the indefatigable Princess Sturdza, she explained to us that she never watered new shrubs again once they were planted, having given such thorough preparation as I have described, followed by watering them in well, and giving them a thick top mulch of leafmould or pine needles to retain the moisture.

A water feature, such as a pool or a fountain, brings another dimension to the garden and can provide interest particularly in the late summer period. The pond at Foggy Bottom – for one can hardly consider it a lake – was created towards the lower part of the garden, which seemed to make eminent sense but, although it might fill up in winter, without a butyl liner it would empty in summer. After two years with a dry pond we managed in 1978 to get a patchwork butyl liner made to cover the island and fit the rather uneven natural shape. Remarkably, within a few years the pond became the natural feature which an informal garden of six acres needed. What I failed to do at the time, however, was to allow sufficient liner to overlap the adjacent moisture beds which I was to plant three or four years later. When the time came to plant, it was obvious that there was little to hold the moisture in these beds adjoining the pond – the soil is so well drained in summer that many plants have been disappointing and in due course we will need to tackle the problem properly by adding an extension to the liner.

I learned another lesson when planting down near the pond. I was anxious to have in the garden a rather unusual spring-flowering moisture-loving perennial, *Peltiphyllum peltatum*, with its large summer leaves; thinking that my father would let me have some from his group

in the Dell Garden, I dug up a fair-sized chunk in mid-winter (with his permission, I hasten to add). Only later did I realize that it contained some all too healthy roots of a dreaded weed, the perennial horsetail. Despite all our efforts, we have so far failed to stop its establishment, so that is another problem to be tackled before it gets totally out of hand. There must be a moral there somewhere.

Despite these problems, the water feature has given year-round appeal as well as a place for fish to breed, herons to feed and wild duck to shelter and nest. Summer, winter and other seasons are reflected in the water, and on occasion we have taken a canoe out on it, and also skated round the island on thin ice in winter. In the late summer of 1987 the bottom third of the garden was flooded which, despite its serious after-effects in terms of loss of plants, had some benefit in that it enabled us to canoe around the garden. And some say that nothing happens in the garden in August!

This flooding in particular highlighted the adaptability of one of the best of the hardy perennials, *Rudbeckia* 'Goldsturm' or, to give its true title, *Rudbeckia fulgida* var. *sullivantii* 'Goldsturm'! This black-eyed susan is a North American native which brightens up the late summer garden with its deep yellow flowers highlighted by a black central cone, over the abundant deep green foliage. When the rains came, the group of rudbeckia was in full flower in a reasonably well-drained sunny spot, but soon only the flowers were showing above the flood level. Throughout the ten days the plants were under water, the flowers continued to bloom, and for another month afterwards as the water receded. To me, brought up in the knowledge that this was a sun lover, if not for dry soil then for ordinary, well-drained conditions, its performance was remarkable. It was only after I looked it up in reliable botanical reference books that I learned that it was native to low-lying, moist meadows.

Though 'Goldsturm' is a popular perennial in North America, it is surprising how little used this glorious plant is in Britain. There is also a quite different, but lesser known rudbeckia which deserves a place in more gardens. *Rudbeckia laciniata* 'Goldquelle', like 'Goldsturm', was raised in Germany, and its finely cut, light green leaves produce 60cm/2ft high stems with fully double heads of clear yellow, with overlapping petals. I have these two rudbeckias close to each other beside some contrasting ornamental grasses. Blue with yellow always seems to work well and *Festuca glauca* 'Blueglow' ('Blauglut'), another German selection, has the brightest blue leaves or needles; 'Elijah Blue' is another example. I have found these fescues invaluable in creating low-growing groups for the front of a border to enhance other, contrasting plants; they look their best if they are divided every few years.

Ornamental grasses

Ornamental grasses have certainly added a whole new dimension to gardening as far as I'm concerned. I have not only developed a passion for collecting them to try out at Foggy Bottom, but I have also experimented by using them in different situations in the garden where they seem to give greater impact to many other types of planting. Ornamental grasses fit in perfectly well with hardy perennials and generally have a much longer period of interest than most individual types of perennial.

Take *Stipa gigantea*, for instance: I have copied a combination found in the Dell Garden using this majestic yet airy grass with *Phlox paniculata* 'Franz Schubert', a pleasing soft lilac phlox which grows to 120cm/4ft. The stipa in spring makes a large, grassy hummock with narrow, dark green leaves, whose early flowers emerge on panicles like delicate heads of oats, but much more widely spaced. The plumes turn from green to beige in early to mid-summer, then to golden brown later in the summer, at the time *Phlox paniculata* 'Franz Schubert' reaches the peak of its flowering performance. The plumes of the stipa have by now reached 180-240cm/6-8ft and the burnished golden heads make a stunning contrast to the phlox – as though both had come to the harvest festival together. I have no qualms about copying combinations or ideas from other gardens or gardeners and am only too pleased to give credit as to where an idea came from. Some of the best ideas, so we are told, happen by chance and of course this may well be true at times.

Ornamental grasses are undoubtedly now nearing a peak of popularity and as more gardeners realize how they can use them, and how wide the range is, the more widely they will be grown and appreciated. Twenty-five years ago we listed nearly forty varieties of grasses in our Bressingham Gardens catalogue but, although there was some interest, we gradually had to reduce the list through

ORNAMENTAL GRASSES ARE at their most dramatic when light plays on their flowers and foliage. Early morning sun touches the plumes of Molinia altissima *'Windspiel' before lighting up the plants around it* (left)

lack of sales. However, following the lead by German nurserymen and gardeners and some innovative work in the U.S.A. in using and publicizing this group of plants, British gardeners are now developing a new interest. This is largely due to the ever-increasing range of newly discovered, bred or selected species and varieties available.

Many of these grasses come from Japan originally and one, with a name once heard, never forgotten (though remembering it is the difficult part) – *Hakonechloa macra* 'Alboaurea' – has been in demand ever since its introduction to Britain thirty or more years ago. Growing to only 30cm/1ft at most, this slow growing, clump-forming grass has narrow-golden-yellow leaves, striped irregularly with green, which arch gracefully over each other, giving the appearance of a golden sea. We grew it in the garden for a number of years, where it needs a friable soil which does not dry out, but it wasn't until I had seen it growing in a large container in a garden centre in Japan, that I realized its true vocation was probably as a patio or container plant. Back in England I potted plants up for our patio and for the last several years this plant has been one of the star exhibits of our Chelsea Flower Show stand.

Some grasses are at their best in early summer, such as *Calamogrostis* × *acutiflora* 'Overdam', with striking pink-flushed, variegated leaves and *Deschampsia flexuosa* 'Tatra Gold', whose tussocks of foliage shine with gold early in the season, followed by wispy flowers. Others with variegated foliage, like some of the miscanthus, make a pleasing foil to other plants. In this respect few can match the adaptability of *Miscanthus sinensis* 'Variegatus' which seems happy in half shade or full sun and can make as good a combination with a hosta or a fern as it can with a sun-loving kniphofia or crocosmia. Of narrower leaf but every bit as effective is the graceful 'Morning Light'. However, for me the outstanding "finds" in recent years are some of the miscanthus hybrids, bred and selected by Ernst Pagels. Until Herr Pagels' numerous introductions, many of which are listed in the Directory of Plants (see page 78), very few cultivars of *Miscanthus sinensis* flowered in the cooler summers of northern climates. We are only recently aware of what we have been missing, and although other excellent foliage forms have recently come from Japan and North America, we certainly owe a debt to this German nurseryman.

These strains, of which there are now almost too many to choose from, offer interest from early summer to the following spring, though they are most spectacular from late summer until late autumn. With heights ranging from 1m/3ft to 2.4m/7ft, with grassy foliage of green and silver and plumes of varying sizes and forms, and with colours ranging from crimson to silver and changing from one to the other, they are plants which have come to add an exciting new form to the garden. And, as will be seen in the chapter on the smaller garden (see page 60), they are suitable not only for the large plot.

MISCANTHUS SINENSIS 'Morning Light' lives up to its name as the morning sun strikes its narrow variegated leaves, gracefully arching out from an upright centre. It looks equally effective through winter as its leaves and stems turn light brown (right)

LATE-FLOWERING PERENNIALS

Just as the ornamental grasses have in themselves brought a new dimension to summer colour (and autumn and winter too), so they have highlighted so many other good plants with which they can be associated. Some of those I have used include plants with South African origins – the kniphofias, agapanthus and crocosmias, plants with mostly bold colours and interesting flowerheads. Late- or long-flowering broad-leaved perennials such as *Polygonum* (now *Persicaria*) *amplexicaule* 'Taurus' can be equally striking.

The common name for kniphofias – red hot pokers – is certainly a misnomer these days, for recent breeding and selection has widened the range from the original South African species to include sizes from 30cm/1ft to over 2m/6ft and colours which range from white through yellow, orange and pink as well, of course, as all shades of red. Some have tight buds which open from green, brown or bronze, then change as the flowers open to yellow, then white, so that it can be an oversimplification to describe a cultivar by one colour only. Take *Kniphofia* 'Innocence', for instance; it starts tight in bud with true poker-like heads in green and bronze, the flowers as they open turning to orange, then yellow and lastly fading to white from the base. The bees can't wait to dive into the opening flower buds to draw out the nectar – another attraction of kniphofias as garden plants.

A FINE CONTRAST IN colour and form is provided by two plants in close proximity. Scabiosa caucasica *'Blue Seal' and* Kniphofia *'Bressingham Comet' provide colour from late summer into early autumn* (left)

THE VOLCANO BED

I believe one should try and have some fun with garden plants and I recently had the opportunity to experiment with an idea I had had for creating an association of kniphofias with grasses. In the late spring I dug up some failing heathers which had been badly damaged by spring frosts as well as by recent dry summers. This left a slightly sloping area between conifers and heathers, into which I planted a meandering line of glowing orange-red flowered *Kniphofia* 'Bressingham Comet' to represent a stream of lava, while the wavy ornamental grasses *Stipa tenuissima* on either side were the land through which it flowed. This, which we named the volcano bed, has been surprisingly effective with other plants being added later to continue the year-round appeal.

This species of stipa is a marvellous plant, with bright green, narrow leaves in spring producing delicate sprays in summer which, en masse, reflect the light and movement of every breeze. In autumn the faded plumes are bleached white, but dew and frost settling on them continue their attraction into winter. Though it seeds itself happily around, this is never a nuisance and indeed often a bonus.

Provided you select carefully, you can achieve enough colour to see you through the late summer months without difficulty, though in areas with extremely hot summers the flowering periods are often reduced. But I believe that wherever you live there is a plant or several plants that can be found to fit a purpose.

Late summer in the early years at Foggy Bottom meant almost exclusively summer-flowering and foliage heathers, which were planted in large groups among the winter-flowering types and contrasting conifers, to provide ever more colour as well as height, scale and structure. But nothing is for ever, and although many of these original plantings are still effective others, which have given of their best for twenty years or so, have gradually been replaced by perennials and shrubs.

In late summer the bergamots (the monardas) are good value, their mop-like heads in brilliant colours attractive to bees. And in recent years penstemons have also come back into fashion, helped along by milder winters, since most of the hartwegii types will not take severe winter temperatures. These plants produce stems in mid-summer from which hang developing buds, opening to both brash reds, crimson and purple flowers often with white or speckled throats, as well as delicate pastel shades. They will flower for most of the summer, and if they are cut back after the main flush, they will repeat-bloom until the autumn.

Good blues are not always easy to come by at this time of year, but plants like *Aster* × *frikartii* and its dwarfer cousin, *Aster* × *thompsonii* 'Nana' flower for several weeks at the end of the summer and will continue into the autumn. These trouble-free asters are essential ingredients for creating colour and contrast, so I make no apology for having two or three groups in the garden. The *Aster* × *frikartii* selections have proved themselves over many years to be one of the best groups of perennials, let alone of asters – and I will always have a particularly soft spot for them because they were introduced not long before I worked at the Frikart nursery in Stafa in Switzerland, by the shores of Lake Zurich, during the spring and summer of 1961.

SEDUM 'AUTUMN JOY' can always be relied on to produce a beautiful show. In the foreground is Ajuga reptans *'Braunherz'* (above)

Phlox paniculata 'Mother of Pearl' shows delicate toning in both sun and shade (above)

This grouping has a warm glow on a late summer's afternoon: the Joe Pye weed, Eupatorium, *on the left surrounded at the base by* Rudbeckia fulgida *var.* sullivantii *'Goldsturm'. Ripening seedheads of* Stipa gigantea *tower behind, partially obscuring* Phlox paniculata *'Franz Schubert'* (above top)

Aster x frikartii, with a similar hybrid Aster × frikartii 'Monch', are among the finest perennials ever raised. Hardy, free- and long-flowering, they are very useful for late colour (above)

LATE FLOWERING SHRUBS

In late summer there are still shrubs to provide colour, though they are fairly limited in number – until you start to list them! Many hebes are at their best now and shrubby potentillas start to rebloom more strongly as cooler nights arrive. The blues of ceratostigma, perovskia and caryopteris are welcome alongside those of abelia, lavatera and lesser-known plants such as lespedeza, while many roses will continue to flower for weeks yet.

Buddlejas are a group of popular shrubs enjoying something of a revival. This revival was started, as is often the way, by the introduction of a new variety. In this case it was *Buddleja davidii* 'Pink Delight' which arose from a breeding programme in Boskoop, Holland; it has proved a winner, being compact in habit, and the closest to pink yet seen. Hypericums used to be relied upon to give us flowers throughout the summer, followed by mostly crimson, red or black fruits. Unfortunately some have become susceptible to rust which can ruin, and sometimes kill, the plant. A dwarf and admittedly free-seeding North American species, *H. prolificum*, which is very hardy and seems immune to this disease, deserves to be more widely used. It grows to 1m/3ft or so and has small, bright green leaves and masses of tufted golden-yellow flowers all summer long.

Hydrangeas should also be mentioned, both for the garden and for containers. Unfortunately, in Foggy Bottom spring frost seems to damage the flowering shoots of the mophead and lacecap forms of *Hydrangea macrophylla*, so I have increasingly been using those that flower on the new season's growth. *Hydrangea arborescens* and *H. paniculata*

BUDDLEJA DAVIDII 'PINK DELIGHT' is flowering away in the background, standing above the heathers or lings in the foreground. One can almost hear the bees going about their work on this late summer's day (above)

are the species to look for: though limited in flower colour, if pruned back each spring they will produce heads of white flowers in late summer. *H. arborescens* 'Annabelle' is a favourite, with large, green rounded heads opening to brilliant white, while *H. paniculata* 'Kyushu' and 'Pink Diamond', whose white florets turn pink with age, are some of the worthiest selections.

We are still skimming the surface in selecting plants to provide late summer colour which will drift into early autumn. In Foggy Bottom we may start to get autumn colour even before autumn begins, once the cooler nights arrive, bringing mist and sometimes fog with the still evenings. At this time the conifer background is at its most colourful, the heathers at their best and, being low-lying, the cooler air gathers to bring some wonderful misty mornings, with the dew hanging onto leaf surfaces and the plumes of the grasses.

The flowers of asters, rudbeckias, sedums, kniphofias, some crocosmias and agapanthus, solidagos, ceratostigmas, perovskias and many, many more are there to brighten late summer and take us into autumn. The coloured foliage of many shrubs – cotinus, berberis, cornus and corylus can create striking backgrounds, quite apart from the conifers. Flashes of light come through the waving grasses as the sun takes a lower arc in the sky. There are fruits on the sorbus (the mountain ashes), cotoneasters and pyracanthas, while crimson autumn colour is already appearing on the leaves of *Euonymus planipes*, its yellow seedheads held enticingly open for the birds to collect from the crimson capsules that surround them. Colour is all around – summer garden glory may be over, but autumn and winter garden glory are about to begin.

AS A FINE FOLIAGED and free-fruiting shrub, Sorbus koehneana *has considerable merit, with bunches of glossy white fruits in late summer* (above)

HYDRANGEA ARBORESCENS 'Annabelle' makes quite a spectacular show for much of the summer with its large ball-shaped flowerheads (left)

Summer in the Smaller Garden

SUMMER COLOUR IN THE SMALLER GARDEN

At Foggy Bottom I am continually attempting to change and develop the garden and to fill any seasonal gaps with plants of interest, whether for the effect of their flowers or their foliage. In a six-acre garden there is of course room to grow a much wider range of plants than in the small garden and I can create cameos or scenes in one area without even disturbing the rest of the garden.

In the smaller plot it is essential to be selective in the use of plant material to create year-round interest and a careful choice needs to be made according to the length of display. Although there may be fewer varieties of plants that give winter colour, many of those plants will give a longer period of interest than plants selected for summer colour. Shrubs like the dogwoods – *Cornus alba* and *Cornus sanguinea* – will offer leaf colour in autumn then, when the leaves have dropped, will provide coloured stems until spring when new growth begins.

STRUCTURE AND SCALE

For late spring and summer we need another selection of plants, a different balance; it is important to remember that part of the structure of the garden, including many of the plants which have given winter colour, will remain, though by now they mostly provide a supporting role. Certain evergreen foliage plants, such as hollies, elaeagnus, euonymus and conifers, continue to be invaluable. And the ornamental grasses like carex and perennials such as bergenias and ophiopogons are equally attractive in summer as they are in winter.

THIS DWARF BIRCH, Betula 'Trosts Dwarf', has many of the attributes of a dwarf Japanese maple: slow growing with finely cut foliage and able to take full sun. Viola 'Boughton Blue' grows beneath it in mid-summer (left)

Scale is another important consideration in the small garden. In Britain many gardeners seem frightened of planting trees – and in a garden 5m x 5m (20ft x 20ft) or less, one can understand that reluctance. In North America, where gardens are usually larger and most summers considerably hotter, "shade trees" are often a necessity. But there are trees which can give structure to the small garden: trees with a fastigiate habit will not give much shade, but won't take over either, while other trees can be pruned to keep them within bounds. These days it is popular to plant pendulous "top worked" trees where, for example, a weeping willow or cotoneaster is grafted onto a stem to cascade down. But although there are more dwarf trees which will provide periods of flower or fruit – crataegus, prunus and sorbus, to name but three – it is true to say that most of the flower power in a small garden will be provided by shrubs and perennials (here I include plants like crocosmias which are strictly bulbs).

Though they look nothing in winter, shrubby potentillas, especially *P. fruticosa*, are generally good value, most being relatively dwarf and flowering from late spring until autumn, depending on the climate. Many of the more common shrubs, such as philadelphus and deutzia, have a limited period of flower, but there are selections with mottled or variegated foliage to extend their interest. Spiraeas too are one of the most trouble-free shrubs and many of the *S. japonica* cultivars, like 'Gold Mound' and 'Golden Princess', not only have a display of pink flowers, but offer summer-long colour with their golden or yellow leaves. Foliage is all-important for providing colour in the smaller garden, both in its own right and as effective contrast to other plants.

In selecting plants for the small garden a useful exercise is to go through books and catalogues and initially to list far more plants than you will probably need; then, against those names, note when the flowering period is and how long it lasts, plus any other features it may have at other times of the year. Make sure that your selection covers the seasons adequately and in this way you will start to whittle down your selection to those plants that will give you most value throughout the year. Always include a few of your favourite plants, albeit it those which last but a moment. Gardening should not all be done on a scientific basis: impulse and flair must be allowed for if it is to be enjoyed.

THE STAR PLAYERS

Against the more static trees, shrubs and conifers, we have already seen that

BENEATH THE ACER BED a moist, shady area offers a home for Dicentra *'Pearl Drops',* Corydalis flexuosa *'Purple Leaf' and* Trillium ovatum, *whose white flowers have faded to a pretty pink* (above)

perennials, alpines and ornamental grasses provide not only the ebb and flow of the garden but also the summer highlights. There are vast numbers of species and varieties to fit almost any site or situation – though extremes of shade, drought and moisture will narrow down the choice significantly. As with structural planting, look for plants which give a long period of interest, preferably with a mixture of foliage and flower – there are good examples of multi-purpose plants in the two small suburban front gardens featured later in this section, while others are described in the Directory of Plants (see page 78).

SOME SMALL-GARDEN PLANTS WITH A LONG PERIOD OF INTEREST

DWARF SHRUBS

Shrubby potentillas are deciduous, but give months of flower; dwarf hebes such as 'Red Edge' *have flowers and attractive foliage;* Choisya ternata *'Sundance' has bright yellow leaves and fragrant flowers.* Ceratostigma willmottiana *flowers for weeks late in the summer.* Berberis thunbergii *'Dart's Red Lady' has deep purple leaves and crimson autumn colour, 90-120cm/3-4ft in height;* 'Bagatelle', *reddish-purple, is more dwarf. Useful variegated evergreens include euonymus, pieris, cotoneaster, ivy; for certain areas, the larger growing aucubas, elaeagnus and ilex can be used and pruned accordingly. Deciduous shrubs which have flowers and coloured leaves include spiraeas such as S. japonica 'Gold Mound' and 'Golden Princess', S. thunbergii 'Mt. Fuji' and 'Pink Ice',* Weigela florida *'Praecox Variegata',* Caryopteris *'Worcester Gold' and* Fuchsia genii. *Some of the dwarfer ground cover roses are excellent value for long flowering periods in summer.*

Weigela florida *'Praecox Variegata'*

HEATHS AND HEATHERS

*Remember that summer-flowering heathers need an acid soil. The lings, callunas and bell heathers (*Erica cinerea*) all have dwarf varieties which have flowers in summer and golden foliage in winter.* Calluna vulgaris *'Sir John Charrington' is outstanding and* Erica cinerea *'Rock Pool' or 'Windlebrooke' can be recommended.* Erica carnea *'Aurea', 'Westwood Yellow' and 'Foxhollow' have golden foliage in summer, pink flowers in winter. All are best in sun.*

Calluna vulgaris *'Allegro'*

PERENNIALS

Most spring-flowering perennials may have a long period of flower, but most summer-flowering perennials, depending on climate, are over relatively quickly. The pulmonarias are an exception and flower for weeks in spring, then many have attractive leaves later in summer, lasting well into autumn. My recommendations include Pulmonaria angustifolia *'Highdown' (also known as 'Lewis Palmer') with strong blue flowers and large spotted leaves;* P. officinalis

'Sissinghurst White', smaller, with silver-spotted leaves'; P. rubra *'David Ward' has variegated, white-margined leaves and red flowers;* P. saccharata *'Leopard', red flowers, dark green silver-dotted foliage;* P. longifolia *'Roy Davidson' has smaller, narrower, spotted leaves and light blue flowers;* P. saccharata argentea, *with almost fully silver-grey leaves.*

Perennials with evergreen foliage include the Japanese "black mondo grass", Ophiopogon planiscapus *'Nigrescens', with narrow black leaves, sparse lilac-white flowers and black berries in autumn; planted against blue, silver or yellow, it can make a stunning year-round combination. Some bergenias with broad, cabbage-like leaves are a bright green in summer but turn purple or ruby in winter providing a show of flowers in late winter.* Bergenia purpurascens, B. *'Bressingham Ruby', 'Eric Smith' and 'Wintermarchen' are all recommended. In recent years new heucheras have been introduced with coloured leaves – purple, bronze or silver – which give summer-long foliage attraction, adding to the briefer season*

Diascia rigescens × integerrima lilacina

of flower: 'Palace Purple', 'Bressingham Bronze' and 'Pewter Moon' fit into this category. Hostas give ample choice for shade; some excellent smaller-leaved varieties give foliage effect in the small garden.

Perennials with longer periods of flower are much in demand. New varieties of diascia will flower for most of the summer, including D. 'Blackthorn Apricot', D. 'Salmon Supreme' and D. rigescens × integerrima lilacina'. Several hardy geraniums can be relied upon to flower for months; best for a small garden are: G. 'Ann Folkard' which is vigorous but can climb less attractive shrubs in late summer, G. × riversleanum 'Russell Prichard' and 'Mavis Simpson', and G. oxonianum 'Bressingham's Delight', 'Little Gem' and 'Sea Spray'. Dwarf scabious have a succession of flower in sunny spots; recommended are S. 'Pink Mist' and 'Butterfly Blue', lesser known but equally attractive S. graminifolia and S.g. 'Pincushion'. Certain coreopsis, dicentras and rudbeckias have long flowering periods. Other perennials, such as euphorbias, sedums, ajugas, artemisias, thymes and dianthus, have a worthwhile mixture of flower and foliage.

ORNAMENTAL GRASSES

Ornamental grasses should have a place in most gardens, however small, provided they are sunny. In summer the grasses and sedges act as a foil to other plants, their brown, bronze, green, silver and blue leaves contrasting well with flowering and foliage plants. Grasses such as pennisetum, deschampsia, stipa and miscanthus have dwarf or compact selections with plumes or panicles which develop and ripen through the summer, going on to create wands which dew and frost can enhance in autumn and winter. One of the most valuable grass-like plants for year-round colour is Acorus gramineus 'Ogon', whose low, mounded habit of golden leaves is actually brighter in winter than summer.

CONIFERS

Conifers of course give year-round colour and a selection for the smaller garden must be made on the basis of habit, colour, scale and suitability to climate. Rate of growth is another important factor, so always study books or seek advice from garden centres. There are many fascinating and colourful dwarf conifers to choose from, and they can be fitted in with other plants, as I have shown at Foggy Bottom and in the small front gardens featured in this chapter.

Geranium sanguineum *var.* striatum 'Splendens'

Pennisetum orientale

MID-APRIL. The shade provided by the acer creates the right environment for some woodland plants from North America and China. In the foreground is Corydalis flexuosa *'Purple Leaf', the purple-flowered* Trillium sessile *and white* Trillium ovatum. *Behind and under the stems of the tree are the white lockets of* Dicentra *'Pearl Drops' and the yellow heads of daffodils*

LATE APRIL. Acer shirasawanum aureum *is sheltered from the morning sun, which protects it from spring frosts as it comes into leaf. The snowdrops at the base of the tree are in full growth. Daffodils, pulmonarias and violas show flower as well as dicentras, bergenias and* Phlox × divaricata

Over the years, as our garden at Foggy Bottom developed, I have tried to remain aware of the need to create smaller areas and plant associations which could be readily 'transported' to smaller gardens. In fact, going back to 1975 when I created my first year-round garden, mostly using conifers and heathers, I have attempted to show by example that almost all gardens, however small, can benefit from displays of plants carefully used and designed. One of the best examples of this at Foggy Bottom is the area we have called the acer bed, an oval-shaped bed about 3 x 4m (10 x 13ft), first planted in 1967. It began with two main plants, *Acer shirasawanum aureum*, a wonderful Japanese maple, and *Picea pungens* 'Globosa', the dwarf blue spruce which we surrounded by heathers.

For nearly twenty years this bed was a picture from the house, providing glorious colour all year round, the maple with its golden leaves in summer contrasting brightly with the blue-grey needles of the spruce. But inevitably, as the plants grew, it became obvious that unless both were to spoil, one tree would have to be moved. It was decided it should be the picea, by now less of a dwarf than the books had indicated! On a frosty midwinter morning in 1985 the operation began to remove the picea, with a good rootball, to another site. It was hoisted on a large fork lift and successfully established elsewhere. I then replanted the bed, using a much wider range of plants that would adapt to shade and sun to create a new effect. In this small area choices had to be made to give year-round interest without using evergreen shrubs and conifers. Some of the plants and planting associations are shown on these pages as the seasons develop through the year of 1994.

MID-MAY. Seen from another angle, the acer is now in full fresh golden leaf, sparkling in the midday sun. A mound of greenery and flowers cover the ground and there is a strong contrast from the Acer palmatum *'Garnet' behind. Golden-leaved hostas contrast vividly with* Phlox divaricata *'Blue Dreams'*

MID JUNE. The foliage plants in the centre foreground now take a lesser role than in March, the Bergenia *'Bressingham Ruby' now with leaves turned green. A seedling white foxglove lights up the left foreground and* Geranium × oxonianum *'Bressingham's Delight' the right*

EARLY AUGUST. The flowers have diminished with just the geranium showing touches of colour, but now the foliage of ferns, bergenias, ophiopogons, pulmonarias and hostas becomes more important

DECEMBER. The framework of branches of Acer japonicum *'Aureum' are momentarily clothed with hoar frost, giving it an ethereal appearance. The evergreen bergenias, ophiopogons and acorus hardly show but the old flower sprays of* Stipa tenuissima *are also lit up with frost*

SUMMER COLOUR IN CONTAINERS

Patio plants have never been more popular, but the selection used is often quite limited. There are far more plants which will grow in containers than most people imagine: many trees, shrubs, perennials and ornamental grasses all make excellent patio subjects and there is sufficient choice to suit both sun and shade. I remember the reaction we had when people saw a *Wisteria sinensis* in full flower in a container in our garden. Grafted wisterias, trained and pruned, will within a few years make impressive container specimens.

Containers are essentially versatile – they can be moved to front or back, to produce new arrangements and different effects, to create their own plant associations. Depending on the size of plant or container, they can be transported from sun to shade, and be taken to a less prominent spot once their main season is over in order for others to be put in the limelight. We use a sack barrow to transport larger pots, which takes some of the physical strain out of this task. Over the years the more established container-grown specimens will tend to get bigger and may need either repotting or root pruning.

One of the most important considerations when growing plants in containers is to adapt the compost to the subject. If you garden on alkaline soil, here is your chance to grow plants which like acid soils – camellias and pieris, for instance – by potting into an ericaceous mix. Clay or terracotta containers will dry out much more quickly than plastic, but on the other hand it is more difficult to overwater plants in them, which is a risk when first planting in a plastic pot, before the plant grows large enough to take up all the moisture in the compost. Feeding and pruning are equally important; knowing how easy it is to forget to

keep up a regular liquid feed, I would always recommend incorporating a slow-release fertilizer which should last the plant a whole season.

Besides the traditional summer-colour subjects for containers– such as pelargoniums, fuchsias and annuals – trees, shrubs, conifers, climbers, perennials and grasses, as well as bulbs, ferns, alpines and even bamboos, can all offer something different and yet will be long-lasting container subjects. Planted as single specimens or as part of a group planted to create an association in a pot, there is no limit to the versatility and effects one can achieve. Pendulous or prostrate-growing plants are particularly attractive when they cascade over the side of the container.

Individual plants such as hostas can give summer-long interest and when grown in containers they are less subject to slug damage. The new American cultivars – 'Francee', 'Wide Brim' and

WISTERIAS ARE MOSTLY seen growing against walls or over pergolas but they can also be trained as a small tree or shrub. This fifteen-year-old specimen of Wisteria sinensis *at Foggy Bottom regularly performs each year in late spring* (left)

CAPTIVES IN CONTAINERS

Wouldn't you be frightened of growing in your garden plants that behave like invasive weeds? There are several plants with attractive foliage which I would hesitate to let loose in the garden but the answer is to grow them in pots, tubs or other containers, keeping them captive by restricting their root run. Simply plant them in container compost, keep them fed and watered like any other plant and they will remain decorative all summer long. Since most of them are vigorous, I would suggest splitting and replanting them at least every other year. Some suggestions are:

Aegopodium podogaria 'Variegata' – a less aggressive form of ground elder which has brightly variegated leaves and will grow in quite deep shade.

Houttuynia cordata 'Chameleon' – a late-shooting plant which is stunning in a herb pot or container; its multi-coloured foliage has a pungent smell. Though a relatively new plant to western gardeners, this was in cultivation in Japan before 1850.

Trifolium repens 'Purpurascens' – a purple-leaved clover which spreads rapidly in a garden situation but makes an attractive mat of purple leaves in a container.

Disporum sessile 'Variegatum' – a choice plant for shade or semi-shade where it will run happily, it is equally satisfied in confinement in a pot to brighten up a dull corner.

Arundinaria viridistriata – a golden-leaved dwarf bamboo which is quite content in captivity.

Phalaria arundinacea var. picta 'Feesey' – this is a brightly variegated selection of gardener's garters, normally extremely invasive, especially in moist soil.

Kalimeris yomena 'Shogun' – another brightly variegated plant which spreads, though not particularly invasively. Related to the aster, it has stiff upright stems and small leaves edged creamy-white, followed by insignificant lilac flowers.

Aegopodium podogaria *'Variegata'*

Disporum sessile *'Variegatum'*

Houttuynia cordata *'Chameleon'*

'Shade Fanfare' – are recommended, but top of my list, both for the garden and for containers, is a selection of a Japanese native, *Hosta fluctuans* 'Variegated', whose leaves present a sculptural quality. Unfortunately it is still rare and highly priced as well as prized – but probably the technique of micropropagation will alter that in time. On this page are but a few examples of plants used in containers at Foggy Bottom to provide summer colour or form.

MIXED PLANTING FOR YEAR-ROUND COLOUR
THE PUTTS' GARDEN FROM LATE SPRING TO LATE SUMMER

By almost any standard, 6m x 6m (20ft x 20ft) is a small front garden. Yet how many people make the most of their front gardens, which, although they are generally not places to sit or relax in, are walked past by the home owner at least a thousand times a year!

Of course the situation of a garden, its type of soil and aspect, whether it is in a city or a more open location, will all have an effect on what can be grown. Personal preference also plays a significant role – some may prefer a landscaped garden, with very few types of plants – but in both the Putts' and the Johnsons' gardens (see page 70), I was able to concentrate on a wide selection of plants. I used about 80 different varieties in each

garden in fact. In my opinion, plants can provide interest and excitement all year round, and with careful initial selection and a degree of control, can last for years without a great amount of work.

Although the Putts' garden was planned particularly for autumn and winter interest, it has colour in spring and summer too, though it is less spectacular than the next-door Johnsons' garden during these seasons of the year. Foliage plays an important part too, and bulbs, alpines, perennials and shrubs all contribute something during their flowering period. There is a feeling of informality in the design of this garden, which looks almost like a scaled-down part of Foggy Bottom! And where in my

THIS SCREE BED HAS been planted with dwarf conifers for year-round colour (some of which will need thinning out in due course) and interplanted with dwarf perennials or alpines. Spots of colour can be provided by dwarf bulbs in spring and early summer but in mid-summer when this photograph was taken, Geranium cinereum *'Laurence Flatman', dianthus and thymes provide flower, the bronze* Ajuga reptans *'Braunherz' strongly contrasting with* Juniperus × media *'Gold Sovereign'. Including the bed behind, this front garden measures only 6m x 6m (20ft x 20ft) and contains 80 different species and cultivars (below)*

own garden I would have used groups of between five and twenty of certain plants, here it is primarily singles or threes, and the effect is similar, though on a considerably smaller scale. We have had to make good use of the secateurs to prune the few faster-growing shrubs, but that is good and necessary husbandry in such a small garden and allows a wide variety of interest to be added by smaller plants such as bulbs and some perennials which still have room to put on a flowering display in between the woodier plants.

After five years the Putts' garden has matured, without looking overgrown, though before too long one or two conifers will need to be removed from the scree bed to somewhere in the larger back garden.

This garden is certainly as maintenance-free as was the original lawn: Maggie Putt estimates that she spends barely half an hour a week on it, even during the spring and summer, though no doubt more time could be spent if desired. And there is always something happening or about to happen from January to December, which can be enjoyed either by looking out of the window or by walking past each day – each season being fully appreciated as plants grow, flower and fade and as foliage changes its hues and colour through the spring, summer, autumn and winter.

THE ORIGINAL Campanula carpatica *has seeded itself to make this pleasing combination on the scree bed in mid-summer, contrasting with the conifers and purple-leaved* Berberis thunbergii *'Bagatelle'* (below)

WINTER STEMMED DOGWOODS are pushed out of the limelight by Lavandula *'Hidcote' and* Coreopsis verticillata *'Golden Gain', soon to flower, both lasting several weeks.* Microbiota decussata *in the foreground will turn purple-bronze in winter* (below)

A garden Without a Lawn

The Johnsons' Drought-resistant Garden

Planted in spring 1991, Judy and Roy Johnsons' garden was designed to be quite different from the average suburban front garden. A front garden without a lawn was to be planted somewhat mediterranean style with a shingle and pebble covering. Like the Putts' garden next door, it was all planted in one day, but as there are considerably more hours of daylight in May than ther are in November, this gave us longer to apply the finer touches.

The front lawn disappeared, carefully cut away to reveal free-draining, sandy soil. Although the flat area was too small to create much in the way of undulations, we dug an impression curving from the centre of a dried-up "river bed" throughout which, after planting, I placed some larger stones or pebbles to create interest and a natural feel.

The plants were once again the main ingredient. Few shrubs were chosen, except one or two towards the back to soften the lines of the brick wall of the house, and a small shrubby specimen of *Acer negundo* 'Flamingo' in the front to give summer-long colour. Though termed a "drought-resistant" garden, not all the plants I selected would in fact take happily to prolonged drought with intense heat. Droughts in Britain tend to be somewhat gentler affairs than where hot summers are the norm, but with water restrictions from local councils coming in quite early, this is still a concern to many gardeners.

Ornamental grasses, perennials and alpines were the main ingredients in the Johnsons' garden and here the choice was fairly critical in order to select plants to give a long period of summer interest. Bulbs were also used to give spring colour. Apart from their diversity, the perennials and grasses quickly mature to give colour in the first year and to look

totally at home by the second. Some of course can be quite vigorous and those types need to be watched, particularly if rapid top growth starts to smother other smaller or slower-growing plants surrounding them. Even such a small garden can give the opportunity to create some attractive plants combinations and associations. Although 80 varieties of plants might seem like an extravagance which would lead to a rather congested mess, this does not have to be the case – as hopefully some of the plant groups on these pages show.

The shingle or gravel mulch works very well at helping to retain moisture and ideally it should be kept in a layer as thick as 2in (5cm) to control weeds. The larger the grade of shingle the fewer weeds will prosper, but too large a grade may look heavy in a small garden. Seedlings from weeds and plants alike will enjoy the benefits of protection offered by the shingle while germination takes place. It is best to look for annual weeds regularly and ensure that they are not allowed to seed, and to check that plants which seed freely, like the *Carex comans, Campanula carpatica* and origanum, are not allowed to grow in all the wrong places. But despite the potential drawbacks, this garden has been a success and is greatly enjoyed by the Johnsons, who can certainly claim to have their own summer garden glory right outside their front door!

ANOTHER EXAMPLE of a successful partnership is the white-flowered Dicentra *'Snowflakes' intermingling with* Geranium × cantabrigiense *'Cambridge' (far left)*

THE IMPRESSION IS of a much larger garden with this vista across from the neighbouring garden. Acer negundo *'Flamingo' is this side of the boundary.* Diascia elegans *contrasts with the grey foliage of* Artemisia nutans, *while* Campanula carpatica *'Forester's Blue' is sandwiched between* Geranium *'Ann Folkard' in the distance and* Geranium × riversleaianum *'Russell Prichard' in the centre (left)*

PLANTING ASSOCIATIONS FOR SUMMER COLOUR

Planting to create interesting, even exciting plant combinations is, to my mind, the most rewarding of all gardening challenges – and success in this area can often be elusive. There are many factors to bear in mind before you start, in relation to your site – whether you have a clear "green field" site or whether you are planting against a fence, wall or hedge, or underneath existing trees and shrubs. You need to decide whether it is desirable or necessary to build a plant association into an existing framework, or whether it is better to try and start from scratch.

Starting from scratch, as I have assumed for many of the following association ideas, is, at least in theory, much easier. The soil can be prepared to suit the plants chosen and there is no competition from existing structures or plantings. Planting around existing specimens can not only create immediate microclimates of sun or shade, but the developed root systems demand water and space, so that new plantings may need considerable assistance in establishing their own root system.

You must then think about the effects you would like to achieve, and decide on the best plants to create that effect, given the aspect and soil conditions of your site. Are you looking for spring, summer, autumn or winter appeal or hoping to achieve a combination of interest in all seasons?

Taking advice from a garden designer or following suggested plans in books will give you a guide and a starting point, but in a way it is more fun working out ideas for yourself after doing some basic reading and research. just as with cookery recipes, the information you glean can give you ideas which will enable you to change some of the ingredients to create your own association or design.

The illustrations and outline plans on the following pages come mostly from associations and plants which I have used at Foggy Bottom. Some 'artist's licence' has been used in conveying compatible flowering periods in the illustrations but none will vary by more than a few weeks. Remember that if suggested plants are unavailable in your area, others may well fit the bill.

SUMMER BRILLIANCE IS PROVIDED in this mixed planting of perennials in front of the steel-blue foliage of the Juniperus chinensis *'Blue Alps'.* Agapanthus *'Bressingham Blue' interplanted with* Crocosmia *'Lucifer', contrasts strongly with the clump of* Rudbeckia fulgida *var.* sullivantii *'Goldsturm' behind.*

A SMALL ISLAND BED FOR CONTINUAL COLOUR

The fairly dwarf plants in this narrow bed, shown here in mid-summer, are colourful during all other seasons too. The purple-leaved shrub *Berberis thunbergii* 'Dart's Red Lady' is the only shrub, though several of the other plants will offer autumn, winter and early spring interest before the berberis even comes into leaf. The *Stipa calamagrostis* will reach a height of 120cm (4ft) or so, the plumes remaining attractive well into winter, when the steely-blue leaves of *Euphorbia myrsinites* will contrast vividly with *Bergenia* 'Bressingham Ruby', whose leaves turn from summer green to ruby red. The grass *Festuca glauca* 'Blueglow', dotted around the bed to contrast with the surrounding plants, forms a strong juxtaposition with the summer purple of the berberis. Summer-long interest at this end of the bed is offered by the silver leaves and white flowers of *Lamium maculatum* 'White Nancy', the white, pink and red flowers on *Persicaria affinis* 'Dimity', and *Geranium × riversleanum* 'Mavis Simpson' which with its grey leaves and soft pink flowers, knitting in with their neighbours and offsetting the strong colour of the berberis. *Iris pallida* 'Argentea' with erect, sword-like leaves remains a bright focal point, enhanced in midsummer by pale blue flowers. The diascia, with its creeping habit and striking flowers, will flower all summer long to contrast in late summer with one of the best, yet most underrated perennials, *Aster thompsonii* 'Nana'. This in turn makes the classic yellow and blue combination with the dwarf day lily, *Hemerocallis* 'Stella de Oro'.

This bed should be in full sun, most of the plants requiring reasonable drainage.

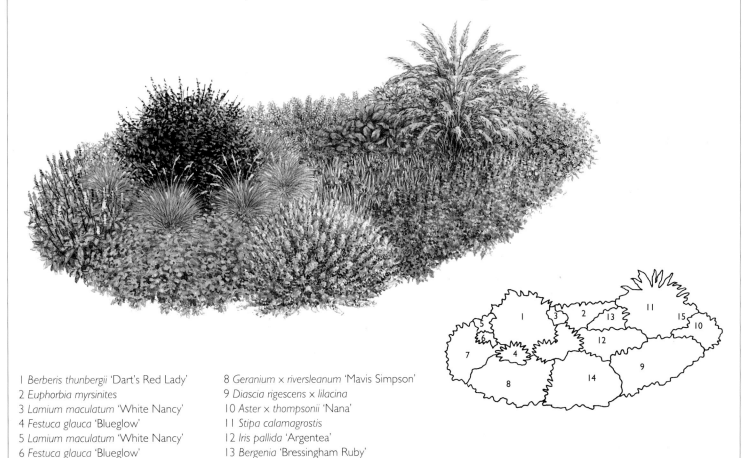

1 *Berberis thunbergii* 'Dart's Red Lady'
2 *Euphorbia myrsinites*
3 *Lamium maculatum* 'White Nancy'
4 *Festuca glauca* 'Blueglow'
5 *Lamium maculatum* 'White Nancy'
6 *Festuca glauca* 'Blueglow'
7 *Persicaria* (syn. *Polygonum*) *affinis* 'Dimity'
8 *Geranium × riversleanum* 'Mavis Simpson'
9 *Diascia rigescens × lilacina*
10 *Aster × thompsonii* 'Nana'
11 *Stipa calamagrostis*
12 *Iris pallida* 'Argentea'
13 *Bergenia* 'Bressingham Ruby'
14 *Nepeta racemosa*
15 *Hemerocallis* 'Stella de Oro'

AN ASSOCIATION FOR LIGHT SHADE WITH SOME MOISTURE

While the background to this association is provided by trees here, sites and situations will vary, and the shade could be afforded by a high canopy of trees some distance from the bed or even by the high boundary wall of the garden or the wall of the house. With younger trees of lower height, the roots may be a problem, taking the moisture from the soil. It is always difficult to achieve a balance of shade and the right amounts of moisture. But root pruning of trees by digging a trench every two or three years may help, besides digging in well-rotted compost and mulching the whole bed, plus irrigation if available, will all help to maintain the ideal conditions.

A great many shade-loving woodland plants flower in spring, including trilliums, uvullaria, epimediums and the startling blue *Corydalis flexuosa* cultivars. Other bulbs can be added here, including hardy cyclamen, erythronium, woodland anemones, snowdrops and aconites. But in this association most plants provide foliage or flower interest for a long period in summer. Plants such as hostas, *Rodgersia pinnata* and

Dryopteris erythrosora create a background against which other foreground plants can be shown off to advantage. The blue flowers on the spreading *Geranium himalayense* form a natural contrast to the white and green leaves of *Hosta* 'Francee' and the soft pink spikes of × *Heucherella* 'Bridget Bloom'. The flowers of the latter remain in bloom for many weeks but these will be fading before the pretty pink plumes of *Astilbe* 'Sprite' make a show. The deschampsia will tolerate sun or shade and its grassy green leaves will create an effective backcloth to the attractive variegated Jacob's ladder (*Polemonium caeruleum* 'Brise d'Anjou').

Contrast exists too between *Lysimachia nummularia* 'Aurea', the golden-leaved creeping Jenny and the powder-blue foliage of *Hosta* 'Krossa Regal', long-flowering *Dicentra* 'Snowflakes' and *Persicaria* (formerly *Polygonum*) *milletii*. By summer the bronze fronds of *Dryopteris erythrosora* will give a foliage contrast to the silver-spotted leaves of *Pulmonaria* 'Roy Davidson', whose light blue spring flowers have long finished.

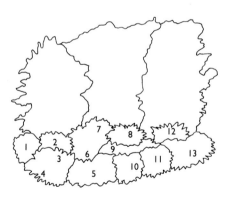

1 *Geranium himalayense*
2 *Hosta* 'Francee'
3 × *Heucherella* 'Bridget Bloom'
4 *Astilbe* 'Sprite'
5 *Polemonium caeruleum* 'Brise d'Anjou'
6 *Deschampsia caespitosa* 'Golden Dew'
7 *Rodgersia pinnata* 'Elegans'
8 *Hosta* 'Krossa Regal'
9 *Lysimachia nummularia* 'Aurea'
10 *Dicentra* 'Snowflakes'
11 *Persicaria* (syn. *Polygonum*) *milletii*
12 *Dryopteris erythrosora*
13 *Pulmonaria* 'Roy Davidson'

A Mediterranean-style Garden in Full Sun

Much publicity has been given in recent years to the potential effects of global warming, and a succession of milder winters in northern Europe, parts of North America and Britain. At the same time, more people visiting countries with a mediterranean climate has led to the increasing popularity of plants formerly considered appropriate only for coastal and warmer districts. "Mediterranean" plants may come from any part of the world with a similar climate, be it South Africa, Australasia or California but the many new introductions may include an even wider range of plants that like the same conditions of sun and good drainage.

This bed, shown here in late summer, could be freestanding or backed by a hedge. Height is provided by the *Eucalyptus niphophila*, the Mount Etna broom (*Genista aetnensis*) and eventually by *Arbutus unedo*, the adaptable strawberry tree. A mixture of shrubs and perennials make up the rest of an interesting association of flowering and foliage plants. *Lavatera* 'Barnsley' will rapidly grow to about 2.4m(8ft) but will eventually be surpassed by the genista, which may reach a height of 3m(10ft) or more. By summer, spent flowers should be cut off the euphorbia, leaving grey-green foliage. The compact *Scabiosa graminifolia* has shiny silvery leaves and a succession of powder-blue flowers, while *Cosmos atrosanguinea*, though not reliably hardy, will provide a dark contrast to both the scabious and the grey-leaved non-flowering *Artemisia* 'Powis Castle'. The flat heads of the sedum are an ideal counterpoint to the spiky, erect, sword-like yucca and the rounded, deep blue umbels of the hardy *Agapanthus* 'Bressingham Blue'. Along the front of the bed, the rich pink *Geranium* 'Alan Bloom' vividly offsets the soft yellow of *Molinia caerulea* 'Variegata' and *Coreopsis verticillata* 'Moonbeam'. Coupled with both the azure blue of the spiky perovskia and the soft pink of the penstemon, this should provide more than enough colour for most people. There is also sufficient structure to keep this bed looking interesting into autumn and even winter.

The bed needs to be mulched with a mixture of fine and coarser gravel to help retain moisture but allow free drainage on the surface as well as offering some degree of weed control.

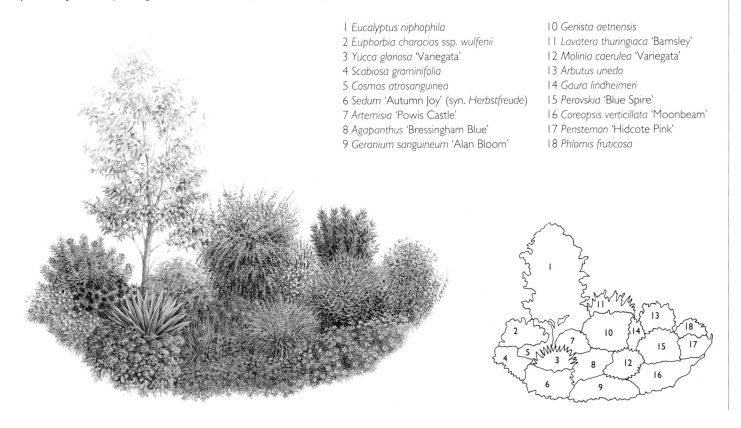

1 *Eucalyptus niphophila*
2 *Euphorbia characias* ssp. *wulfenii*
3 *Yucca gloriosa* 'Variegata'
4 *Scabiosa graminifolia*
5 *Cosmos atrosanguinea*
6 *Sedum* 'Autumn Joy' (syn. *Herbstfreude*)
7 *Artemisia* 'Powis Castle'
8 *Agapanthus* 'Bressingham Blue'
9 *Geranium sanguineum* 'Alan Bloom'
10 *Genista aetnensis*
11 *Lavatera thuringiaca* 'Barnsley'
12 *Molinia caerulea* 'Variegata'
13 *Arbutus unedo*
14 *Gaura lindheimeri*
15 *Perovskia* 'Blue Spire'
16 *Coreopsis verticillata* 'Moonbeam'
17 *Penstemon* 'Hidcote Pink'
18 *Phlomis fruticosa*

PERENNIALS WITH ORNAMENTAL GRASSES

In recent years hardy perennials have made a tremendous comeback and are now probably the most popular group of garden plants. The popularity of ornamental grasses is even more recent and owes much to the efforts of German and American nurserymen, garden designers and plantspeople. Initially, grasses tended to be used on their own but their real value lies in the contrast in form, foliage, light and movement that they offer to more brilliant flowering and non-flowering plants. The wide variety of ornamental grasses now available has given even greater opportunities to create pleasing combinations. The period of interest of ornamental grasses extends well beyond summer, and most continue to look attractive through autumn and winter, before they are cut back to encourage them to rejuvenate.

There are no invasive grasses in this bed, which could be an island bed or a bed against a wall, hedge or shrubs. However this plant association idea is adapted, always remember the importance of allowing light to pass round it all year. In the reflected view, with light flashing through stems or plumes, you will derive much enjoyment. A position in full sun is recommended and a fertile, but reasonably well-drained soil will suit most plants.

Three different miscanthus provide the most height, along with *Stipa gigantea*, and although the wispy plumes of the latter will reach 1.8m(6ft) or more by mid-summer, the full height of miscanthus foliage and flower will not be achieved until a month or more later. Spots of colour and bright contrast will be provided by this bed throughout summer, though late summer will be its peak season, as shown here. The late flowers of rudbeckia, *Aster × frikartii*, persicaria, kniphofia, scabious, diascia and anthemis continue well into autumn – particularly if earlier flowers are cut back after their first main flush of flowering in mid-summer.

This bed could be mulched with gravel.

1 *Stipa gigantea*
2 *Miscanthus sinensis* 'Flamingo'
3 *Aster × frikartii*
4 *Persicaria* (syn. *Polygonum*) 'Taurus'
5 *Pennisetum alopecuroides* 'Hameln'
6 *Diascia vigilis*
7 *Kniphofia* 'Bressingham Comet'
8 *Miscanthus sinensis* 'Variegatus'
9 *Carex comans* 'Bronze'
10 *Agapanthus* 'Isis'
11 *Miscanthus sinensis* 'Klein Silberspinne'
12 *Crocosmia* 'Bressingham Beacon'
13 *Anthemis tinctoria* 'E.C. Buxton'
14 *Scabiosa caucasica* 'Clive Greaves'
15 *Festuca glauca* 'Blueglow'
16 *Rudbeckia fulgida* var. *sullivantii* 'Goldsturm'
17 *Agapanthus* 'Bressingham White'
18 *Salvia × sylvestris* 'Blauhugel'
19 *Calamagrostis* 'Overdam'
20 *Phlox paniculata* 'Franz Schubert'

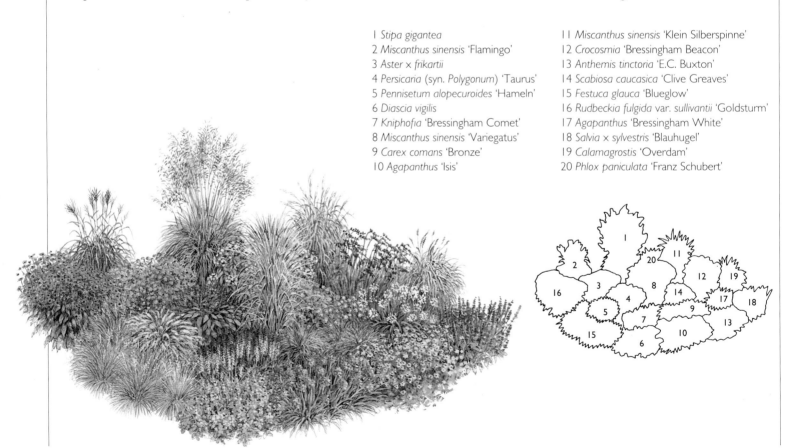

A Mixed Border of Summer-long Colour

From my experience at Foggy Bottom, I believe that some structure is important in a garden – and for most gardeners it already exists when they move into another property. This illustration, which shows the bed in mid- to late summer, shows some striking associations including small trees, shrubs and conifers, as well as ornamental grasses and perennials. Even if some of these plants are not available to you, similar forms and colours may be sought. Always think of the year-round aspect, the foliage colours as well as those of the flowers and – as mentioned time and again – consider what is likely to succeed in your own conditions, soil and climate.

Spring-flowering bulbs can be added for an earlier effect, and if I was planning with year-round colour in mind, I might wish to add a red- or orange-stemmed dogwood against the blue spruce. Highlights in this border will certainly include the bright reddish-pink *Geranium sanguineum* 'John Elsley' against the three golden spires of *Thuja orientalis* 'Golden Sceptre' –

but do not plant them too close together or it will spoil the conifer foliage. The silver-leaved pear, *Pyrus salicifolia* 'Pendula', will make a pleasing backdrop to the bed. Though *Acer negundo* 'Flamingo' can be grown as a tree on a stem, it is far better to keep it as a shrub at less than 3m(10ft), by pruning regularly. This multi-coloured, easily grown maple will offer good contrasts to both the pear and to the *Picea pungens* 'Hoopsii' behind, a striking silver-blue spruce.

Completing the shrubs is one I rate highly for its broad purple leaves, *Cercis canadensis* 'Forest Pansy'. If this is not available, a purple smokebush (*Cotinus coggygria* 'Purpureus') would be a good substitute. Various long-flowering perennials complete the colourful picture in the front of the bed, with the golden-yellow *Coreopsis verticillata* 'Golden Gain' and *Lavandula* 'Blue Cushion' creating a splash in mid- to late summer. This combination of shrubs and perennials would suit a sunny bed or border for most soils.

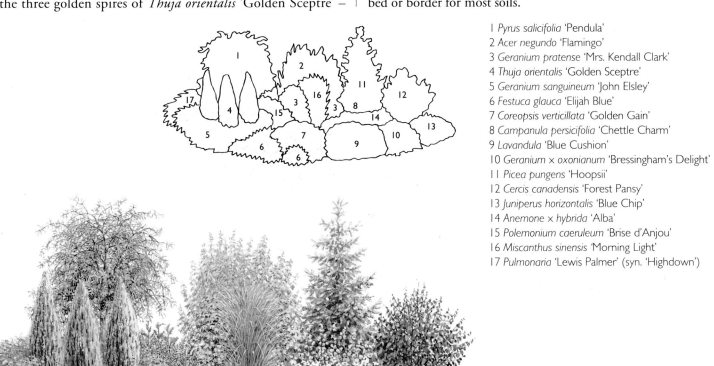

1 *Pyrus salicifolia* 'Pendula'
2 *Acer negundo* 'Flamingo'
3 *Geranium pratense* 'Mrs. Kendall Clark'
4 *Thuja orientalis* 'Golden Sceptre'
5 *Geranium sanguineum* 'John Elsley'
6 *Festuca glauca* 'Elijah Blue'
7 *Coreopsis verticillata* 'Golden Gain'
8 *Campanula persicifolia* 'Chettle Charm'
9 *Lavandula* 'Blue Cushion'
10 *Geranium* × *oxonianum* 'Bressingham's Delight'
11 *Picea pungens* 'Hoopsii'
12 *Cercis canadensis* 'Forest Pansy'
13 *Juniperus horizontalis* 'Blue Chip'
14 *Anemone* × *hybrida* 'Alba'
15 *Polemonium caeruleum* 'Brise d'Anjou'
16 *Miscanthus sinensis* 'Morning Light'
17 *Pulmonaria* 'Lewis Palmer' (syn. 'Highdown')

DIRECTORY
OF PLANTS

DIRECTORY OF PLANTS

This directory is a personal selection of hundreds of plants recommended to provide colour and interest in the garden from late spring through to late summer. While it includes both popular and unusual plants, and species for all situations in the garden, it is necessarily selective rather than comprehensive – there are just too many plants from which to choose.

CULTURAL REQUIREMENTS

Most of the plants listed are "hardy" in Europe and the British Isles (Zones 7-9 in the USA hardiness zones – see below) and will adapt to most garden soils except where a specific need is stated. A soil testing kit enables you to determine whether your soil is acid or alkaline.

Soil Unless you already have good, friable, fertile soil, you will probably need to dig thoroughly to a depth of 35-45cm (14-18in). Mix in some organic material, such as well-rotted garden compost or manure. This will help to retain moisture in light soils and to aerate heavier soil types.

Planting Before planting, soak plants in their containers – for an hour or two if the compost is dry or a few minutes if it is moist. Dig the hole deep enough for the level of the soil in the container to come just below the surface of the soil. Add some fertilizer: select a slow-release type for conifers, shrubs or trees, but use a faster-acting, balanced one if you are planting perennials.

After planting, fill the hole in with soil, firming gently on heavy soils but more firmly on lighter soils. Do not compact the soil too much. Water in the plant, then mulch to retain moisture, protect new roots from frost and keep down weeds. Water regularly until the plant is established; for a tree that means for at least a year.

SIZE AND RATE OF GROWTH

The approximate size of each tree, shrub and conifer after ten years is given at the end of its description. Always remember that geographical situation, climate, soil conditions and pruning will affect a plant's size as well as its precise flowering times and sometimes even a plant's appearance.

HARDINESS ZONES

Though hardiness zones are generally used little in Europe and the British Isles, they are commonplace in horticultural reference works, catalogues and labels in North America. The plant hardiness zones given in the chart below are determined by the United States Department of Agriculture and are based on the average annual minimum winter temperatures for each zone. Hardiness zones are of particular relevance in the USA, where considerable variation in climate occurs across the country. In the British Isles, such variation is much less: Zone 7 covers the eastern Scottish Highlands; Zone 8 includes most of inland and eastern Britain and Ireland; and Zone 9 covers the western coastal areas of Britain and Ireland.

Each plant in the directories has been allocated a zonal range (for example, Z7-9) within which it is most likely to thrive. However, these zones can give only an approximate indication of appropriate climate for the plants listed. Within any one zone several local microclimates can occur, and other factors, such as site, aspect and soil, may also affect a plant's growth. Heat and humidity are other factors affecting a plant's performance, and the protection afforded by, for example, sunny walls, provides an exception to every rule. Please use the hardiness zones as a guideline only.

HARDINESS ZONES

Zone	Range of temperatures
1	Below -45°C/-50°F
2	-45° to -39°C/-50° to -40°
3	-39° to -35°C/-40° to -30°F
4	-35° to -29°C/-30° to -20°F
5	-29° to -23°C/-20° to -10°F
6	-23° to -18°C/-10° to 0°F
7	-18° to -12°C/0° to 10°F
8	-12° to -6°C/10° to 20°F
9	-6° to -1°C/20° to 30°F
10	-1° to 4°C/30° to 40°F
11	Above 4°C/40°F

KEY TO SYMBOLS

☼	full sun
❋	semi-shade
✳	shade
◻	dry soil
◪	moist soil
■	well-drained soil
⊖	alkaline soil
⊕	acid soil
☆	most soils
✫	fertile soil
★	humus-rich soil

TREES DIRECTORY

MANY GARDENERS ARE HESITANT TO PLANT TREES, particularly if their garden is small – but there are many small trees which can provide foliage, flower, bark or catkins to enhance rather than take over the garden. In warmer climates trees provide some shade in summer. In spacious plots trees help to provide the garden's structure and framework, furnishing a backcloth to other plants. Many trees can be pruned to keep them within the limits required – but this is a subject for another book! The selection made here is primarily for late spring and summer colour.

Planting trees
Make the planting hole two or three times the width and depth of the rootball; on heavy soils break up the clay at the bottom to avoid possible waterlogging. Provide a sturdy stake for anything over 90cm/3ft and use proper tree ties. Leave a circular ridge of soil just beyond the circumference of the rootball and fill with a good mulch.

H: Approximate height after 10 years
W: Approximate width after 10 years
F: Months usually in flower
Z: Relevant suggested hardiness zone(s) – see page 80

Cornus controversa 'Variegata'

ACER Maple

Deciduous. For further selections and more detail see Shrubs Directory, page 84.

A. griseum Paperbark maple. Year-round interest. With age, slowly flaking bark reveals orange-brown beneath. Trifoliate green leaves, often colouring well in late autumn. H3-4m/10-13ft, W1.5-2m/5-6ft. Z5. ✿ ❋ ✳

A. hersii (syn. *A. grosseri hersii*) Snake-bark maple. Small, shapely tree for autumn colour. Smooth, grey-green, silver-streaked or marbled bark. Broadly ovate leaves. On mature specimens, pendulous greenish flowers in spring and greenish-yellow fruits in autumn. ✿ ❋ ☆ (where not too dry).

A. negundo Box elder (though not an elder). Fast growing, adaptable tree with light green, pinnate leaves. More garden worthy and slower in growth are the cultivars '**Elegans**', green with irregular bright yellow margins, '**Flamingo**' whose leaves are multi-coloured pink, cream and green, and '**Kelly's Gold**', with bright yellow foliage. All can be pruned as shrubs and grown as patio

Acer platanoides 'Princeton Gold'

specimens. All (unpruned) H5-7m/16-23ft, W4-6m/13-20ft. Z3-9. ✿ ☆

A. platanoides '**Crimson Sentry**'. A selection of the Norway maple. Narrow, columnar habit, rich crimson-purple leaves, a striking form. H5m/16ft, W75cm-1m/30in-3ft. '**Princeton Gold**', broader habit, bright yellow leaves in spring and early summer, yellow-green later. Both H6-7m/20-23ft, W4-5m/13-16ft; both Z3-8. ✿ ☆

A. pseudoplatanus

'**Brilliantissimum**'. An ornamental, slow-growing sycamore whose spring buds unfurl to reveal shrimp-pink leaves paling to cream then deepening with age to green in summer. Usually good autumn colour. H4m/13ft, W2-2.5m/6-8ft. Z4-8. ✿ ❋(in hot climates), ☆

CORNUS CONTROVERSA 'VARIEGATA'

A choice plant which slowly makes a magnificent wide, spreading tree with layered branches bearing creamy-white and green leaves. H3m/10ft, W2-3m/7-10ft. Z5-8. ✿ ❋ ✳

EUCALYPTUS Gum tree

Evergreen trees with aromatic foliage. ✿ ✳ ★

E. niphophila Snow gum. One of the hardiest and most ornamental, and one of the few eucalyptus that can be classed as a small tree. Leathery, oval, grey-green juvenile leaves become grey, narrow and lance-shaped as plant matures. Main stem usually develops a "lean", the smooth, grey-green bark flaking to reveal creamy-white, green and brown. Grown from seed, like all the gums, it is best planted as a young pot-grown plant so that early roots

establish quickly to support the rapid growth. The foliage is excellent for flower arranging and, if cut back by hand or frost, vigorous new shoots will emerge from the base. H10m/33ft, W5-6m/16-20ft. Z7-9.

FAGUS SYLVATICA Beech

Among the many forms of the common beech are some suitable for the smaller garden. They are very adaptable trees for acid or alkaline soils and some are extremely ornamental in habit and foliage. Z4-8 (dislikes extreme heat). ✿ ❋ ☆

Eucalyptus niphophila

Gleditsia triacanthos 'Sunburst'

'**Aurea Pendula**'. Though rare, this is worth looking out for, for its pendulous habit, slow early growth and golden leaves. Best in half shade when young. Train up a cane in early years. H3-4m/10-13ft, W1.5-2m/5-6ft. '**Dawyck Gold**', attractive, narrow column, leaves light yellow in spring, greeny-yellow in summer; '**Dawyck Purple**' is similar but broader in habit with dark purple foliage, making a striking accent plant. Both approx. H5-6m/16-20ft, W1-1.5m/3-5ft. '**Purpurea Pendula**', the weeping purple beech, makes a strong accent plant for a small garden. Top-grafted on a stem, it cascades downwards; its leaves fade in late summer. H usually 2-3m/6-10ft, W2m/6ft.

GLEDITSIA TRIACANTHOS 'SUNBURST'
Golden honey locust
Small to medium tree with thornless branches. Bright yellow, finely cut new leaves, older leaves green then brighter yellow again in autumn. Light, airy appearance. H5-6m/16-20ft, W3-4m/10-13ft. Z3-9. ☀ ☆

MALUS **Crab apple**
Some of the most ornamental flowering and fruiting deciduous

Malus 'Liset'

trees, including many suitable for the small garden. Flowers appear in mid- to late spring, often creating clouds of blossom and later colourful fruits. All Z5-8. ☆ (neither very dry nor very wet).
M. '**Evereste**'. Good-value small tree with large white flowers, red in bud, deep green foliage and a profusion of orange-yellow fruits in autumn.
M. floribunda. The Japanese crab makes a broad-headed small tree, its arching branches carrying red buds which open pink, fading to white, and small yellow fruits. H5-6m/16-20ft, W3-4m/10-13ft. F4-5.
M. hupehensis. Erect branching habit. Pink buds open to smother the tree in fragrant white blossom. Yellow fruits tinted red. H5-6m/16-20ft, W2-3m/6-10ft.
M. '**Liset**'. Striking small tree. Deep crimson buds open to rosy-red flowers; purple young foliage; small red fruits. H4-5m/13-16ft, W2-3m/6-10ft. F4-5.
M. '**Maypole**'. An ornamental crab for the smaller garden forming a narrow column; carmine-pink flowers, bronze foliage tints; reddish-purple crab apples, good for jelly. H5-6m/16-10ft, W30-45cm/12-18in.
M. '**Royalty**'. Wine-red flowers and

shining dark red-purple leaves make this a tree of long-term appeal, the leaves turning red in autumn. Deep red fruits. H4-5m/13-16ft, W2-3m/6-10ft. F4-5.
M. '**Van Eseltine**'. Flowering crab apple forming an excellent columnar tree. Large semi-double flowers, rose-red in bud opening pale pink; yellow fruits. H5-6m/16-20ft, W2-3m/6-10ft. F4-5.

POPULUS ALBA 'RICHARDII'
Slower growing form of the white poplar. Maple-like leaves with white undersides and bright golden-yellow upper sides – a brilliant combination, especially where wind can ruffle the foliage, giving flashes of silver and gold; green winter stems; eventually a suckering habit. Can be pruned as a shrub or small tree. H8m/26ft, W4m/13ft. Z5.

PRUNUS
Many of the cherries make excellent trees both for flower and autumn colour, though some become large in time. Plums, almonds, peaches and laurels as well as "flowering cherries" all come under this genus. Most are adaptable to a wide range of soils, including alkaline and chalk soils. The few forms listed here have been selected for flower and foliage. ☀ (preferred), ✳
P. '**Accolade**'. Though eventually too large for the smaller garden, this is a graceful, wide spreading tree with arching branchlets. Clusters of pendulous rich pink flowers, fading gradually to almost white.

Prunus 'Accolade'

Outstanding. H5-6m/16-20ft, W4-5m/13-16ft. F3-4. Z5-8.

P. 'Amanogawa'. Considered one of the most suitable for smaller gardens with its narrow columner habit, but on heavier soils attains some size. Fragrant, semi-double, light pink flowers, good autumn colour. H5-6m/16-20ft, W1-2m/3-6ft. F4-5. Z5-8.

P. cerasifera 'Pissardii'. Purple-leaved plum. White, pink-budded flowers wreathe the branches in spring; red young shoots and leaves turn deep purple in summer. Good for hedging too. H3-4m/10-13ft, W2.4-3m/8-10ft. F3-4. Z2-8.

P. 'Cheal's Weeping'. One of the most popular of weeping Japanese cherries, also known as 'Kiku-shidare Sakura'. Deep pink double flowers adorn the branches. Bronze-tinted shoots, glossy green leaves in summer. H2.4-3m/8-10ft, W2-3m/6-10ft. F4-5. Z5-8.

P. 'Mount Fuji'. Formerly known as P. 'Shirotae', a famous Japanese cherry with horizontal, slightly pendulous branches which in spring are clustered in large, fragrant snow-

Pyrus salicifolia 'Pendula'

white flowers. Distinctive. H6-7m/20-23ft, W4-5m/13-16ft. F4-5, Z4-8.

P. *padus* 'Colorata'. This form of the bird cherry has bronze-purple shoots and purplish-green leaves, contrasting elegantly with pendulous racemes of fragrant lilac-pink flowers. Leaves in summer deep green. H6-8m/20-26ft, W3-4m/10-13ft. F4-5. Z3-8.

P. 'Spire' (P. × *hillieri* 'Spire'). First-class hybrid between P. *sargentii* and P. *incisa*. Erect, vase-shaped branching habit, light pink flowers and good autumn colour. H5-6m/16-20ft, W2-3m/6-10ft. F3-4. Z4-8.

PYRUS SALICIFOLIA 'PENDULA'
Weeping form of the willow-leaf pear makes a striking accent plant, with branches sweeping to the ground, creamy-white flowers in spring and silvery-grey leaves all summer. Prunes well. H3-4m/10-13ft, W2-3m/6-10ft. F4. Z4-8. ☼ ☀ ☆

ROBINIA PSEUDOACACIA 'FRISIA'
A selected form of the false acacia with bright golden-yellow pinnate leaves all summer and into autumn. Grow as a tree or shrub; the latter will need annual pruning in spring. Prefers well drained soil. H6-7m/20-23ft, W3-4m/10-13ft. Z4-8. ☼ ■

SALIX Willow
S. *alba* 'Sericea'. Though quite a large tree if unpruned, this selection of the white willow can be kept as a small tree by annual pruning. Bright, silvery leaves shimmer in the wind. A striking foliage background plant. H7-8m/23-26ft, W3-4m/10-13ft. Z2-8. ☼ ☀ ☆

S. *exigua* Coyote willow. Graceful shrub or small tree. Long slender stems, somewhat suckering habit, narrow silvery-grey leaves. H3-4m/10-13ft, W2.1-3m/7-10ft. Z6-8.

From left to right: *Eucalyptus niphophila* x *canadensis, Populus* 'Aurea', *Fagus sylvatica* 'Dawyck Purple', *Robinia pseudoacacia* 'Frisia'.

SORBUS
Popular trees for the smaller garden. Two distinct types: the whitebeams, grown primarily for their broad green or grey leaves, and mountain ashes, grown for their fruits and

Salix alba 'Sericea'

finely cut, often showy foliage.. ☼ ■

S. *aria* 'Lutescens'. Selected form of the round-headed common whitebeam, with brighter, creamy-white upper oval leaves in spring, becoming green with white beneath. White flowers in spring, bunches of crimson fruits in late summer. Withstands wind even in coastal areas. H6-7m/20-23ft, W3-4m/10-13ft. Z5-8.

S. *aucuparia*. Mountain ash or rowan. Relatively small trees whose pinnate leaves turn tints of orange-red and yellow in autumn. White, early summer flowers are quickly followed by often heavy bunches of orange or red fruits. Many selections exist with somewhat different habits. and fruits from crimson and red to orange and yellow. H5m/16ft, W2-3m/6-10ft. F5. Z3-9.

S. *thibetica* 'John Mitchell' (syn. S. *mitchellii*). One of the most striking foliage trees; strong growing, large, silver-backed leaves, a broad head, few fruits. H7-8m/23-26ft, W3-4m/10-13ft. Z5-8.

SHRUBS DIRECTORY

SHRUBS INCLUDE BOTH DECIDUOUS AND EVERGREEN woody plants and climbers. Like trees, they provide structure in the garden and it is important to aim for a balance of shrubs in order to provide year-round interest. Luckily, many of the dwarfer shrubs provide long flowering periods or attractive foliage, so even for the smaller garden there is ample choice. Apart from their structural role, flower and foliage need to be assessed in choosing shrubs and climbers that will create late spring and summer-long appeal. The selection offered here includes some of the lesser known as well as the more popular shrubs.

Planting shrubs
Always assess the requirements of a particular plant with regard to soil and aspect prior to planting (see page 80 for cultural requirements and hardiness zones). After planting it is a good idea to mulch around newly planted shrubs, particularly shallow- or fibrous-rooted ones, and then mulch annually or every two years. Apply a general, slow-release fertilizer in spring if shrubs lack colour or vigour. Protect susceptible new shrubs from wind or frosts with close-woven or shade netting.

H: Approximate height after 10 years
W: Approximate width after 10 years
F: Months in flower
Z: Relevant hardiness zone(s)

ABELIA
Bright-foliaged evergreen or deciduous shrubs, late flowers. Best grown in a warm, sheltered position. Trim or prune as required in spring. ☼ ■ ☀
A. × grandiflora. This glossy shrub has oval, shiny green leaves and pale pink, softly fragrant flowers for many months. **'Francis Mason'** offers yellow variegated leaves and **'Gold Sport'** brighter golden-yellow foliage, the colour of both brightest in full sun. All H1.2-1.5m/4-5ft, W1.2-1.5m/4-5ft, F7-10, Z7-9. A recent introduction, **'Confettii'** promises equally striking foliage, but is a more compact plant, the leaves prettily edged cream and pink. H90-120cm/3-4ft, W90-120cm/3-4ft. F7-10. Z7-9.

ACER Maple
Most maples are trees (see page 81) but some can be considered shrubs, mostly the Japanese maples, which are outstanding for their attractive and colourful foliage and autumn colour. They are happiest on moist, neutral to acid soil though will succeed, given shelter from cold winds, if non-acid soils are thoroughly prepared with humus or leafmould. ☼ ☀ ■ ☀ ⊝
A. japonicum 'Aureum' – see **A. shirasawanum** 'Aureum'.
A. palmatum Japanese Maple. A very wide selection is available from specialists including: **'Atropurpureum'**, with rounded head and purple leaves, colouring red in autumn; **'Aureum'**, light yellow; **'Bloodgood'**, striking reddish-purple; **'Butterfly'**, erect branches, green leaves edged pink and cream; **'Trompenburg'**, purple-red, deeply lobed leaves, rounded at the margins, turn greener in summer, red in autumn. Average H1.8-3m/6-10ft, W1.5-1.8m/5-6ft. F4-5. Z5-8.
Dissectum group. Shrubby, spreading pendulous branches, fern-like leaves. **'Atropurpureum'**, **'Garnet'** and **'Inaba Shidare'** all strong purple, red in autumn;

Berberis temolaica

'Viridis', fresh green leaves. Average H1.2-1.5m/4-5ft, W1.5-2.1m/5-7ft. Z5-8. **'Linearilobum'**, green-leaved, and **'Linearilobum Atropurpureum'**, purple-leaved, form broad-headed shrubs with leaves that have widely spaced, finger-like lobes. Both H1.5-1.8m/5-6ft, W.1.5-1.8m/5-6ft. Z5-8. **'Ribesifolium'** (syn. 'Shishigashira'), very slow growing, with greenish stems and deep green, finely cut leaves, golden in autumn.
A. shirasawanum 'Aureum' (syn. *A. japonicum* 'Aureum'). Very slow growing, with bright yellow leaves all summer, which can scorch in full sun. H1.2-1.5m/4-5ft, W90-120cm/3-4ft. F4-5. Z6-8.

ACTINIDIA KOLOMIKTA
Striking foliage climber for walls, pergolas or through shrubs, its oval leaves are irregularly splashed with white and pink. Small, white, scented flowers. Deciduous. H3-4m/10-13ft, W3-4m/10-13ft. F6. Z5-9. ☼ ☀

AESCULUS PARVIFLORA
Bottlebrush buckeye
Spreading deciduous shrub, whose erect stems make a rounded dome. It has light green leaves and candle-like heads of white flowers in summer. H2.4-3m/8-10ft, W2.4-3m/8-10ft. F7-8. Z5-9. ☼ ☀ ☆

AKEBIA QUINATA
Vigorous semi-evergreen twining climber. Five-fingered leaves, clusters of scented chocolate-purple flowers in spring; after hot summers, sausage-shaped purplish fruits appear in autumn. H.6-7m/20-23ft, W6-7m/20-23ft. F3-5. Z5-9. ☼ ☀ ☆

Acer palmatum 'Aureum'

Berberis thunbergii 'Bagatelle'

Buddleja globosa

ARTEMESIA

Silver- or grey-leaved shrubs revel in full sun with good drainage. *A.* 'Powis Castle' is particularly recommended, with its non-flowering mound of finely cut silver-grey foliage, semi-evergreen in mild localities. H90-120cm/3-4ft, W90-120cm/3-4ft. Z5-8. ☼ ☆

BERBERIS

A wide range of deciduous and evergreen adaptable shrubs, many with coloured foliage as well as showy flowers and fruits; some very thorny. Most withstand pruning. ☼ ☆

B. darwinii. Popular evergreen shrub with arching branches, dark green leaves, racemes of orange-yellow flowers in late spring, sometimes again in autumn, and plum-coloured fruits. Prune if required after early flowering. H1.5-2.1m/5-7ft, W1.2-1.5m/4-5ft. F4-5. Z7-9.

B. × *stenophylla*. Three distinct selections are all excellent: 'Corallina Compacta', an underrated dwarf shrub with coral-red buds, deep orange flowers. H30-45cm/12-18in, W60-75cm/24-30in. F4-5. 'Cream Showers', vigorous, arching branches, dark green leaves, creamy-white bell-like flowers. Prune after flowering. H1.5-1.8m/5-6ft, W1.5-1.8m/5-6ft. F4-5. Z6-9. 'Etna', dense, medium-sized shrub with green-bronze leaves, red buds, orange flowers. H90-120cm/3-4ft, W90cm/3ft. F4-5. Z6-9.

B. temolaica. A superb flowering and foliage plant with large, striking blue-grey leaves and vigorous growth. Difficult to find and to propagate. Keep compact by pruning away one-third of stems in spring. H2.4-3m/8-10ft, W1.5-2.1m/5-7ft. F5. Z7-9.

B. thunbergii. The biggest group of cultivars come from this hardy Chinese deciduous species, all thorny; foliage colours of purple, red, green, yellow, some variegated. Except where indicated, all H1.5-1.8m/5-6ft, W1.2-1.5m/4-5ft. F4-5. Z5-8. Purple-leaved forms need sun to colour well but not too much. 'Atropurpurea', arching branches, red-purple leaves, free fruiting, with good autumn colour. 'Atropurpurea Nana' (syn. 'Crimson Pygmy', 'Little Favourite'), with congested branches, compact habit, dark purple leaves. H45cm/18in, W45cm/18in. 'Aurea', a first-class contrast plant, with bright yellow leaves in spring and summer, yellow-green in shade; can scorch by late

summer. H60-75cm/2-3ft, W60-75cm/2-3ft. 'Bagatelle', dense dwarf bush with small purple leaves, copper-red new shoots, rounded habit; ideal with dwarf shrubs or alpines. H30cm/12in, W30-45cm/12-18in. 'Bonanza Gold', dwarf golden-leaved selection to match 'Atropurpurea Nana', yellow leaves, tinged red in summer. H30-45cm/12-18in, W45-60cm/18-24in. 'Dart's Red Lady', excellent contrast shrub with dark, glossy purple leaves, broad habit, good autumn colour. H60-75cm/24-30in, W75-90cm/30-36in. 'Helmond Pillar', an erect form, narrow when young, vase-shaped when older, with deep purple leaves. H1.2-1.5m/4-5ft, W30-45cm/12-18in. 'Rose Glow', similar to 'Atropurpurea' but new summer growth attractively mottled and splashed with cream and pink; 'Harlequin' is similar.

BUDDLEJA Butterfly bush

Free-flowering shrubs, mostly deciduous in cool, temperate climates. Many hybrids are renowned for their summer colour and attractiveness to bees and butterflies. Prune annually in early spring to 30cm/12in from the ground to produce strong flowering shoots. Wide variety, some growing quite large. ☆ where not too wet.

B. davidii. Cultivars have fragrant flowers. All F7-9. Z5-9. 'Black Knight', erect habit, with deep violet-blue trusses. H2.4m/8ft, W2.4m/8ft. 'Dartmoor', striking form with arching branches, large panicles of magenta flowers. H2.4m/8ft, W2.4m/8ft. 'Harlequin', creamy variegated leaves contrast with purple-red flowers. H1.2-1.5m/4-5ft, W1.2-1.5m/4-5ft. Var. *nanhoensis alba*, 'Nanho Blue' and 'Nanho Purple' are all small-leaved, dwarfer in habit with arching branches and give a succession of flowers. All H1.2-

1.5m/4-5ft, W1.2-1.5m/4-5ft. 'Pink Delight', excellent compact selection with large lilac-pink flowers. H1.8-2.1m/6-7ft, W1.8-2.1m/6-7ft. 'Royal Red', compact habit, purple-red flowers. H1.8m/6ft, W1.8m/6ft. *B. globosa*. Unusual early-summer-flowering species with rounded heads of orange-yellow flowers. Prune after flowering. H2.4-3m/8-10ft, W2.4-3m/8-10ft.

BUXUS

Adaptable slow-growing, small-leaved evergreen shrubs, often used for topiary. All withstand clipping well. Many introductions, some dwarf and compact, others upright, some pendulous. Ideal for containers and formal dwarf hedges. Some have colourful variegated leaves. ☼ ☀ ☆ *B. sempervirens* 'Elegantissima'. A selection with green and creamy-white variegated leaves, fits well with other plants. H45-60cm/18-24in, W45-60cm/18-24in (eventually much more). Z7-8.

CALLUNA – *see* HEATHS AND HEATHERS

CARPENTERIA Tree anemone
C. californica. A delightful evergreen shrub for milder climates, often

Caryopteris × clandonensis 'Heavenly Blue'

grown as a wall shrub. Pure white, saucer-shaped flowers with yellow anthers produced in summer on old wood. H2.1m/7ft, W1.8m/6ft. F7-8. Z8-9. ✿ ■ ☆

CARYOPTERIS Bluebeard, blue spiraea

Aromatic, deciduous, mostly dwarf or low-growing shrubs. Bright blue flowers produced in late summer. Prune each spring to 10-15cm/4-6in from the ground. In cold climates, grow against a wall facing the sun. Plant in spring. ✿ ■

C. × clandonensis. 'Arthur Simmonds', hybrid with grey-green leaves, profuse bright blue flowers. 'Heavenly Blue', more compact, with deep blue flowers. 'Worcester

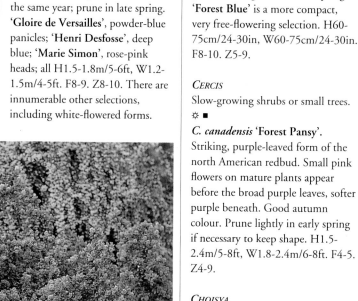

Ceanothus 'Blue Mound'

Gold', greenish-gold leaves, bright blue flowers, less hardy. All H60-75cm/24-30in, W60-75cm/24-30in. F8-9. Z6-9.

CEANOTHUS

Popular evergreen and deciduous shrubs, some quite tender, often used as wall shrubs. Good seaside plants but need shelter from cold winds and frost. The evergreens are mostly spring-flowering and less hardy than the deciduous summer-flowering forms. Best planted in spring. Prune larger spring-flowering evergreens after flowering but not into old wood. ✿ ■

C. 'Autumnal Blue'. Glossy evergreen leaves, deep blue flowers, quite hardy. H1.5-1.8m/5-6ft, W1.5-1.8m/5-6ft. F8-9. Z8-10.

C. 'Blue Mound', evergreen mound of small, shiny leaves, light blue flowers. H60-75cm/24-30in, W60-90cm/2-3ft. F5. Z8-10.

C. delinianus. Deciduous French hybrids, flowering on wood made in the same year; prune in late spring. 'Gloire de Versailles', powder-blue panicles; 'Henri Desfosse', deep blue; 'Marie Simon', rose-pink heads; all H1.5-1.8m/5-6ft, W1.2-1.5m/4-5ft. F8-9. Z8-10. There are innumerable other selections, including white-flowered forms.

Cercis canadensis

CERATOSTIGMA Hardy plumbago

The two species listed behave like perennials in cool, temperate climates. Both late-flowering, bright blue, periwinkle-like flowers. ✿ ■

C. plumbaginoides. Dwarf, spreading, with leaves that turn reddish in autumn, contrasting with blue flowers. H15-20cm/6-8in, W30cm/1ft. F7-9. Z5-8.

C. willmottianum. Twiggy, upright stems, bright deep blue flowers; prune to the ground in late spring. 'Forest Blue' is a more compact, very free-flowering selection. H60-75cm/24-30in, W60-75cm/24-30in. F8-10. Z5-9.

CERCIS

Slow-growing shrubs or small trees. ✿ ■

C. canadensis 'Forest Pansy'. Striking, purple-leaved form of the north American redbud. Small pink flowers on mature plants appear before the broad purple leaves, softer purple beneath. Good autumn colour. Prune lightly in early spring if necessary to keep shape. H1.5-2.4m/5-8ft, W1.8-2.4m/6-8ft. F4-5. Z4-9.

CHOISYA

Evergreen shrubs with glossy leaves. ✿ ❂ ☆

C. 'Aztec Pearl'. Free-flowering evergreen hybrid with narrow aromatic leaves; pink buds open to

appealing display of fragrant white flowers late spring/early summer, sometimes again in late summer. H1.5-1.8m/5-6ft, W1.2-1.5m/4-5ft. F5-6. Z7-9.

C. ternata Mexican orange blossom. Popular evergreen shrub, bright green leaves, makes a rounded bush. White fragrant flowers. Prune lightly after flowering, though will take harder pruning in early spring. H1.5-1.8m/5-6ft, W1.2-1.5m/4-5ft. F5-6. Z7-9. 'Sundance', a popular selection with bold yellow leaves, ideal for patio containers. Slightly less hardy; foliage not so bright in less sun. H1.2-1.5m/4-5ft, W1.2-1.5m/4-5ft. F5-6. Z7-9.

CISTUS

A group of evergreens from the mediterranean regions, splashy in flower and needing sun and good drainage for longevity. Many are tender, but provide bright, colourful single rose-type flowers in summer. These are mostly white, pink or purple, often with contrasting patches on the inside of the papery petals, and yellow stamens. Grey or green leaves. Sometimes short-lived, not breaking easily from old wood. Many species and varieties available, including two closely related genera, *Halimium* and *Halimiocistus*. Plant

Choisya 'Aztec Pearl'

Clematis 'Jackmanii Superba'

in late spring or early summer. F6-7. Z7-9. ✿ ■

CLEMATIS

Indispensible climbers for spring and summer colour for use on pergolas, walls, fences, up into trees, over shrubs or as container plants. Best if roots are shaded, and planted with well rotted compost. ✿ ☆

C. alpina. Perfect for walls and fences, masses of pendant flowers in early summer, followed by silky seedheads. Little or no pruning needed. Named forms include **'Columbine'**, pale blue, **'Pamela Jackman'**, mid-blue, **'Ruby'**, purple-pink, **'White Moth'**, double white. All H2.4m/8ft, W1.8-2.4m/6-8ft. F4-5. Z5-9.

C. macropetala. Related, but more vigorous than *C. alpina*. Light green divided leaves, nodding lavender-blue flowers, attractive seedheads. ✿ ☆. **'Markham's Pink'**, rose-pink and **'White Swan'**, white, widen the choice. All H3m/10ft, W3m/10ft. F5-6. Z5-9.

C. montana. Vigorous species for climbing up walls or trees, flowers white to deep pink, ✿ ☆ roots preferring moisture. **'Alexander'**, fragrant white flowers, yellow stamens; **'Elizabeth'**, pale pink, heady fragrance; **'Marjorie'**, creamy-pink, semi-double flowers; **'Tetrarose'**, bronze foliage, large

rose-pink flowers. No pruning needed except to control size. H10m/33ft, W10m/33ft. F5-6. Z6-9.

C. orientalis. Vigorous scrambler or climber with finely dissected leaves, fragrant yellow pendant flowers for weeks, fluffy seedheads. Larger-flowered selection, **'Bill Mackenzie'**, is outstanding. Almost identical is the species *C. tangutica*. All if required can be pruned back in early spring, but not necessary for flowering. All H5-6m/16-20ft, W5-6m/16-20ft. F7-9. Z6-9.

C. viticella. Species variable but excellent for scrambling over fences, through shrubs and up trees. Prune in early spring only if required. Abundance of nodding wine-red, dark-veined flowers, **'Alba Luxurians'**, white, flushed mauve, green markings; **'Etoile Violette'**, violet with yellow anthers; **'Kermesina'**, deep red-purple; **'Polish Spirit'**, velvety purple-violet; **'Purpurea Plena Elegans'**, nodding double violet flowers. All H3m/10ft, W3m/10ft. F7-9. Z5-9.

Large-flowered hybrids. In general the spread is roughly the same as the height. A great choice exists but ten recommendations follow. All Z4-9. **'Ascotiensis'**, bright blue, green stamens, H3m/10ft. F7-9. **'Daniel Deronda'**, free-flowering with large, purple-blue semi-double and single

flowers, good seedheads. H2.4m/8ft. F6. **'Dr. Ruppel'**, deep rose-pink flowers, darker bar. H2.4m/8ft. F6. **'Duchess of Edinburgh'**, large double white, scented flowers. H2.4m/8ft. F6-7. **'Jackmanii Superba'**, rich purple flowers, reliable performer. H3m/10ft. F8. **'Marie Boisselot'**, excellent large white flowers, long season. H3m/10ft. F6-7. **'Mrs Cholmondeley'**, free-flowering, with lavender-blue flowers, good seedheads. H2.4m/8ft. F6-8. **'Mrs. N. Thompson'**, blue with red bar, striking. H2.4m/8ft. F6-7. **'Niobe'**, ruby-red, velvety flowers, long season. H3m/10ft. F6-8. **'Will Goodwin'**, attractive pale blue flowers, long season. H3m/10ft. F6-8.

CLETHRA

Acid-loving, mostly deciduous shrubs bearing fragrant flowers in late summer. Best in hot summers. ✿ ❋ ☆

C. alnifolia Sweet pepper bush. Erect branches, bottlebrush heads of fragrant white flowers. **'Paniculata'** has larger panicles, **'Pink Spire'** and **'Rosea'** both pink fading to white. All H1.5-1.8m/5-6ft, W90-120cm/3-4ft. F8-9. Z4-9.

COLUTEA ARBORESCENS Bladder senna

Underrated shrub, member of the

Clematis tangutica

pea family, ✿ ❋ ■ Small yellow flowers all summer continue as green bladder-like pods develop.

C. × *media* **'Copper Beauty'**. Bluish-green leaves, copper-orange flowers. Both H1.8-2.4m/6-8ft, W1.8-2.4m/6-8ft. F7-9. Z6-8.

CORNUS Dogwood

Deciduous shrubs attractive for their summer foliage, flowers and winter stems.

C. alba Red-barked dogwood. These plants have year-round appeal. All have white flowers and bluish-white fruits on the second-year wood. **'Aurea'** is first-class, with golden leaves all summer, good red twigs in

Cornus alba 'Aurea'

winter; **'Elegantissima'**, grey-green leaves splashed with silvery-white and maroon stems; **'Kesselringii'**, dark purple-green shoots, deep green leaves, purple-black winter stems; **'Sibirica Variegata'**, small, dark green leaves, cream margins, deep red stems. **'Spaethii'**, golden variegated leaves. Prune all for best stem colour in early spring. H1.5-2.4m/5-8ft, W1.5-2.4m/5-8ft (without pruning). F5-6. Z3-9.

C. alternifolia **'Argentea'**. A choice shrub or small tree. Layered purplish, twiggy branches covered in small, white-variegated, light green leaves. Needs shelter. H1.5-2.4m/5-8ft, W1.5-2.4m/5-8ft. F5-6. Z5-8. ☼ ◣

C. florida Flowering dogwood. Slow-growing shrubs and small trees. Seldom performs as well in Europe as in its native North America where flowers or bracts of white, pink and red make a spectacular show in late spring or early summer. **'Rainbow'** has bright golden-yellow and green variegated leaves, which have longer appeal. H1.8-2.4m/6-8ft, W1.8-2.4m/6-8ft. F5. Z5-9. ☼ ✹ ⊝

C. mas **'Variegata'** Cornelian cherry. This selection is an excellent, though little-known, slow-growing shrub with striking white and green summer foliage. Bare stems covered with tiny yellow flowers in early spring, red fruits in autumn. H1.5-1.8m/5-6ft, W1.2-1.5m/4-5ft. F2. Z6-9. ☼ ✹ ☆

C. stolonifera (syn. *C. sericea*). Closely related to *C. alba*, with similar habit and requirements. Two good selections offer colourful summer foliage: **'Kelsey Gold'**, a sport on the green-leaved **'Kelsey's Dwarf'**, has bright yellow leaves, dwarf habit. H45-60cm/18-24in, W60-90cm/2-3ft. Z3-8. **'White Gold'** has yellow winter stems, green and golden-yellow leaves which turn

Cytisus battandieri

creamy-white. H1.5-1.8m/5-6ft, W1.5m/5ft. F5-6. Z3-8.

CORYLUS **Hazel**
Large deciduous shrubs or small trees, easy to grow in most soils. Two or three are worth growing for their striking colourful foliage.
C. avellana **'Aurea'**. Dense bush with large round or oval leaves, bright yellow throughout the summer. Long yellow male catkins on older plants in late winter. H3-4.5m/10-15ft, W3-4.5m/10-15ft. F2-3. Z5-9.
C. maxima **'Purpurea'**. Bold, deep purple leaves on vigorous, erectly branching bush; colour fades to green in hot climates. Purplish catkins. H3-4.5m/10-15ft, W3-4.5m/10-15ft. F2-3. Z5-8.
'Te Terra Red' is a more dwarf form with smaller reddish-purple leaves. H1.5-1.8m/5-6ft, W1.2-1.5m/4-5ft. Z5-8. ☼

COTINUS **Smoke bush, Venetian sumach**
Several selections of these deciduous shrubs are outstanding for summer foliage as well as for fluffy, plumed, beige-pink panicles which turn smokey-grey in late summer. Prune lightly in late spring; severe pruning will lose the season's flowers. ☼ ☆ ■

Cotinus 'Grace'

C. coggygria. **'Foliis Purpureis'**, **'Notcutt's Variety'** and **'Royal Purple'** are all purple-leaved selections providing summer-long colour, though the purple effect diminishes in hot summers. Reddish-purple and crimson autumn tints. All H2.4-3m/8-10ft, W2.4-3m/8-10ft. F7-8. Z5-9.
C. **'Grace'**. Strong-growing hybrid with large purple-red leaves, good autumn colour, imposing pinkish inflorescences. H3-5m/10-16ft, W3m/10ft. F7-8. Z5-9.

COTONEASTER
Large group of deciduous and evergreen shrubs and small trees. While attractive in summer for their small white flowers, most are grown for their late summer and autumn displays of fruits varying from crimson to scarlet-orange and yellow, even to pink. Some have attractive silver-backed leaves. One of the best is *C. horizontalis* **'Variegata'** which seldom fruits, but makes up for it with small green cream-edged leaves with pink tinges in autumn. Good for a wall or a bank. H60-75cm/24-30in, W1.2-1.5m/4-5ft. F6-7. Z5-8.

CYTISUS **Broom**
Easily grown, sun-loving members of

the pea family with narrow, evergreen stems and leaves. Most species are yellow-flowered, in late spring and early summer, but there is a wide range of colours in selected cultivars. Prune with a sharp knife if necessary immediately after flowering, but not into old wood. ☼ ■

C. ardoinii. Showy dwarf, smothered in creamy-white flowers. H30cm/12in, W60-90cm/2-3ft. F5-6. Z6-8.
C. battandieri. Morocco Broom is quite distinct, with silvery-grey oval leaves and bottlebrush heads of golden-yellow, pineapple-scented flowers. Train against a wall or as a freestanding shrub. Trim regularly after flowering. Needs a warm, sheltered position. H3-5m/10-16ft, W2.4-3m/8-10ft. F7. Z8-9.
C. praecox Warminster broom. Compact, free-flowering species, with creamy-yellow flowers. **'Albus'**, taller, white; **'Frisia'**, striking, with white-pink, lilac, yellow and brown flowers; **'Hollandia'**, showy cream and cerise blooms. All H1.2-1.8m/4-6ft, W1.2-1.5m/4-5ft. F4-5. Z6-9.
C. scoparius Common broom. Though it looks evergreen from the appearance of its green stems, this yellow-flowered species is deciduous.

Daphne burkwoodii 'Somerset Gold Edge'

Deutzia × *hybrida* 'Strawberry Fields'

Many selections include: 'Andreanus', large yellow and brown pea flowers; 'Burkwoodii', red, brown and yellow; 'Goldfinch', crimson, pink and yellow; 'Killiney Red', brightest red; 'Windlesham Ruby', popular carmine-red. All H1.5-1.8m/5-6ft, W1.2-1.5m/4-5ft. F6. Z7-9.

Hybrids. Some of the best for the smaller garden include: 'Compact Crimson', broadly spreading, with rich crimson flowers, H90-120cm/3-4ft, W90-120cm/3-4ft. F5-6. Z7-9; 'Dukaat', bushy, upright habit, bicolor gold and creamy-white, H45-60cm/18-24in, W30-45cm/12-18in. F5-6. Z7-9; 'Lena', spectacular crimson and yellow, contrasting with dark green foliage, H90-120cm/3-4ft, W60-90cm/2-3ft. F5-6. Z7-9.

DAPHNE
Choice fragrant shrubs, deciduous and evergreen. Contains both dwarf, prostrate and taller growing shrubs, some flowering in late winter/early spring, most in late spring/early summer. Berries are poisonous. Most prefer good drainage but not extremes of wet or dry. Of many choice species the easiest are: *D.* × *burkwoodii* 'Carol Mackie', 'Somerset Variegated', 'Somerset Gold Edge' and 'Astrid', all with

variegated leaves which follow the fragrant white, suffused pink, flowers. All H90-120cm/3-4ft, W90-120cm/3-4ft. F5-6. Z5-9. ☀ ◧ ■

DEUTZIA
Deciduous shrubs, showy in flower but mostly dull for the rest of the summer. Easy to grow. Prune immediately after flowering if necessary, thin out old stems in winter. ☀ ☀ ☆ ■

D. crenata 'Nikko'. Pleasing dwarf shrub, with clusters of white flowers. H45-60cm/18-24in, W60-90cm/2-3ft. F5-6. Z5-8.

D. × *elegantissima* 'Rosealind' (syn. *D.* × *hybrida* 'Rosea Plena'). Excellent broadly spreading shrub, with arching branches laden with carmine-red and pink scented flowers. H90-120cm/3-4ft, W1.2-1.5m/4-5ft. F6-7. Z6-8.

D. × *hybrida*. 'Magicien', vigorous, erect shrub with purple-red buds opening to carmine-pink flowers with white-edged petals. 'Mont Rose', clear pink, starry flowers; 'Pink Pompon', with arching branches, rounded clusters of double pink flowers, fading to white. 'Strawberry Fields', large flowers, with crimson outside petals, white, suffused pink, inside. All H1.8-

2.4m/6-8ft, W1.5-1.8m/5-6ft. F6-7. Z6-9.

D. scabra. Vigorous upright species with erect white flower clusters on narrow spikes, peeling bark on old plants. 'Candidissima', double white, 'Pride of Rochester', rosy-pink outer petals, white inside. All H1.8-2.4m/6-8ft, W1.5-1.8m/5-6ft. F6-7. Z5-8.

ERICA – see HEATHS AND HEATHERS

ESCALLONIA
Colourful shrubs originating from South America. Evergreen in warmer coastal or mild localities, deciduous in colder areas. Excellent near coasts. Glossy green leaves, usually masses of small tubular flowers lasting for weeks from early summer. Many selections, most flowering on previous year's wood. Most F6-8. All Z8-9. ☀ ☀ ☆

E. 'Apple Blossom'. Free-flowering,

Escallonia 'Apple Blossom'

Exochorda macrantha 'The Bride'

with glossy leaves, mostly single pink, white-eyed flowers. H1.5-1.8m/5-6ft, W1.2-1.5m/4-5ft. F7-9. 'Donard Brilliance', large-leaved, vigorous shrub with profuse, rich crimson flowers. H1.5-1.8m/5-6ft, W1.2-1.5m/4-5ft. 'Donard Radiance', bushy habit, rosy-pink flowers. H1.2-1.5m/4-5ft, W1.5-1.8m/5-6ft. 'Gwendolyn Anley', hardier variety with small leaves, masses of small, shell-pink flowers and a spreading habit. H60-90cm/2-3ft, W60-90cm/2-3ft.
E. laevis. 'Gold Brian', large, golden

Fremontodendron californicum

leaves draw the eye, making a dramatic background to rosy-red flowers. H60-75cm/2ft 6in, W60-90cm/2-3ft. 'Red Elf', a compact, upright shrub with glossy green leaves and crimson flowers. H90-120cm/3-4ft, W90-120cm/3-4ft. F6-9.

EUONYMUS
Some evergreen selections of these hardy shrubs, particularly those with variegated leaves, offer year-round colour. Very adaptable as to soils, including chalk. Some are grown as ground cover and climbers. ✿ ❋ ❋☆
E. fortunei. Many selections and species have green foliage, but the year-round colour of 'Emerald Gaiety' cannot be bettered, with green and white margined leaves, and of 'Emerald 'n Gold', with green and gold leaves, pinkish-tinged in winter, and bright gold new shoots. Both will climb into other plants or up trees and walls, given a little encouragement. Prune in late spring if required. H60-75cm/2ft-2ft 6in, W90-120cm/3-4ft. Z5-9.

EXOCHORDA Pearlbush
Deciduous shrubs, striking in flower.
E. macrantha. 'The Bride' is the outstanding selection, a broad, spreading pendulous bush covered in pure white flowers in late spring/early summer. H1.2-1.5m/4-5ft, W1.5-1.8m/5-6ft. F5. Z5-8. ✿ ❋ ☆

FOTHERGILLA
Early-flowering, acid-loving shrubs worth including for their autumn colour too. Honey-scented bottlebrush flowers are borne on bare branches in late spring and early summer.
F. gardenii (syn. *F. alnifolia*). Dwarf, twiggy stems and small, fragrant, white bottlebrush flowers. Dull green, oval summer leaves turn yellow, orange and fiery red in

autumn. H45-60cm/18-24in, W45-60cm/18-24in. F5. Z5-9.
F. major (syn. *F. monticola*). Erect, picturesque shrub, variable in habit, which can reach 3m/10ft. Congested branches, small, white scented, cylindrical flowers. Most have yellow, orange and crimson autumn colour, sometimes on the same leaf. H90-120cm/3-4ft, W75-90cm/30-36in. F5. Z5-9.

FREMONTODENDRON CALIFORNICUM
Often listed as a climber, this spectacular Californian evergreen or semi-evergreen shrub needs a sunny south or west wall, sheltered from cold winds. Vigorous growth, with light brown, woolly branches and shiny green, lobed leaves, their undersides covered in hairs. Large, golden-yellow, saucer-shaped flowers continue for months. Tie or train against a wall and prune regularly to shorten outward growth. Selections to look for are 'California Glory' and 'Pacific Sunset'. H3-5m/10-16ft, W2.1-3m/7-10ft. F6-9. Z8-10. ✿ ■

FUCHSIA
Of this vast group of shrubs, small trees and climbers, only "hardy fuchsias" are listed below. The long-flowering shrubs, some with colourful gold or variegated leaves, all give a display of pendulous flowers for several months and are ideal for containers as well as in the garden. Deciduous, except in mild localities, they make excellent seaside plants. Cut old wood to the ground in spring. All Z8-10. ✿ ◢ ■
F. magellanica. Dwarfer selections, most having arching stems and long, narrow flowers, with scarlet sepals and purple petals. 'Aurea', bushy and spreading, has deep yellow leaves and red flowers. H90-120cm/3-4ft, W90-120cm/3-4ft. F6-10. 'Pumila', dainty dwarf, with crimson and purple flowers.

Genista pilosa 'Lemon Spreader'

H30cm/1ft, W30cm/1ft. F6-10. 'Versicolor', grey-green leaves, flushed pink, and creamy-white, purple and red flowers. H90-120cm/3-4ft, W90-120cm/3-4ft. F6-10.
Hybrids. There are innumerable hardy hybrids. Recommendations include: 'Alice Hoffman', bushy, purple-tinged foliage, white petals, rosy-red calyx. H90-120cm/3-4ft, W90-120cm/3-4ft. F6-10. 'Chillerton Beauty', pale pink and purple. H1.2-1.5m/4-5ft, W90-120cm/3-4ft. F6-10. 'Dollar Princess', free-flowering, double purple and cerise. H75-90cm/30-36in, W60-75cm/24-30in. F5-10. 'Genii', golden-yellow leaves in sun, small red and purple flowers. H90-120cm/3-4ft, W90-120cm/3-4ft. F6-10. 'Madame Cornelissen', bushy, semi-double white and scarlet. H1.2-1.5m/4-5ft, W1.2-1.5m/4-5ft. F6-10. 'Mrs. Popple', one of the hardiest, masses of crimson and violet blooms. H1.2-1.5m/4-5ft, W1.2-1.5m/4-5ft. F6-10. 'Tom Thumb', a true dwarf, bushy, with crimson and purple flowers. H30-45cm/12-18in, W30-45cm/12-18in. F6-10.

Calluna vulgaris 'Dark Beauty'

Daboecia cantabrica

GENISTA Broom

Sharing the same common name as *Cytisus*, to which they are closely related. All have yellow blooms and can be very showy. Tolerate a wide range of soils, preferring ☼ ■
G. aetnensis Mount Etna broom. Eventually a large shrub or small tree, with wispy, pendulous branches. A good background shrub with golden-yellow flowers for many weeks in summer. Prune, only if necessary, after flowering but not into old wood. H3m/10ft, W3m/10ft. F7-8. Z9-10.
G. lydia. Dense, twiggy bush with slender green stems swathed in small, bright yellow flowers in early summer. H45-60cm/18-24in, W90-120cm/3-4ft. F6. Z7-9.
G. pilosa. Prostrate, deciduous bush which looks evergreen. Best selections are '**Lemon Spreader**' and the more compact and ground-hugging '**Vancouver Gold**', covered in sheets of golden-yellow flowers in early summer. Excellent on banks or over walls. Both H15-30cm/6-12in, W1.2-1.5m/4-5ft. F6. Z6-8.

HALIMIOCISTUS and HALIMIUM – see CISTUS

HEATHS and HEATHERS

I have put both these groups of shrubs together for easy reference and because they associate so well together. Where they can be grown successfully they offer year-round colour from both flower and foliage. Acid soil is required for the majority of summer-flowering types, but there are many lime-tolerant winter-flowering ones that also have colourful foliage in summer. Heaths (*Erica*) and heathers (*Calluna vulgaris*) grow well in cooler temperate or alpine regions, but resent cold, drying winter winds as well as high heat and humidity. Best planted in groups, but a wide range can offer flower almost every month of the year. They can be used on their own, in foreground groups to shrubs or conifers, or with ornamental grasses. Well over 500 cultivars are currently in cultivation, and wider selections can be obtained from specialists. Those recommended below are primarily for summer colour. As a guide to planting densities, the approximate width or spread of heathers after only 3-4 years' growth are given, after which time the plants will have

carpeted together. All do best on well-drained but moisture-retentive soil, responding well to a surface mulch of composted bark.

CALLUNA Common heather, ling

C. vulgaris. Hundreds of cultivars of this heathland plant offer an amazing range of colours, shapes and sizes. Prune all except the dwarfest and very prostrate types in early to mid-spring, before growth really begins. All flowers are single unless otherwise stated. All Z5-7. ☼ ⊖
'**Allegro**', a profusion of deep red flowers, with dark green foliage. H45-60cm/18-24in, W45cm/18in. F8-10. '**Anne Marie**', bushy habit, dark green foliage; flowers open bright pink, gradually deepening to brilliant carmine-rose. H23-30cm/9-12in, W45cm/18in. F8-11. '**Beoley Gold**', one of the best yellow-foliaged cultivars, with bushy year-round foliage, contrasting with white flowers. H30-45cm/12-18in, W45cm/18in. F8-9. '**Boskoop**', superb, dense, feathery foliage, golden-orange in summer, bronze-red in winter; light mauve-purple flowers. H30-45cm/12-18in, W45cm/18in. F8-9. '**Dark Beauty**', compact, bushy plant with dark green foliage, bright crimson flowers over a long period in autumn. H30cm/12in, W30-45cm/12-18in. F8-10. '**H.E. Beale**', vigorous, with strong, erect spikes of soft, double silver-pink flowers lasting for weeks. H30-45cm/12-18in, W50cm/20in. F9-11. '**Robert Chapman**', foliage changes from gold to yellow, orange to bronze and red; lower winter temperatures enhance the colour intensity; purple flowers. H30-45cm/12-18in, W45cm/18in. F8-9. '**Sir John Charrington**', arguably the best foliage cultivar, compact and bushy, with golden-yellow summer foliage, orange with bright red and crimson tips in winter; excellent in bloom, with short spikes of crimson

flowers. H30-45cm/12-18in, W40cm/16in. F8-9.

DABOECIA Irish bell heather

Summer-flowering, needs acid soil. ☼ ❋ ◪ ⊖
D. cantabrica. Long flowering period, glossy green leaves and bell-shaped flowers. Resent drought almost as much as severe frost, but where they can be grown offer a contrast to other heathers. Many cultivars available from specialists; stronger-growing ones can get straggly with age and should be pruned each year, either lightly once the flowers have finished in late autumn, then more severely in spring, or all in spring. All Z7-9.
'**Atropurpurea**', one of the hardiest and most reliable, with bronze-green leaves, rich purple flowers. H60cm/2ft, W50cm/20in. F6-10. '**Snowdrift**', bright green foliage, masses of white bell flowers; '**Alba**' is similar. Both H45cm/18in, W45cm/18in. F6-10.
D. × *scotica* '**William Buchanan**'. One of several dwarf hybrids between *D. azorica* and *D. cantabrica*. Glossy green leaves, masses of crimson flowers. One of

Erica cinerea 'Rock Pool'

the hardiest cultivars. H30cm/1ft, W30cm/1ft. F5-10. Z7.

ERICA Heath

E. carnea (syn. *E. herbacea*). Winter heaths are among the most valuable garden plants. Most cultivars are low-growing with a bushy or spreading habit, and flower from late autumn to late spring, some lasting several months. Very few need pruning, except to prevent spreading into other plants or to tidy them occasionally. Those listed below have colourful summer foliage. All Z5-8. Acid soil, some alkaline soil. '**Ann Sparkes**' slowly makes a compact bush of deep orange-yellow foliage, tipped bronze-red; deep carmine-red flowers. H15cm/6in, W25cm/10in. F2-4. '**Foxhollow**', low-growing, spreading habit, brilliant golden-yellow foliage in late spring and summer, deep gold in winter, often flecked with red; in low-lying areas, new growth can be caught by late spring frost; pale pink flowers, rarely borne. H15-25cm/6-10in, W45cm/18in. F2-4. '**Vivellii**' (syn. 'Urville'), dark, bronze-green attractive foliage, ideal against gold, silver or blue evergreen plants; deep carmine-red flowers. H10cm/4in, W35cm/14in. F2-3. '**Westwood**

Yellow', similar to '**Foxhollow**' but more compact, flowering more freely. H15cm/6in, W40cm/16in. F2-4.

E. cinerea Bell heather. Grows on cliffs by the sea and on moorlands, surviving with less moisture than most species. Wide range of cultivars, some with golden foliage, others with startling flowers and a long flowering period. Prune in spring, just as new growth begins. ☼ ◑. All Z7-9. '**Alba Minor**', compact, with bright green foliage and short spikes of white bell flowers. H15cm/6in, W25cm/10in. F6-10. '**Atrosanguinea Smith's Variety**', excellent, free-flowering, with dark green leaves, intense scarlet blooms. H15-20cm/6-8in, W25cm/10in. F6-9. '**C.D. Eason**', reliable old cultivar, with darker green foliage glowing red-pink. H23-30cm/9-12in, W30cm/1ft. F7-9. '**C.G. Best**', tall, with erect, clear salmon-pink flower spikes. H30cm/1ft, W40cm/16in. F7-8. '**Eden Valley**', compact and bushy, with soft lavender and white bicolored flowers. H15-20cm/6-8in, W25cm/10in. F7-10. '**Foxhollow Mahogany**', deep green foliage, rich mahogony-red flowers. H25-30cm/10-12in, W35-40cm/14-16in. F7-9. '**Hookstone White**', vigorous, long-lived, slightly loose in habit, with a profusion of white flowers. '**Hookstone Lavender**', similar, with pale lavender flowers. Both H30-45cm/12-18in, W40cm/16in. F7-10. '**My Love**', striking luminous blue-mauve flowers, dark foliage. H23-30cm/9-12in, W30cm/1ft. F6-9. '**Pink Ice**', outstanding, compact mound, masses of bright pink flowers. H23-30cm/9-12in, W23-30cm/9-12in. F6-9. '**Purple Beauty**', reliable and showy, spreading, with dark green leaves, large, bright purple flowers. H30cm/1ft, W40cm/16in. F6-10. '**Rock Pool**', low spreading habit,

Erica erigena 'Irish Dusk'

deep golden-yellow in summer, copper-bronze in winter, occasional purple-red flowers. H15cm/6in, W25cm/10in. F6-9. '**Velvet Night**', one of the darkest-flowered bell heathers, with dark green foliage, deep maroon-purple flowers. H30cm/1ft, W30cm/1ft. F6-9. '**Windlebrooke**', excellent foliage plant, with yellow foliage in summer, orange-yellow in winter, purple flowers. H25-30cm/10-12in, W30cm/1ft. F7-9.

E. × darleyensis. Easily grown, long-flowering hybrids which flower from late autumn to late spring; lime-tolerant. Though new growth on many cultivars is quite colourful, only one, '**J.H. Brummage**', an attractive and reliable cultivar, has yellow year-round foliage. '**J.W. Porter**' has cream and red shoots. All need full sun for best flowering. Prune if necessary to tidy plants just as flowering finishes in spring and new growth begins. Most H30-45cm/12-18in, W45-60cm/18-24in. F11-4. Z7-8.

E. erigena. The Irish heath is lime-tolerant, flowering in late spring and early summer, but is less hardy than other winter-flowering heaths. Both the variable species and the many selected cultivars are honey-scented.

All Z8. '**Golden Lady**', dense bush of bright yellow foliage, with white flowers; can scorch, so best in slight shade. H45-60cm/18-24in, W35cm/14in. F4-5. '**Irish Dusk**', compact and bushy, erect habit, deep green foliage, intense salmon-pink flowers. H45-60cm/18-24in, W40cm/16in. F12-5. '**W.T. Rackliff**', dense, rounded, deep green bush, white flowers. H60-75cm/24-30in, W40cm/16in. F3-5.

E. tetralix Cross-leaved heath. Acid loving, best where some moisture exists. Flowers held in terminal clusters on erect shoots. Prune in spring, by cutting back old flowerheads and a-third of the stem. All Z6-8. '**Alba Mollis**', silver-grey, downy foliage and white flowers. H20-25cm/8-10in, W35cm/14in. F6-9. '**Con Underwood**', grey-green hummocks, large crimson flowers. H20-25cm/8-10in, W30cm/1ft. F6-10. '**Pink Star**', soft pink, star-like flowers on compact, silver-grey bushes. H20-25cm/8-10in, W25cm/10in. F6-9.

E. vagans Cornish heath. Valuable group for year-round interest. Will tolerate some lime; grow in full sun or light shade. Old flower spikes attractive through the winter; prune away in mid-spring. All Z7-8. '**Lyonesse**', light green leaves, white flowers with golden anthers. H30-45cm/12-18in, W45cm/18in. F8-10. '**Mrs. D.F. Maxwell**', neat habit, with attractive spikes of deep cerise flowers. H45-60cm/18-24in, W45-60cm/18-24in. F8-10. '**Valerie Proudley**', bright yellow leaves, few white flowers; can scorch in exposed positions, try in light shade. H15-20cm/6-8in, W35cm/14in. F8-9.

TREE HEATHERS

Taller species which mostly flower in late spring or early summer. Some, like *E. australis*, *E. lusitanica* and *E. × veitchii*, are not completely hardy

Erica arborea 'Alpina'

but all are reasonably lime-tolerant. *E. arborea* is best represented by the selection '**Alpina**' which makes a tall evergreen shrub with green foliage and masses of fragrant white flowers in late spring. H1.5-2.4m/5-8ft, W60-75cm/24-30in. F4-5. '**Albert's Gold**' is an excellent, quite hardy selection with bright yellow year-round foliage and white flowers on older plants. H60-75cm/24-30in, W45-60cm/18-24in. F3-5.

HEBE

A wide range of evergreen shrubs originating from the southern hemisphere. The more dwarf, smaller-leaved varieties tend to be hardier than taller, large-leaved types. Tolerant of seaside conditions and cool, temperate climates but not extremes of cold, heat or humidity. Prune as required to keep shape or cut away old or dead wood; plants will mostly break from the base. ☼ ☀ ☆

H. albicans. Attractive bush with glaucous, oblong leaves, white flowers. H45cm/18in, W60cm/2ft. F6-8. Z8-11.

H. '**Autumn Glory**'. Purple-tinged foliage, short spikes of bluish-purple flowers. H60cm/2ft, W90cm/3ft. F8-9. Z8-11.

H. cupressoides. '**Boughton Dome**' is the best form of this species with grey-green, scale-like foliage making a compact bush, bright green in summer; seldom flowers. H45-60cm/18-24in, W45-60cm/18-24in. Z8-10.

H. '**Emerald Green**' (syn. 'Emerald Gem'). Few richer greens exist than this dense compact bush; white flowers; ideal for a container. H30cm/1ft, W45cm/18in. F6-8. Z8-10.

H. × *franciscana*. '**Blue Gem**' is small and dome-shaped, with green leaves, bright blue flowers. Hardier than the brighter-foliaged '**Variegata**', whose leaves are margined creamy-white. H1.2m/4ft, W1.2m/4ft. F6-8. Z8-10.

H. '**Glaucophylla Variegata**', slender shoots, small grey-green leaves, prettily edged with creamy-white, white flowers. H60-75cm/24-30in, W60cm/2ft. F7-8. Z8-10.

H. '**Great Orme**'. Lance-shaped leaves, tapering racemes of deep pink flowers. H90cm/3ft, W90cm/3ft. F6-9. Z8-10.

H. '**Margret**', hardy dwarf, with deep green leaves, bright blue flowers fading to white. H30cm/1ft, W30-45cm/18-24in. F6-9. Z8-10.

H. '**Midsummer Beauty**'. Large leaves, red beneath, and profuse lavender-purple flowers. H1.2m/4ft, W1.5m/5ft. F7-10. Z8-10.

H. pinguifolia. '**Pagei**', compact, glaucous-leaved cultivar, with small, round leaves, white flowers. H15cm/6in, W30-45cm/12-18in. F6-7. Z8-10. '**Red Edge**', good year-round foliage, grey green, red-tipped through winter to late spring; lilac flowers fade to white. H45cm/18in, W45cm/18in. F6-8. Z8-11. '**Rosie**', free-flowering selection, rosy-pink flowers fading to white. H30-45cm/12-18in, W60cm/2ft. F6-8. Z8-10.

HEDERA Ivy

Adaptable evergreen shrubs, grown as ground cover or climbers, many

Hibiscus syriacus 'Pink Giant'

with variegated leaves. Ideal for hanging baskets and containers, especially in autumn and winter when less colour is available. For larger-leaved types, *H. colchica* '**Dentata Variegata**' and *H. c.* '**Sulphur Heart**' (syn.'Paddy's Pride'), both selections of the Persian ivy, would be good choices, the former with broad green leaves margined creamy-yellow, the latter with an irregular golden splash in the centre of the leaf. Both H30cm/1ft, W1.8-3m/6-10ft. Z6-9.

H. helix Common ivy. There are innumerable selections of this species with variegated foliage, and other attractive green-leaved forms with deeply cut or lobed leaves. Excellent as ground cover in sun or shade, or grown as climbers. Green forms mostly Z4-9, variegated forms Z6-9.

HIBISCUS Mallow

H. syriacus Tree hollyhock. From eastern Asia, these medium-sized deciduous shrubs are showy in flower during late summer in hot weather, with a succession of exotic trumpet-shaped blooms. Seldom need pruning. ☼ ☆ ■ '**Admiral Dewey**', double white; '**Bluebird**' (syn. 'Oiseau Bleu'), deep violet-

blue, with darker centres; '**Diane**', single white; '**Duc de Brabant**', reddish-purple, double; '**Hamabo**', white or pink flushed white, crimson eye, single; '**Pink Giant**', bright rose-pink, dark centre, single; '**Red Heart**', white, red-centred, single; '**Russian Violet**', vigorous leafy habit, violet, single; '**Woodbridge**', pink, red-centred, single. All H1.5-1.8m/5-6ft, W1.2-1.5m/4-5ft. F7-10. Z6-9.

HUMULUS

H. lupulus '**Aureus**'. The golden hop is a hardy herbaceous climber, useful for climbing up trees or over a roof, wall or fence – wherever its clinging tendrils can reach. Coarse, bright yellow leaves in full sun, flowers insignificant; attractive autumn hops can be used for making beer. Cut away old foliage after winter dieback. H5-6m/16-20ft, W5-6m/16-20ft. F7-8. Z6-9.

HYDRANGEA

Indispensable deciduous shrubs for summer flowers – unless you happen to live in a frost pocket like Foggy Bottom! Frosts can damage some flowering shoots enough to prevent them flowering the same year, but other forms which flower on the

Hydrangea arborescens 'Annabelle'

Hydrangea paniculata 'Pink Diamond'

same year's growth will escape. Selections range from dwarf to large, some with spectacular flowerheads; the "mopheads", with large, rounded heads, and the lacecaps come in a considerable range of colours. ☼ ✳ ◼ ⊖

H. arborescens. Easy in full sun or light shade, any soil, flowering on same year's growth; prune by half or to the ground in early spring. 'Grandiflora', large round heads of creamy-white, sterile flowers, attractive in winter. H1.2-1.5m/4-5ft, W1.5-1.8m/5-6ft. F7-9. Z3-9. 'Annabelle' has even larger heads, sometimes as much as 30cm/1ft across, but on shorter stems; especially striking when early green florets turn to brilliant white. H90-120cm/3-4ft, W1.2-1.5m/4-5ft. F7-9. Z3-9.

H. aspera. The species is variable but 'Villosa' is a good selection. Shade-loving, slow-growing, erect woody shrub, sometimes tender when young. Soft, dark green felted leaves, flat flowerheads of tiny bluish-purple flowers with lilac florets; attractive bark on older plants. ◼. Prune to tidy or remove dieback. H1.5-1.8m/5-6ft, W1.5-1.8m/5-6ft. F8-9. Z7-9.

H. macrophylla. This Japanese species includes the mopheads and lacecaps, both dense bushes with erect branches, often weighed down by flowers. ☼ ✳ ★. Buds can be damaged by winter or spring frost; mature plants are more resistant but an autumn mulch of composted bark, leafmould or rotted manure helps. Prune in spring, removing only the previous year's dead flowerheads and, on older plants, a few woody stems from the base if congested. Both mopheads and lacecaps make good container plants. Some *H. macrophylla* types can change colour; very acid soils produce real blue, neutral or alkaline soils pink or red. To achieve blue flowers on neutral or alkaline soils, add aluminium sulphate.

Lacecaps have small flowers surrounded by large, showy, flat ray florets. Most H1.2-1.5m/4-5ft, W1.2-1.5m/4-5ft. F6-9. Z6-9. 'Blue Wave' needs shade; blue fertile flowers, pink ray florets on alkaline soils, blue on acid soils. 'Geoffrey Chadbund', deep crimson, purple on acid soils. 'Lanarth White' and 'Mariesii', dwarf (H90cm/3ft), the former pink or blue with white ray florets; the latter, rose-pink ray florets, blue on acid soils. 'Tricolor' has flowers like 'Mariesii', leaves splashed green, grey and pale yellow. 'White Wave' (syn. 'Mariesii Alba'), large heads, pink on limey soils, blue on acid soils, with white ray florets.

Mopheads or Hortensias have round heads of sterile florets in various colours, some changing according to soil. Dried flowerheads attractive when cut. Most H1.2-1.5m/4-5ft, W1.2-1.5m/4.5ft. F6-9. Z7-9. ☼ ✳ 'Altonia', rose-pink, deep blue on acid soils. 'Ami Pasquier', dwarf, crimson turning purple. 'Europe', vigorous, deep pink, changing to mid-blue. 'Generale Vicomtesse de Vibraye', pink, clear blue on acid soil; needs shade. 'Madame Emile Mouillere', slightly tender, serrated white florets with a pink or blue central spot according to soil. 'Masja' has deep crimson heads. For containers or sheltered gardens, 'Pia', pink, and 'Tovelit', bright pink (both H30-45cm/12-18in).

H. paniculata. Easily grown shrubs flowering on new season's growth. White flowers rounded or pyramidal, some quickly fading to pink. ☼ ✳ ◼ Prune in spring if required to restrict growth or initiate stronger flowering shoots, by as much as half the shrub's height. 'Grandiflora', sometimes pruned to a standard with few flowers to achieve grotesquely huge pyramidal flowers. 'Kyushu', more compact, has glossy leaves and profuse long panicles of creamy-white florets. 'Pink Diamond', large, creamy-white heads, turning pink, finally red-brown. 'Unique', with large, erect heads, turns rosy-pink in autumn. All H2.4-3m/8-10ft, W2.4-3m/8-10ft. F7-10. Z4-8.

H. 'Preziosa' (syn. *H. serrata* 'Preziosa'), one of the best raised; deep green, later bronze, foliage and domed pink flowerheads, turning crimson. ☼ ✳. H75cm/30in, W60-90cm/2.3ft. F6-9. Z6-8.

H. quercifolia Oak leaf hydrangea. Responds best to hot summers. Large, dark green oak-type leaves turn bronze to purple in autumn. Small, erect, long-lasting greeny-white flower panicles flop with age. 'Snowflake', double flowered, with a spreading habit. Both require a warm, sheltered position for best flowering. H90-150cm/3-5ft, W1.2-1.5m/4-5ft. F6-8. Z5-9. 'Snow Queen', erect habit, large leaves,

free-flowering in hotter climates. Large panicles of white florets, later tinged pink; bronze-purple leaves in autumn. A good container plant. H1.2-1.5m/4-5ft, W1.2-1.5m/4-5ft. F6-8. Z5-9.
H. serrata. Variable species rarely exceeding 90cm/3ft high; allied to *H. macrophylla* and needing similar conditions. '**Bluebird**', dense, erect habit, deep blue flowers, large ray florets, crimson-purple on alkaline soils, deep blue on acid ones. '**Blue Deckle**', '**Blue Diadem**', both dwarf forms, pink on alkaline soils, blue on acid ones. All H60-90cm/2-3ft, W60-90cm/2-3ft. F6-9. Z6-8.

HYPERICUM

A family containing woody shrubs and semi-woody alpines; most deciduous but some evergreen in mild winters, all with yellow flowers. Long flowering period, some with attractive red or black fruits. Prune back by a third of the previous season's growth in spring, occasionally on older plants more severely, to rejuvenate. Some are prone to rust which can be difficult to eradicate. ☼ ☀
H. androsaemum Tutsan hypericum. Adaptable species used for ground cover. Dark green leaves, small yellow flowers with prominent stamens; red-brown fruits turn black in autumn. '**Gladys Brabazon**', attractive selection with new leaves splashed with cream-yellow flowers, bright red fruits; seeds quite freely. '**Hidcote**', dense, free-flowering bush with profusion of large, saucer-shaped yellow flowers; non-fruiting. H1.2-1.5m/4-5ft, W1.5-1.8m/5-6ft. F7-10. Z6-9.
H. prolificum. Showy species, densely branched, with slender upright stems and a profuse show of small, tufted, bright yellow flowers; adaptable and very hardy. H60-75cm/2ft-2ft 6in, W60-90cm/2-3ft. F7-9. Z5-8.

Indigofera heterantha

INDIGOFERA

Includes some valuable summer- and autumn-flowering plants, with pinnate leaves and racemes of pink, white or purple long-lasting flowers. Except in mild climates, most die back to the ground in winter, the new shoots emerging in late spring or early summer. Prune semi-evergreen shoots back in spring. ☼ ☀ ■
I. decora (syn. *I. incarnata*). Rare Chinese and Japanese species makes a beautiful dwarf shrub with low, arching stems and large pink flowers. '**Alba**', also impressive, with white flowers. Both H45-60cm/18-24in, W45-60cm/18-24in. F7. Z7-9.
I. heterantha (syn. *I. gerardiana*). The most popular indigo makes a twiggy, upright bush with small green leaves and purple-pink flowers. H1.8-2.4m/6-8ft, W1.2-1.5m/4-5ft. F7-9. Z7-9.

JASMINUM Jasmine

Popular as wall plants and climbers, many species also make adaptable freestanding or sprawling shrubs, ideal to cover a fence, wall or a stump. Most are deciduous but their green stems create an evergreen effect. The trumpet-like flowers are sweetly fragrant. Those grown as climbers or wall shrubs require careful tying in and training against firm supports. ☼ ☀ ■
J. officinale. Summer jasmine, with fragrant white flowers. Mostly used as a wall climber where it can reach 10m/33ft in mild areas. '**Aureum**', with gold-splashed leaves, is slower: left to its own devices it will sprawl, but as a wall shrub it can reach 1.8-2.4m/6-8ft, W1.8-2.4m/6-8ft. '**Fiona Sunrise**', a recent introduction with golden-yellow leaves makes quite an impact; will reach a height and spread of 6m/20ft against a wall. Of similar growth rate is '**Grandiflorum**' which has larger flowers than the species. All F7-9. Z8-11.

KALMIA

Spring- and summer-flowering, mainly evergreen shrubs requiring acid soil and similar conditions to rhododendrons.
K. angustifolia. The sheep laurel forms a thicket of small, bright green leaves, grey-green when mature, with dense clusters of deep rose-red flowers. '**Rubra**' is more compact and showy; '**Candida**' has white flowers. All H60-75cm/24-30in. F5-6. Z2-7.
K. latifolia Calico bush. The species grows wild in central and north-eastern U.S.A. but recent hybridizing has produced some spectacular flowers which in summer make up for the shrub's woody, untidy appearance. Named cultivars include '**Bullseye**', with white, purple-banded flowers and reddish foliage; '**Candy**', with white flowers striped pink and red; '**Carousel**', pink in bud opening white with vivid purple-cinnamon banding; '**Olympic Fire**', with deep crimson buds and light pink, white-centred flowers; '**Ostbo Red**', red buds and

Kalmia latifolia 'Ostbo Red'

deep pink blooms; '**Silver Dollar**', with profuse, large white flowers. H1.2-1.5m/4-5ft, W90-120cm/3-4ft. F5-6. Z5-9.

KERRIA JAPONICA

Deciduous shrub with upright, graceful, arching branches, light green serrated leaves and yellow, saucer-shaped spring flowers. Use freestanding, massed or against a wall. The green-leaved forms are suckering. All have distinctive green stems, attractive in winter, but these become congested; prune older branches from the base immediately after flowering. '**Golden Guinea**', similar to the species but with larger, single, golden-yellow flowers. Both H1.5-1.8m/5-6ft, W1.5-1.8m/5-6ft. F3-5. Z5-9. '**Pleniflora**', showy, taller form, with more upright stems and double yellow flowers; needs regular pruning. H1.8-2.4m/6-8ft, W1.8-2.4m/6-8ft. F3-5. Z5-9. '**Variegata**' (syn. '**Picta**') is slower-growing and more spreading, with its green leaves irregularly edged creamy-white and with single yellow flowers. H1.2-1.5m/4-5ft, W1.5-1.8m/5-6ft. F3-5. Z5-9.

Kolkwitzia amabilis

KOLKWITZIA

K. amabilis. The deciduous beauty bush is a hardy, trouble-free, flowering shrub from China. It has densely erect, later arching, branches, light green leaves and freely borne clusters of trumpet-shaped, pale pink flowers with yellow throats. It makes a good specimen or background plant where space permits. Very little pruning needed, but remove some older stems of specimen shrubs to the base, thinning out congested branches, immediately after flowering. 'Pink Cloud' has deeper pink flowers. Both H1.8-2.4m/6-8ft, W1.8-2.4m/6-8ft. F5-6. Z5-8. ✿ ✾ ☆

LAVANDULA Lavender

Indispensable summer-flowering shrubs. Can be used for groups, edging or low hedges, renowned for its flowers and fragrance. Silver-grey, mostly aromatic foliage, blue or violet flowers. A wide choice but some species much hardier than others; many selected cultivars. Unless tender, most species are long lived, their longevity improved by pruning by half each spring or every two or three years. ✿ ✾ ■ ⊖ ⊕.

L. angustifolia. The old English or common lavender from which most garden lavenders derive. Narrow grey leaves, spikes of deep purple flowers. Excellent for seaside, herb, silver or grey gardens and mixed planting. H60-75cm/24-30in, W60-75cm/24-30in. The following selections all F6-8, Z6-9. 'Alba' is a robust, white-flowered form. 'Grappenhall', equally robust, is lavender-blue. Both H90-120cm/3-4ft, W90-120cm/3-4ft. The best and most popular, 'Hidcote', is compact, with violet-blue spikes. H60-75cm/24-30in, W60-75cm/24-30in. 'Hidcote Pink', 'Loddon Pink' and 'Rosea' are tinged pink, quickly fading. All H60-75cm/24-30in, W60-75cm/2ft-2ft 6in. The more compact 'Munstead' has grey-green foliage and blue flowers. H60-75cm/24-30in, W60-75cm/24-30in. 'Nana Alba' makes a compact bush of grey leaves and white flowers. H30cm/1ft, W30-45cm/12-18in. 'Vera', the Dutch lavender, has large grey leaves and long spikes of lavender-blue flowers. H90-120cm/3-4ft, W90-120cm/3-4ft.

Lavandula 'Blue Cushion'

L. 'Blue Cushion'. A compact, mound-forming hybrid with grey-green leaves, free flowering, deep blue. H30-40cm/12-15in, W45-60cm/18-24in.

L. 'Fragrant Memories'. Considered an old hybrid. Robust habit, large silvery-grey, strongly aromatic leaves, a long succession rather than a mass of tall spikes bearing lavender-blue flowers. H60-75cm/24-30in, W75cm/30in. F7-10.

L. stoechas. French lavender. Native of south-west Europe, Greece and North Africa. Not reliably hardy, requiring warm, well-drained positions. Flowers appear in early summer on short spikes, their ovoid heads surmounted by purple bracts. Several selections now available: 'Album' has white flowers; 'Helmsdale', compact habit, bronze tinges to deep mauve-purple flowers; 'Marshwood', large flowers, purple-pink bracts with a distinctive twirl. All 30-45cm/12-18in, W45cm/18in. F6-7. Z8-9. 'Pedunculata', a showy lavender which seems hardier than the species, has grey-green aromatic, foliage and usually a striking show of flowers topped by wispy lilac-blue bracts. H45-60cm/18-24in, W45-60cm/18-24in. F6-7. Z7-9.

Lavatera 'Candy Floss'

LAVATERA Mallow

Whatever the botanical classification there are some fine flowering plants among these deciduous, semi-woody plants providing colour throughout the summer and into autumn. Leafy foliage provides a backcloth to a succession of cup-shaped flowers. Plants may die back in winter or even be killed in hard winters, but even if grown as annuals they give a long period of colour. Prune back to 30-45cm/12-18in in late spring. Good near the sea. All below F6-10. Z8-10. ✿ ☆ ■

L. 'Barnsley'. Vigorous, a sport of 'Rosea', with white, red-centred flowers fading to a delicate pink. Sometimes flowers revert to pink and these should be cut out. 'Burgundy Wine', wine-red flowers, compact habit, free flowering. H1.8m/6ft, W1.5-1.8m/5-6ft. 'Candy Floss', pale pink saucer-shaped flowers, open habit. H1.8-2.1m/6-7ft, W1.5-1.8m/5-6ft. 'Pink Frills', dense upright habit, pretty pale pink frilled flowers over a relatively short period. H1.5m/5ft, W1.2m/4ft. F7-8.

LIGUSTRUM Privet

Common and often condemned, but some selections of this family are quite showy and highly adaptable. Some have colourful variegated or golden foliage and most if unpruned produce heads of white tubular flowers followed by black fruits. Many are used for hedging but are quite hungry feeders so site with care. Prune as necessary, but for hedges two or three times in the growing season. ✿ ❀ ☆

L. lucidum. The Chinese privet is relatively tender but vigorous and large leaved. The species has glossy leaves and erect panicles of white scented flowers. '**Excelsum Superbum**' has variegated white and yellow leaves, '**Tricolor**' has leaves margined white flushed pink when young. All H3m/10ft, W3m/10ft. F8. Z8-11.

L. vicaryi. I rate this semi-evergreen privet for its striking yellow foliage, white flowers and in autumn a good display of black fruits, the leaves then purplish. H2.1-3m/7-10ft, W2.1-3m/7-10ft. F7-8. Z6-8. ✿

L. vulgare Common privet. A hardy adaptable shrub growing in poor, dry soil. Deciduous, loose habit with dullish white flower plumes, black fruits. '**Aureum**' has dull yellow leaves. Both H3m/10ft, W3m/10ft. F7-8. Z5-7.

Lonicera periclymenum

LONICERA Honeysuckle

This family includes both free standing deciduous and evergreen shrubs grown for foliage and winter flowers as well as the more usual climbers or scramblers. The climbers are renowned for their fragrance, but not all are scented. They are tolerant of a wide range of soils, but usually prefer their roots in shade. Prune climbers after flowering to remove old wood if necessary and reduce growth.

L. × americana. Glossy green leaves, showy clusters of erect, sweetly fragrant flowers, purple in bud opening to yellow, then fading to cream. Red fruits. Train and prune in early spring. H5m/16ft, W5m/16ft. F7-9. Z5-9.

L. korolkowii. The blue leaf honeysuckle is an excellent, easily grown foliage shrub with intensely blue leaves in summer. Pretty small pink flowers on the shoot tips are followed by red fruits. A good background shrub. Trim after flowering to keep compact. H3m/10ft, W2.4-3m/8-10ft. F6-7. Z5-8.

L. periclymenum Common honeysuckle or woodbine. Grows wild in British hedgerows. A deciduous, scrambling, twining climber, happy in most soils where not too dry. Fragrant yellow or purplish flowers with a mostly white centre in early summer followed by red fruits. '**Belgica**', the early Dutch honeysuckle, has purple-red buds, opening yellow in late spring for several weeks. '**Graham Thomas**', found in a Warwickshire hedgerow by the distinguished English plantsman, has large yellow flowers, a wonderful plant. '**Harlequin**' adds a new note with long-season interest from cream- and pink-variegated leaves. Although there may be several forms of '**Serotina**', the late Dutch honeysuckle is the best, with purple-tinged leaves, deep purple,

Magnolia × liliflora × stellata 'Jane'

red-budded flowers opening creamy-white and is deliciously fragrant; worth searching for. All H3-4m/10-13ft, W3-4m/10-13ft. F5-9. Z5-9.

MAGNOLIA

Aristocratic trees and shrubs, both deciduous and evergreen, and mostly spring flowering. Magnolias are relatively trouble-free on suitable soils. Ideally they like any good, moist but well drained loam including those containing lime, but not thin, dry or chalky soils. They will benefit from the annual addition of a mulch of composted bark, acid leafmould or well rotted compost. Most spring shoots and flowers are susceptible to damage from spring frosts, so if possible site near a tree or a wall to protect plants from the early morning sun. Little or no pruning required. Some worthwhile later-flowering varieties are described below.

M. grandiflora. This handsome evergreen species makes a large tree in warmer climates but in cooler temperate zones is often used as a wall plant where it will get more heat and protection to induce it to flower. Dark green, glossy leathery leaves have cinnamon-brown felt beneath. Large, fragrant cup-shaped

creamy-white flowers in summer are an inspiring sight. Plants from seed will take several years to flower, but many selections have been made which are propagated by cuttings and these will flower much earlier, so go for named cultivars. '**Exmouth**' and '**Goliath**' are but two but many new selections are being introduced from the United States. Average ten year growth rate of the species and two cultivars above: H2.4-3m/8-10ft, W1.5-1.8m/5-6ft. F7-9. Z7-9. ✿ ◢

M. × kewensis '**Wada's Memory**'. An erect bush with fragrant white, somewhat drooping white flowers which appear before the leaves. Good for a small garden. H3m/10ft, W1.5-1.8m/5-6ft. F7-9. F4-5. Z4-8.

M. × liliflora (syn. *M. discolor*). The lily magnolia is ideal if untidy for a small garden, its tulip-like flowers appearing with the leaves, so mostly avoiding frost damage; it continues in flower for several months. Flower petals wine-purple outside, white inside. '**Nigra**' has larger, darker flowers, flushed rose-purple inside. H1.5-1.8m/5-6ft, W1.5-1.8m/5-6ft. F5-7. Z6-8.

M. × liliflora × stellata. Although many are similar, the hybrids made from various crosses between these two species have proved valuable garden plants. All have girls' names; most resemble *M. liliflora* in flower, some are fragrant but are generally bushier and freer flowering. These include '**Ann**', '**Betty**', '**Jane**' (my favourite), '**Judy**', '**Pinkie**', '**Randy**', '**Ricki**' and '**Susan**'. All H1.5-1.8m/5-6ft, W90-120cm/3-4ft. F5-6. Z5-8.

OLEARIA Daisy bush

A large family of Australasian evergreen shrubs and small trees, known as tree asters or tree daisies, but they seldom make trees in cooler temperate climates. Useful summer-

Olearia 'Waikariensis'

flowering shrubs even if their panicles or clusters of daisy-like flowers are mostly white or cream. Most are tender but thrive in mild coastal districts, withstanding gales and salt spray. In cold inland regions grow against a sunny south-facing wall. Best on well-drained soils including chalk. Cut back hard old, untidy or frost-damaged bushes in spring as new growth begins, since they break freely from old wood. Two of the hardiest are described but wider ranges can be obtained from specialists.

O. × *haastii*. Rounded bush with sage green, leathery leaves, silver-grey beneath and clusters of fragrant white flowers in summer. Good hedging shrub in milder areas. H1.2-1.5m/4-5ft, W1.2-1.5m/4-5ft. F7-9. Z8-10.

O. 'Waikariensis'. Compact evergreen, leaves glossy green above with silver-grey undersides. Clusters of white daisy flowers, a good plant for the sunny "mediterranean" garden. H90-120cm/3-4ft, W120-150cm/4-5ft. F7-8. Z8-10.

OSMANTHUS
Related to the olive, though some of these evergreens look more akin to hollies. Grown for their foliage and

small fragrant flowers, those listed below make attractive summer foliage plants for sheltered positions or patios.

O. heterophyllus (syn. *O. ilicifolius*). Large, round, dense shrub or small tree in mild climates. Shining, holly-like leaves, some spined, but mature leaves smooth-edged and oval. Small clusters of fragrant white flowers in hot climates, followed by blue berries. All selections can be tender, especially when young. H1.8-2.4m/6-8ft, W1.8-2.4m/6-8ft. F9-11. Z7-9. '**Aureomarginatus**', leaves edged in yellow. '**Aureus**', bright gold summer leaves, greeny-yellow in winter. '**Latifolius Variegatus**', wide leaves edged silvery-white. '**Purpureus**', striking, purple young shoots and leaves in spring. '**Tricolor**' (syn. 'Goshiki'), dark green, white and pink leaves. '**Variegatus**', creamy-white margins. Average H1.2-1.8m/4-6ft, W1.2-1.8m/4-6ft. F9-11. Z8-9.

OXYDENDRUM
O. arboreum. Deciduous. May reach 15m/50ft in its native eastern U.S.A. but seldom more than a large shrub in climates with cool summers. Open, erect branches with long, narrow, graceful leaves, turning yellow or crimson in autumn, given

Paeonia delavayi

Osmanthus heterophyllus 'Tricolor'

an open situation. Long, pendulous racemes of white, fragrant flowers. H1.5-2.4m/5-8ft, W1.2-1.5m/4-5ft. F7-8. Z5-9.

PAEONIA Tree peony
The woody plants of this genus seldom reach tree size, mostly forming irregular, gaunt, often untidy deciduous shrubs but they can be attractive in leaf and spectacular in flower. All are frost-hardy in winter but can be susceptible to damage from spring frosts, so avoid planting in frost pockets and protect from early morning sun. Best if given fertile but well drained loam that stays moist in summer. Add well rotted compost to the soil and mulch in spring. ☼ ❊

P. delavayi. A variable, Chinese species, mostly red-tinged, deeply divided new leaves and deep crimson cup-shaped flowers with golden anthers. H1.2-1.5m/4-5ft, W90-120cm/3-4ft. F5-6. Z5-8.

P. lutea. Variable from seed and similar in leaf to *P. delavayi* though generally a lighter green. Small saucer-shaped, often semi-double, canary yellow flowers partly hidden by foliage. *P.l. ludlowii* is a superior, more vigorous form with larger, slightly earlier flowers. Both

somewhat shy to flower but foliage is effective. Both 1.5-1.8m/5-6ft, W1.2-1.5m/4-5ft.

P. suffruticosa. The Japanese or Chinese "moutans" have a fascinating history going back to the 6th century. Spectacular single and double flowers both have attractive stamens and can be up to 30cm/1ft across; 15cm/6in is more usual and even these can weigh the branches down when wet. Colours range from white through pink, carmine red, purple, orange and yellow. Most that are sold now will be grafted, so plant with the visible graft union 10cm/4in below ground level and cover with soil – the plant should in time then make its own roots. Expect flowers on named varieties within two years of planting. Little or no pruning required, except to cut out any dead wood, best done after flowering. Average H1.2-1.5m/4-5ft, W90-120cm/3-4ft. F5-6. Z5-8.

PASSIFLORA Passion flower
This Brazilian species is the hardiest and most popular of the genus of woody and herbaceous climbers native to South America. Evergreen and woody in mild localities, elsewhere herbaceous. Extremely

Philadelphus 'Beauclerk'

vigorous, clinging by means of tendrils. Unusually striking white or pink flowers are flattened and star-shaped with a raised circular crown of blue or purple and white filaments, followed in hot summers by orange-yellow fruits. Protect from cold winds. '**Constance Elliott**', an equally vigorous grower, has white flowers. Both H5m/16ft. F7-8. Z8-9. ☼ ❋ ■

PEROVSKIA Russian sage

Indispensable deciduous sub-shrubs. Long, late display of shimmering blue flower spikes. Quite hardy, but young stems can die back in cold winters, new shoots appearing from the base. Prune to 15-30cm/6-12in from the ground in spring to promote new flowering growth.
P. atriplicifolia. Aromatic, downy, grey-green, serrated leaves, white stems and hazy panicles of lavender-blue flowers. '**Blue Spire**', more deeply cut leaves and larger flowerheads. H90-120cm/3-4ft, W90-120cm/3-4ft. F8-10. Z6-8.

PHILADELPHUS Mock orange

Popular, deciduous hardy shrubs though, except for foliage forms, a short flowering season and not much to recommend them for the rest of

the year. Small, medium and large types, generally densely branched. Light green leaves darken in summer; white, fragrant single or double flowers with yellow stamens, the centres sometimes stained purple. On older plants, old branches can be thinned out after flowering, others shortened if required. ☼ ❋ ☆
P. coronarius. Sweet mock orange denotes the heavy fragrance of this species which is seldom offered in its green-leaved form, being surpassed by modern hybrids. Coloured foliage forms are well worth growing for their longer period of interest. They include '**Aureus**' with bright yellow leaves turning yellow-green and even green in hotter climates, and '**Variegatus**', with grey-green leaves irregularly edged creamy-white and single or semi-double, scented flowers. Both best in part shade and less vigorous than the species. H1.8-2.4m/6-8ft, W1.8-2.4m/6-8ft. F6. Z5-8.
Hybrids. All F6-7, Z5-8 unless otherwise indicated. '**Avalanche**', profuse small, single, heavily fragrant white flowers on arching branches. H1.5m/5ft, W1.5m/5ft. '**Beauclerk**', creamy-white single, saucer-shaped, fragrant rose-stained flowers. H1.8m/6ft, W1.8m/6ft. '**Enchantment**', arching branches, fully double, richly fragrant white flowers. H2.4m/8ft, W2-4m/8ft. '**Manteau d'Hermine**' dwarf shrub, small leaves, masses of double or semi-double fragrant white flowers. H90-120cm/3-4ft, W90-120cm/3-4ft. '**Minnesota Snowflake**', vigorous with fully double, sweetly scented white flowers in clusters. H2.4m/8ft, W2.4m/8ft. Z4-8.

PHLOMIS

Large genus of shrubs and sub-shrubs with woody, grey or grey-green leaves and lax spikes with tiers of flowers in whorls or circles around

Phlomis fruticosa 'Edward Bowles'

the stem. They prefer sun and good drainage, thriving against hot dry walls or banks. Prune back a third or a half of the old woody stems as needed in spring as new growth starts.
P. chrysophylla. Attractive compact shrub with grey-green sage-like leaves and golden-yellow flowers. H90-120cm/3-4ft, W1.2m/4ft. F7-8. Z8-10.
P. fruticosa Jerusalem sage. Perhaps the hardiest species, with grey-green woolly leaves and spikes of bright yellow whorled flowers. H90-120cm/3-4ft, W120cm/4ft. F7-8. Z8-11. '**Edward Bowles**', large woolly silver-grey leaves and impressive sulphur-yellow flowers, semi-shrubby. H1.2-1.5m/4-5ft, W1.2-1.5m/4-5ft. F7-9. Z8-11.

PHORMIUM New Zealand flax

Distinctive and colourful foliage plants, classed as shrubs but hardly woody. Sword-shaped leaves are flexible and pithy. Selections are available from 30cm/1ft to 3m/10ft in height. The species and some cultivars produce quite spectacular flowers in hotter climates. Phormiums grow well in most soils where not too dry but vary in hardiness and adaptability. Excellent

for coastal areas. Some make striking accent plants and are ideal for pots and patios, though pot-grown plants will need taking under cover in frosty weather.
P. cookianum (syn. *P. colensoi*) Mountain flax. Variable species with shining green arching leaves. Older plants bear exotic yellow and red flowers on spikes which vary from 90cm/3ft to 1.8m/6ft in height. Foliage H60-90cm/2-3ft, W90-120cm/3-4ft. F7-8. Z9-11. '**Tricolor**', bright green strap-like leaves striped white, margined red. H45-75cm/18-30in, W75-90cm/30-36in. F7-8. Z8-11.
P. tenax. Imposing architectural clump-forming plant, eventually large. Broad, erect sword-like leaves. Flower spikes to 4.5m/15ft with panicles of bronze-red flowers, then reddish seedheads. H1.8-3m/6-10ft, W1.5-3m/5-10ft. F7-8. Z8-11. '**Purpureum**', similar to the species with broad blades of bronze-purple leaves. H1.5-1.8m/5-6ft, W1.2-1.5m/4-5ft. '**Sundowner**', outstanding with leaves striped grey, coppery red and pink. '**Variegatum**', broad green leaves edged creamy-white. Both H1.5-1.8m/5-6ft, W1.2-1.5m/4-5ft.
Hybrids. Parentage between the two species and cultivars. Many cultivars cannot be relied upon to flower but, if they do, F7-8. All Z8-11. '**Bronze Baby**', narrow, bronze-purple leaves. H60-90cm/2-3ft, W45-60cm/18-24in. '**Cream Delight**', sometimes listed under *P. cookianum*, has broad green arching leaves with a central band of creamy-yellow. H60-90cm/2-3ft, W90-120cm/3-4ft. '**Dark Delight**', broad, erect, glossy red-purple leaves, pendulous tips. H90-120cm/3-4ft, W90-120cm/3-4ft. '**Maori Chief**', robust, clump-forming, erect leaves striped bright red, with maroon and bronze drooping tips. H90-120cm/3-4ft, W60-90cm/2-3ft. '**Tom Thumb**',

Physocarpus opulifolius 'Dart's Gold'

Pieris 'Forest Flame'

dwarf with narrow green leaves margined bronze. H30-45cm/12-18in, W30-45cm/12-18in. '**Yellow Wave**', striking, bright yellow arched leaves, some edged green. H75-90cm/30-36in, W90-120cm/3-4ft.

PHOTINIA
Mostly south-east Asian in origin, these make large shrubs or trees, depending on climate. Deciduous types dislike lime but the evergreens thrive in it, even on chalky soil. Both types prefer reasonably moist but free-draining, warm soil. ✿ ✹. In cool summers, the evergreens are shy to flower, but still make excellent foliage plants. The flowers are white, hawthorn-like and borne in clusters or panicles, followed by red fruits. In cold regions the evergreens need shelter rom freezing winds and severe frost. If leaf drop occurs they normally shoot again in spring. For compact, dense growth and ample new colourful shoots, prune leading shoots back by 30-60cm/1-2ft in spring, as new growth commences; hedges or screens might also need a summer trim.

P. davidiana '**Palette**' (syn. *Stransvaesia davidiana* 'Palette'). Foliage shrub, variable, but relatively bushy, leaves irregularly splashed and variegated white, pink and green,

new shoots flushed reddish-pink. White flowers do not always develop into impressive red fruit. H1.5-1.8m/5-6ft, W1.2-1.5m/4-5ft. F6-7. Z7-9.

P. × fraseri '**Birmingham**'. Robust evergreen, glossy dark green leaves, copper-red when young. Denser and hardier than the closely related, more colourful '**Red Robin**', with an almost continuous show of brilliant red new growth all summer. Both make outstanding focal points. H2.4-3m/8-10ft, W1.8-2.4m/6-8ft. F6. Z8-9.

× PHYLLIOPSIS
× *P. hillieri*. '**Pinocchio**', a first class hybrid, a compact rounded bush with green leaves and a long display of deep pink bell flowers. '**Coppelia**', slightly more vigorous with profuse lavender-pink flowers. Ideal for rock gardens or peat beds. Both H30-45cm/12-18in, W38-45cm/15-18in. F5-6. Z5-8. ✿ ✹ ⊖

PHYSOCARPUS Ninebark
P. opulifolius '**Dart's Gold**'. Striking deciduous foliage shrub, brighter and more compact than a similar form '**Luteus**', which will reach 3m/10ft or more. Erect branching habit, the stems attractively peeling with age; bright yellow new shoots

in spring might be mistaken at a distance for a forsythia. Broad lobed, serrated leaves are bright yellow all summer and into autumn. Species and cultivars carry round clusters of pink-tinged white flowers on second-year wood so pruning to keep it compact in spring will remove the chance of flowers, though this is no great loss. Prune in late winter or early spring. '**Diabolo**' is a selection with bronze-purple leaves, and equally striking foliage plant against the right background. Yellow leaves can scorch in full sun or from spring frost, but soon recover. Both 1.5-1.8m/5-6ft, W1.5-1.8m/5-6ft. F6. Z3-7. ✿ ✹ ☆

PIERIS
Evergreen, attractive in flower and foliage and early summer growth often spectacular. Most make slow-growing, mounded bushes, with lance-shaped, glossy leaves. Racemes often develop in autumn, opening in spring, with mostly pendulous, fragrant, bell-shaped white flowers. New growth can be vulnerable to spring frosts. Prune only to tidy up bushes or remove old flowerheads as the new growth begins. Mulch with leafmould or composted bark every two or three years. Needs a peaty soil.

P. '**Flaming Silver**'. One of several selections with variegated foliage and new growth of scarlet or crimson in late spring. Leaves edged silvery-white. H1.2m/4ft, W1.2-1.5m/4-5ft. F3-5. Z5-8.

P. '**Forest Flame**'. One of the best hybrids. Dense flower sprays; scarlet young growth turns pink and white, then green. H1.5m/5ft, W1.5m/5ft. F4-5. Z6-8.

P. japonica. Source of most new European and North American cultivars. Usually glossy leaves, pendulous flower racemes, with waxy, often fragrant, bell-like flowers, showy even in winter as

flowering racemes develop. Most prefer an open, sheltered spot. All F3-5. Most Z6-8. '**Debutante**', dense trusses of white flowers. H75cm/30in, W75-90cm/30-36in. '**Little Heath**', dwarf, compact, variegated form, seldom flowers; small white, pink and copper leaves. H60cm/2ft, W60cm/2ft. '**Mountain Fire**', coppery-red new leaves, sparse white flowers. H90cm/3ft, W90-120cm/3-4ft. '**Red Mill**', glossy wine-red leaves, white flowers. H1.2m/4ft, W1.2m/4ft. '**Variegata**', covers a fast-growing form with white margins, also called '**White Rim**' (H90cm/3ft, W90cm/3ft), and a compact form, with creamy-yellow variegations, which needs shelter. H45-60cm/18-24in. W45-60cm/18-24in.

PIPTANTHUS
P. nepalensis. A Himalayan semi-evergreen with trifoliate leaves and golden-yellow pea flowers. It forms an open bush of flexible stems bearing dark green leaves, with flowers appearing throughout the plant. It makes a good wall plant, but can also be used in the same situations as brooms, enjoying sun and good drainage. There is a form from Bhutan, *P. tomentosus*, with silvery leaves, which promises to be

Potentilla 'Goldfinger'

even more showy. If bushes get untidy, prune stems back after flowering. H3-4m/10-13ft, W2.1-3m/7-10ft. F5-6. Z9-10.

PITTOSPORUM

Evergreen shrubs or small trees grown for foliage, useful for cutting. Few are hardy in cool temperate zones, but for mild and seaside areas there are good species and cultivars, the latter mostly belonging to *P. tenuifolium*. Leaves are rounded and undulating, pale or olive green with more recent variations purple, silver, gold or variegated. Purple or brown flowers, often small and fragrant, on mature plants in warmer climates. In cold, inland areas, grow against a sunny wall. Wet soil and cold, desiccating winds are fatal. If cut back by frost, most make new growth from old wood. Overwinter containerized plants in a greenhouse or conservatory. Plant in late spring. All below F4-5. Z9-11.

P. 'Garnettii'. Hybrid. Grey-green leaves, edged white and tinged pink. H3m/10ft, W1.5m/5ft.

P. tenuifolium. Bushy tree, columnar when young. Glossy, pale, wavy-edged leaves, black stems. Good for hedging. Innumerable cultivars. H3m/10ft, W1.5m/5ft.

'Purpureum', red-purple leaves.

'Silver Queen', white-edged leaves. Both H1.8-2.1m/6-7ft, W1.5-1.8m/5-6ft. 'Tom Thumb', dwarf, purple-leaved form. H1m/39in, W1m/39in.

POTENTILLA Cinquefoil

A valuable range of long-flowering, colourful and adaptable deciduous shrubs for even the smaller garden. Also good for autumn flowers, wide range of colours, some best in cooler weather. Prune established plants annually as new shoots appear. Cut back by a third each year to improve vigour and flowering. Coloured forms may retain deeper hues in shade.

The following are hybrids, mostly listed at one time under *P. fruticosa*, which is the parent of many. All F4-10. Most Z3-8. 'Abbotswood', the best white, profuse-flowering, blue-green leaves. H1.2m/4ft, W1.5m/5ft. 'Elizabeth', bushy, grey-green leaves, golden-yellow flowers, long-flowering. H90cm/3ft, W1.2m/4ft. 'Goldfinger', bright green leaves, golden flowers. H90cm/3ft, W1.2m/4ft. 'Goldstar', erect, open habit, huge yellow flowers. H90cm/3ft, W1.2m/4ft. 'Hopleys Orange', orange flowers. H75cm/30in, W1m/39in. 'Kobold', dense, dwarf, small yellow flowers.

H30-45cm/12-18in, W40-60cm/16-24in. 'Pretty Polly', dwarf, low-growing, light rose-pink flowers. H35-50cm/14-20in, W45-65cm/18-26in. 'Princess', long-flowering, pale pink, then paler, fading to white in heat. H75cm/30in, W1m/39in. 'Red Ace', bright vermilion-flame at best, fading to yellow in heat. 'Red Robin', similar but deeper red. Both H60cm/2ft, W80cm/32in. 'Tilford Cream', low habit, rigid branches, white flowers, can look scruffy. H60cm/2ft, W60cm/2ft.

PRUNUS

Large family of trees and shrubs (see also Trees Directory), most of the latter flowering in early to mid-spring. Some useful for coloured foliage in summer. Deciduous ☀ Evergreens ☀ ❄ All ☆ ■.

P. × cistena (syn. 'Crimson Dwarf'). Deciduous. White flowers, reddish purple foliage. As a hedge, prune after flowering, then regularly through summer. H1.5-1.8m/5-6ft, W1.2-1.5m/4-5ft. F3-4. Z2-8.

P. glandulosa. The Chinese bush cherry, or, in the USA, Chinese dwarf flowering almond, has erect, branched stems with single white or pink flowers, which appear before and with the leaves. Best in warm sun; hard prune the previous year's growth immediately after flowering. There are several ornamental, double-flowered forms, including 'Alba Plena', white, and the densely petalled pink 'Sinensis' (syn. 'Flore Roseoplena'). All H1.2-1.5m/4-5ft, W1.2m/4ft. F4-5. Z5-8.

P. laurocerasus Cherry laurel. Evergreen adaptable shrubs with glossy, leathery leaves. Taller, erect forms are good for screening, hedging and windbreaks, prostrate types for ground cover. Bottlebrush white flowers held above the branches do not last long but are quite showy. Sun or shade on all but thin chalk; take well to pruning after

flowering. All F4-5. Most Z6-8. 'Low and Green', low, free-flowering, glossy green leaves. H90cm/3ft, W2.1-3m/7-10ft. 'Marbled White', broad, spreading; leaves green, grey and cream. H2.4m/8ft, W2.4m/8ft. 'Otto Luyken', broad, semi-prostrate; narrow, shiny leaves, white flowers, often again in autumn, good for hedging. H1.5m/5ft, W1.5m/5ft. 'Renault Ace', erect branching habit, dark green leaves, good flowering performance, excellent for hedges. H1.8-2.4m/6-8ft, W1.8-2.4m/6-8ft. 'Zabeliana', low, spreading ground cover, narrow leaves. H1.2m/4ft, W1.8m/6ft.

RHODODENDRON

Vast range of deciduous and evergreen flowering shrubs requiring (with one or two exceptions) an acid soil. Dwarf and large forms with flowering periods from late winter to mid-summer; a good range of colours, some with striking and exotic blooms. If you are lucky enough to have an acid or even neutral pH soil, the rhododendrons and azaleas will give vibrant spring colours which can fit with other plants. But beware – frost can also damage winter and even late spring

Prunus laurocerasus 'Otto Luyken'

Rhododendron yakushimanum hybrid

Rosa moyesii 'Geranium'

flowers; site plants facing away from early morning sun, under the shade of tall trees and out of a frost pocket. Severe winters or frosts can damage swelling buds. All, except those classed as tender, can be planted throughout the year as long as soil conditions are suitable, early autumn better than late spring for those less hardy for your area.

So large and varied is the selection of rhododendrons that only a brief guide to the types can be given. Consult a book or specialist supplier, or even your nearest garden centre who should be able to advise on the most suitable selections for your area. Rhododendrons tend to be grouped by species, both large and small, and evergreen hybrids, which again can be large or small. The hardy evergreen azaleas and deciduous azaleas are also rhododendrons and among my favourites, since they seem to fit better among other plants. The deciduous aAzaleas flower later, often avoiding spring frost damage and provide good autumn colour too. In recent years breeding work has introduced some excellent varieties of rhododendron for the smaller garden, including hybrids of *Rhododendron yakushimanum*, attractive not only

for flower but for foliage. Almost wherever you live, there will be rhododendrons to suit your climate.

ROSA Rose

No book on "summer garden glory" could be complete without the inclusion of roses, but with limited space only general guidelines can be given and some arbitrary selections made in each main group listed. While shrub, ground cover, climbing and rambling roses are included below, detailed advice and lists of bush roses (hybrid teas and floribundas) patio roses (dwarf cluster roses) and miniature types must be sought elsewhere. All roses are shrubs and although they are often used on their own in rose gardens, today's gardener expects them to mix in with other plants, shrubs and herbaceous in particular. They should also be relatively trouble free from pests and diseases and provide a long period of interest. While gardeners are becoming more demanding, rose breeders are rising to the challenge, with exciting developments coming through. There are roses for climbing wallls and fences, others for rambling over banks and other shrubs; for ground cover or use

among other low growing plants; for hedges, window boxes and tubs. Roses succeed best in sun on rich, loamy soil, and dislike extremes of wet or dry. For best results, add well-rotted compost when planting, and give an annual dressing of fertilizer. Most roses also benefit from mulching with well-rotted compost. Prune as new buds swell in early spring, firstly any thin or dead stems, then to balance the shape; prune just above the bud at an angle of 45 degrees away from it. Brief individual pruning notes are given with each group. Roses are bred, too, for adaptability to different climates, but quite often those which thrive in southern France may not be as happy in northern Europe or cooler areas of the USA, and vice versa. Local experts know what succeeds best in their region.

Shrub roses

Shrub roses can be species or cultivars, tall specimen plants or low, ground-covering types, recent introductions of which provide colour from summer until well into autumn. Prune only to shape or to control size. If the stems of ground-cover types become old or untidy they can be pruned hard to

15cm/6in above the ground every two or three years.

R. 'Ballerina'. Outstanding, with the bold trusses of recurrent, soft pink, white-centred, weather-resistant flowers. Bushy, spreading habit and glossy green leaves. Good ground cover. H1.2m/4ft, W1.2m/4ft. F7-10. Z6-8.

R. 'Bonica'. Popular and versatile, with arching branches and masses of small pink flowers for months. Good ground cover. H90cm/3ft, W90cm/3ft. F7-10. Z4-9.

R. californica 'Plena'. Imposing specimen shrub rose with tall arching branches and a profusion of semi-double, deep pink flowers fading to rose-pink. H3m/10ft, W2.4-3m/8-10ft. F6-7. Z6-8.

R. 'Canary Bird'. An early-flowering, modern shrub rose, which mixes well with shrubs or perennials. Long, arching stems clothed with daintily cut leaves, and freely borne, single, canary-yellow scented flowers. H1.8-2.1m/6-7ft, W1.5-2.1m/5-7ft. F5-6. Z5-9.

R. 'Heritage'. Similar to the above and equally attractive, with blush-pink flowers. H1.2m/4ft, W1.2m/4ft. F6-10. Z4-9.

R. 'Kent'. An award-winning, repeat-blooming, ground-cover shrub with pure white, semi-double flowers. Weathers well. H45cm/8in, W60-90cm/2-3ft. F7-10. Z5-8.

R. moyesii '**Geranium**'. At its peak a glorious sight, the tall, arching, thorny branches ablaze with single, bright scarlet flowers and yellow stamens. Flask-shaped, orange-red hips in autumn. H2.4-3m/8-10ft, W2.4m/8ft. F6-7. Z6-8.

R. '**Surrey**'. Outstanding ground-cover rose with beautiful, soft, double, pink flowers. H90cm/3ft, W1.2m/4ft. F7-10. Z6-8.

Climbing and rambling roses

Use climbing and rambling roses for walls, over fences, pergolas, trellises and arches, or up trees. Most need tying in and training. Plant as for other climbers, ideally at least 45cm/18in away from a wall, so they can more easily obtain moisture. To prune, reduce side shoots by two-thirds in autumn, but only reduce main leading stems if they are too tall. If plants become bare at the base, severely prune one main stem to 30-60cm/1-2ft above ground to encourage new growth. Ramblers can have old stems cut away in late summer as soon as flowering has finished.

R. '**Albéric Barbier**'. An old favourite rambler with vigorous, semi-evergreen, glossy dark green foliage and fragrant, creamy-white, double flowers opening from creamy-yellow buds. Good for a tree or an arch. H3-5m/10-16ft. F6-8. Z5-8.

R. '**Dublin Bay**'. Long-flowering climber with clusters of slightly fragrant, crimson flowers and glossy, dark green leaves. H1.8-2.4m/6-8ft, W1.8-2.4m/6-8ft. F7-10. Z6-8.

R. '**Felicia**'. A hybrid musk rose of considerable merit. Salmon-pink, semi-double, fragrant. H1.5-1.8m /5-6ft, W1.2-1.5m/4-5ft. F6-9. Z6-8.

R. '**Golden Showers**'. Modern shrub

Rosa 'Felicia'

climber with glossy, dark green foliage, clusters of recurrent, large, fragrant, single bright yellow flowers, fading to cream. Upright grower, good for pillars. H2.4-3m/8-10ft, W2.4m/8ft. F6-9. Z5-8.

R. '**Handel**'. Climber, with deep green, bronze-tinted leaves, distinctive semi-double, recurrent cream flowers edged rosy-red, slightly fragrant. H3m/10ft, W3m/10ft. F7-9. Z5-8.

R. '**Iceberg**' **Climbing**. A climbing Floribunda sport with profuse, semi-double, sweetly scented white flowers, sometimes tinged with pale pink. A repeat-bloomer. H3-4m/10-13ft, W3-4m/10-13ft. F7-10. Z4-8.

R. '**Madame Grégoire Staechelin**'. Outstanding, vigorous climber with richly fragrant, large, semi-double, coral-pink blooms, the outer petals splashed with carmine. H5-6m/16-20ft, W3.6-5m/12-16ft. F6-7. Z4-8.

R. '**Mermaid**'. At its best a superb old climber, producing a succession of soft, primrose-yellow, single flowers with amber stamens. Can be difficult to establish, and best against a warm, sunny wall, but worth the effort. H5-6m/16-20ft, W5-6m/16-20ft. F6-11. Z6-8.

ROSMARINUS **Rosemary**

R. officinalis. Aromatic evergreen with narrow, dark green leaves, silver beneath, used extensively in cooking, but excellent foliage and flowering shrubs. A Mediterranean native, it revels in hot sun, but adapts surprisingly well. Light blue flowers appear on growth made the previous year, so unless plants are severely damaged, prune after flowering, usually in mid-summer. It makes an irregular, spreading bush, providing good contrast to silver, sun-loving shrubs. H90-150cm/3-5ft, W1.2-1.8m/4-6ft. F4-6. Z7-9. '**Alba**' is tender, with white flowers. H90-120cm/3-4ft, W90-120cm/3-4ft. F4-6. Z8-9. '**McConnell's Blue**' makes a prostrate mound, useful for tumbling over a path or sunny wall, and hardier than the similar '**Prostratus**' (syn. *R. lavandulaceus*). H45cm/18in, W1.2m/4ft. F4-6. Z7-9. The most popular and hardiest cultivar '**Miss Jessopp's Upright**' (syn. 'Fastigiatus') makes good hedging, with an erect but informal habit. H1.2-1.5m/4-5ft, W90-120cm/3-4ft. F4-6. Z7-9. '**Sissinghurst Blue**', a chance seedling raised at Sissinghurst Castle, Kent, England, has an erect habit and rich blue flowers. H90-120cm/3-4ft, W90-120cm/3-4ft. F5-6. Z7-8.

RUBUS **Bramble**

Many useful for winter stems, two of those below also have attractive summer foliage. These are best cut to the ground in late spring.

R. cockburnianus '**Golden Vale**'. Spreading habit, year-round interest, golden-yellow leaves, silver-white arching branches in winter. H90-120cm/3-4ft, W1.2-1.5m/4-5ft. F6-7. Z5-9.

R. odoratus. Suckering, spreading shrub, erect, thornless stems, large lobed leaves and purple-pink, fragrant flowers, followed by edible

Rubus cockburnianus 'Golden Vale'

red berries. Good in shade. H1.8-2.4m/6-8ft, W1.2-1.8m/4-8ft. F6-8. Z4-9.

R. thibetanus '**Silver Fern**'. Suckering shrub, grey-green, finely cut leaves, arching bright white stems in winter. Unpruned H1.8-2.4m/6-8ft, W1.5-1.8m/5-6ft. F6-7. Z6-9.

SALIX **Willow**

Enormous range of trees (*see* Tree Directory, page 81) and shrubs, attractive for leaves, catkins and winter stems. Most are easy to grow in any but poor dry soil. The few described below are mentioned for foliage effect in the garden.

S. '**Boydii**'. Chance hybrid, a gem for troughs and alpine gardens, with stubby, erect branches forming a miniature tree. Limited grey woolly catkins, silver-grey new leaves. H30cm/1ft, W20-30cm/8-12in. F5. Z4-7.

S. helvetica Swiss willow. Bright dwarf, multi-branched silver-leaved shrub, greyish-white catkins. H60-75cm/24-30in, W60-90cm/2-3ft. F4-5. Z6-7.

S. integra '**Hakuro Nishiki**' (syn. 'Albomaculata'). Twiggy shrub, open habit, renowned for bright shrimp-pink shoots opening to mottled, variegated cream and white leaves. Most effective pruned back annually in early spring and kept dwarf. ✿ ✣ where not too dry. H1.8m/6ft, W1.2-1.5m/4-5ft. F4. Z6-8.

S. lanata. Woolly willow. Low spreading habit, rigid branches, silver-yellow catkins, soft, grey-green downy leaves. H60-90cm/2-3ft, W60-90cm/2-3ft. F4-5. Z4-6.

SALVIA Sage
S. officinalis Common sage. Indispensable evergreen. Plants are best kept young; prune back if required in spring every two or three years. Various coloured-foliage forms, but shy to flower in cool climates. '**Berggarten**', hardy, felted grey leaves. '**Icterina**' (syn. '**Variegata**'), leaves splashed and variegated with creamy-yellow, golden-yellow and light green. '**Purpurascens**', purple younger shoots, older leaves turning soft grey-green. '**Tricolor**', the most tender but colourful, grey-green leaves boldly marked white and pink, new shoots purple, tinged red. H45-60cm/18-24in, W75-90cm/30-36in. F6-7. Z7-9. ✿ ✣ ▪

SAMBUCUS Elder
Some attractive foliage forms among these common deciduous shrubs. Adaptable, growing in acid or alkaline soils both wet and dry. Coloured foliage forms need sun but all tolerate shade. To tidy bushes or to create new growth for foliage colour prune in early spring, perhaps by a third but if necessary to within 30cm/1ft of the ground.

S. nigra. Common or European elder. There are several interesting foliage forms. All respond well to regular annual pruning. '**Albovariegata**', with dark green, white-edged leaves. '**Aurea**', the golden elder, with bright yellow foliage, dulling with age. '**Aureo-**

Salix integra 'Hakuro Nishiki'

marginata', with gold-edged leaves. '**Guincho Purple**' (syn. '**Purpurea**'), with black-purple leaves, in vivid contrast to its white flowers. '**Laciniata**', with graceful, deeply cut green leaves. '**Pulverulenta**', less vigorous, with leaves striped and splashed white. All tend to dislike high humidity. Average H2.4-3m/8-10ft, W2.4-3m/8-10ft. F6-7. Z5-7.

S. racemosa. The red-berried elder, an erect shrub with arching branches and clusters or panicles of relatively small, creamy-white flowers. Red fruits appear in favourable climates in mid-to late summer. Attractive garden forms with striking, golden-yellow foliage include '**Plumosa Aurea**' and '**Sutherland**' (syn. '**Sutherland Gold**'), with finely cut, coppery-yellow leaves, bright yellow in summer. Primrose-yellow flowers are sometimes followed by red fruit, but neither appear if plants are severely pruned. '**Plumosa Aurea**' leaves can scorch, less likely with '**Sutherland**'. All H3m/10ft, W2.4-3m/8-10ft. F3. Z3-6.

SANTOLINA Cotton lavender
Sun-loving, dwarf evergreen shrubs have cypress-like, grey or green foliage on soft, semi-woody stems and make low, spreading mounds. Most have profuse, yellow button flowers. ✿ ▪ They grow quickly and

Sambucus racemosa 'Plumosa Aurea'

can soon look untidy unless pruned annually or every other year in mid-spring. Prune all branches away to just above newly developing shoots.

S. chamaecyparissus (syn. *S. incana*). Popular species, reliably hardy and vigorous, with bright silver-grey, woolly foliage in summer, dull grey in winter, and yellow flowers which last for several weeks. H45-60cm/18-24in, W60-90cm/2-3ft. F7. Z6-9. '**Nana**', a compact, dense bush with smaller leaves and flowers than the species but similarly attractive. H30-45cm/12-18in, W45-60cm/18-24in. F6-8. Z6-9.

S. incana See *S. chamaecyparissus*.

S. virens. This distinct alternative to the grey-leaved forms has bright green foliage, in vivid contrast to its deep yellow flowers. H45-60cm/

18-24in, W45-60cm/18-24in. F7-8. Z7-9.

SENECIO
S. '**Sunshine**'. Often listed as *S. greyi* or *S. laxifolius*. The true *S. greyi* is tender, with soft grey, felted leaves. '**Sunshine**' is hardier, making a compact, later spreading, bush, its white, woolly stems clothed with grey-green, leathery leaves, white beneath. In a warm, sunny position it has masses of golden-yellow, daisy-like flowers. In spring, lightly prune established shrubs annually and older, woody plants to 10cm/4in of the ground every few years for rejuvenation. H90-120cm/3-4ft, W1.2-1.5m/4-5ft. F6-8. Z9-11.

SPARTIUM Spanish broom
S. junceum. The only species in the genus is closely related to *Cytisus* and *Genista*, with similar requirements. Makes a tall, upright shrub, with young, slender stems a deep green. Thrives on chalk and in coastal areas, with large, deep yellow, pea-like flowers. Prune green shoots when quite young to prevent plants becoming leggy, gathering several stems together and cutting with a sharp knife. Flowers on growth made in the same year, so prune to within 2.5cm/1in of the previous year's growth, just as shoots begin to appear in spring. Never prune into

Spiraea japonica 'Golden Princess'

old wood. New shoots will form rapidly, giving a bright display within a few weeks. H2.4-3m/8-10ft, W1.8-2.4m/6-8ft. F7-8. Z7-11. ☼ ■

SPIRAEA

Useful and ornamental hardy deciduous shrubs, particularly for a small garden. ☼ ❋ ☆

S. x arguta (syn. S. 'Arguta'). Popular hybrid, commonly known as bridal wreath, its arching branches carry a mass of dazzling white flowers. Vigorous and tall, it makes an effective hedge. Prune some old stems to the base and shorten others, if required, immediately after flowering. H1.8-2.4m/6-8ft, W1.8-2.4m/6-8ft. F4-5. Z5-8.

S. japonica. The Japanese spiraea cultivars are some of the best garden shrubs, easy to grow, generally dwarf and with flowers that continue for many weeks. The recent addition of many coloured-foliage forms provides added interest, from early spring until autumn leaf-fall. All benefit from annual pruning in late winter, at least by half the length of the previous year's growth. ☼ ❋ New shoots, especially golden-leaved forms, may be damaged by spring frost but soon recover. Can be prone to mildew. All Z4-8. **'Anthony Waterer'**(syn. S. x bumalda 'Anthony Waterer') is vigorous, strong and bushy. Its dark green leaves are sometimes yellow or variegated and its large, flat heads of bright carmine flowers are borne over a long period. H90-120cm/3-4ft, W90-120cm/3-4ft. F7-9. **'Gold Mound'** and **'Golden Princess'** are considerably more colourful than the previously popular **'Goldflame'**; their early shoots are more yellow and bronze respectively, their summer leaves brighter, with no hint of reversion. **'Golden Princess'** is round and compact, with golden-yellow leaves and pink flowers. H60-90cm/2-3ft, W60-75cm/24-30in. F7-8. **'Gold Mound'** is low and more spreading, its leaves brighter yellow and its flowers a brighter pink. H60-90cm/2-3ft, W75-90cm/30-36in. F6-8. **'Goldflame'** (syn. S. x bumalda 'Goldflame') coppery-crimson young shoots and deep golden-yellow leaves in early summer, fading by the time rose-pink flowers appear; prone to reversion to green. H60-90cm/2-3ft, W60-90cm/2-3ft. F6-7. Look for new selections **'Magic Carpet'**, **'Firelight'** and **'Candlelight'**, all striking yellow or gold foliage forms. The green-leaved **'Little Princess'** forms a broad dome of densely congested stems with free-flowering, pretty pink flowers. H45-60cm/18-24in,W60-75cm/24-30in. F6-7. **'Shirobana'** (syn. 'Shibori'), popular, green-leaved Japanese introduction, carries both white and red flowers on the same plant. H90-120cm/3-4ft, W90-120cm/3-4ft. F7-8.

S. nipponica 'Snowmound'. Erect shrub, arching branches festooned with small white flowers in early summer. H1.8-2.4m/6-8ft. F5-6. Z4-8.

S. x vanhouttei 'Pink Ice'. Compact foliage shrub, broad leaves splashed with white and pink. White flowers in mid-summer. H90-120cm/3-4ft, W60-90cm/2-3ft. F6-7. Z3-8.

SYRINGA Lilac

Common spring and early summer flowering deciduous shrubs, known for their fragrance. The common lilac, S. vulgaris and its cultivars are the best known, but all have in common a relatively short period of flower, and unless grown on their own roots, are prone to sucker. ☼ Grow on most soils though preferring heavier alkaline types to acid or peaty soils. They benefit from heavy feeding, and regular topdressing with compost or manure.

Syringa patula 'Miss Kim'

S. x hyacinthiflora. From this hybrid have come many early-flowering selections, mostly upright, with lightly fragrant flowers. **'Alice Eastwood'** has double flowers, deep wine-purple in bud, opoening pale blue. The popular, vigorous **'Esther Staley'** has carmine-red buds, opening pink. All H1.8-2.4m/6-8ft, W1.5-1.8m/5-6ft. F4-5. Z4-7.

S. meyeri 'Palibin' (syn. S. palibiniana). Densely branched shrub, smothered in small panicles of very fragrant, pale pink flowers, even when young. It remains reasonably attractive all year. H1.2-1.5m/4-5ft, W90-120cm/3-4ft. F6. Z4-8.

S. microphylla 'Superba'. Attractive, with deep rose-pink flowers continuing on and off for weeks. H90-120cm/3-4ft, W90-120cm/3-4ft. F7-9. Z4-8.

S. patula 'Miss Kim'. Slow-growing lilac. Freely branching and upright in habit, its pink flower buds open deep lilac, fading to blue. Both floriferous and fragrant. H1.5-1.8m/5-6ft, W90-120cm/3-4ft. F5-6. Z3-8.

S. x prestoniae. The Canadian hybrids are noted for their hardiness and abundant flowers. The large, open panicles are only slightly less fragrant than those of the common lilac. **'Audrey'**, an older cultivar, has deep pink flowers. **'Elinor'**, deep wine-red in bud, opens to pale lavender-pink. **'Isabella'** has large panicles of lilac-pink. A wider range of vigorous cultivars is now available in Canada and the USA. All H2.4-3m/8-10ft, W2.4-3m/8-10ft. F5-6. Z3-7.

S. vulgaris. Species seldom offered but there are numerous cultivars. Lilacs are often unhappy in a container, so these may not look their best at garden centres. They make erect, eventually bushy shrubs, but young plants may not flower for a few years. The single or double flowers are borne in dense panicles in white, violet, blue, lilac, pink, purple and yellow. All cultivars listed below are scented. **'Charles Joly'**, deep purple, double. **'Congo'**, lilac-red, small heads. **'Firmament'**, free-flowering, blue. **'Katherine Havemeyer'**, dense trusses of deep lavender-purple, fading to lilac-pink. **'Madame Lemoine'**, popular double, white, cream in bud. **'Maud Notcutt'**, large, white panicles. **'Michel Buchner'**, lilac-blue, double. **'Primrose'**, small, pale primrose heads. **'Sensation'**, purpled-red flowers, margined white. **'Souvenir de Louis Spath'**, an old cultivar, deep wine-red. All H2.4-3m/8-10ft, W1.5-1.8m/5-6ft. F6. Z4-7/8.

Viburnum × burkwoodii

TAMARIX Tamarisk

Distinctive shrubs often seen in coastal areas, most with narrow, upright, later arching branches, feathery, scale-like leaves and plumes of wispy pink flowers. Plants can become unkempt and straggly, so trim every year or two. Prune late-summer and autumn-flowering species to within 2.5cm/1in of old wood in spring before new growth begins; prune spring-flowering species just after flowering. ☼ ❋ ■

T. parviflora (syn. *T. tetrandra purpurea*). This hardy species has purplish stems, bright green leaves and rose-pink flowers. H1.8-2.4m/6-8ft, W1.8-2.4m/6-8ft. F5/6. Z5-8.

T. ramosissima (syn. *T. pentandra*). This has red-brown branches, bluish-green foliage and clouds of rose-pink flowers. '**Pink Cascade**', shell-pink. '**Rosea**', rosy pink, very hardy. '**Rubra**', deeper pink. All H2.4-3m/8-10ft, W2.4-3m/8-10ft. F8-9. Z3-8.

T. tetrandra. Hardy, early-flowering and rather open and straggly in habit, with arching branches and light pink flowers. H2.4-3m/8-10ft, W2.4-3m/8-10ft. F5-6. Z6-8.

VIBURNUM

Evergreen and deciduous shrubs and small trees, some winter-flowering, most in spring or early summer, early types often fragrant. Generally easy, most grow in any soil, including chalk. Some need moist soil; others, especially evergreens, may need shelter from cold desiccating winds.

V. × burkwoodii. Fragrant, spring-flowering hybrid is now only one of many similar forms, most upright, eventually round, semi-evergreen, often with good autumn colour, the original hybrid nearly deciduous. In winter, round heads of tight, pink buds form, opening white and continuing for many weeks, their fragrance spreading some distance on warm days. Good for cutting. H1.5-1.8m/5-6ft, W1.5-1.8m/5-6ft. F3. Z5-8. '**Chenaultii**', pale pink flowers, fading white. '**Fulbrook**' and '**Park Farm**' are more evergreen, spreading and slightly later flowering.

V. × carcephalum. Similar to *V. carlesii*, one of its parents, but has larger, fragrant flower clusters, pink in bud, opening white. H1.5-1.8m/5-6ft, W1.5-1.8m/5-6ft. F5-6. Z6-8.

V. carlesii. Fragrant, deciduous shrub forms tight clusters of flower buds in autumn, becoming pink before opening to white in spring. Cultivars include '**Aurora**', red flower buds, opening pink, slow-growing. '**Charis**', more vigorous, with flowers fading to white. '**Diana**', compact, with red buds which open to pink. All H1.2-1.5m/4-5ft, W1.2-1.5m/4-5ft. F5-6. Z4-8.

V. davidii. Evergreen, low, spreading shrub, with leathery, narrow, corrugated leaves, dull flowers, but bright metallic-blue fruit in autumn and winter, not always freely produced. Plant several to ensure cross-pollination – many nurserymen offer fruiting female plants with an identifiable male. ❋ ◢ H60-75cm/24-30in, W90-120cm/3-4ft. F6-7. Z8-9.

V. 'Eskimo'. Deciduous or semi-evergreen dwarf shrub, with glossy, dark green leaves and a succession of snowball-white flowers from late spring. Prune after the main flowering to keep density. H1.2-1.5m/4-5ft, W1.2-1.5m/4-5ft. F4-6. Z6-8.

V. opulus. European native, called guelder rose in Britain, and the European cranberry-bush viburnum in the USA. An easy, deciduous shrub, often found in country hedgerows, outstanding in late summer when hung with clusters of succulent, bright red fruit. It prefers moist soil but adapts to drier ones. All selections have maple-like leaves and flat, white, lacecap flowers in early summer. Some have good autumn leaf colour, but fruit appears when leaves are green. '**Aureum**' has bright yellow leaves which can scorch in full sun, but which stay yellow through summer. Red fruit and reddish-brown autumn tints. H1.5-1.8m/5-6ft, W1.2-1.5m/4-5ft. F6-7. Z3-8. '**Roseum**' (syn. '**Sterile**'), the snowball tree, has light green leaves and masses of round, green flowerheads, opening white. Non-fruiting. H2.4-3m/8-10ft, W1.8-2.4m/6-8ft. F6. Z4-8.

V. plicatum. These include snowball and lacecap types, the latter with central flowers surrounded by larger, sterile florets; both often with fruit following. Undeniably showy. The species is now rare, but many fine cultivars are sold. Most Z6-8. ☼ ❋ ◢ '**Cascade**', dense, bushy habit; large, lacecap flowers, often abundant red fruit. H1.5m/5ft, W1.8m/6ft. F5-6. The choice '**Grandiflorum**' needs shade and moist soil, forming an erect shrub with large, pale green, sterile, snowball heads, turning white. H1.5-1.8m/5-6ft, W1.2-1.5m/4-5ft. F5-6. '**Lanarth**' and '**Mariesii**', wide-spreading, horizontally tiered branches with rows of flat, white florets raised above the branches. Both H1.8m/6ft, W2.4m/8ft. F5-6. '**Watanabe**' (syn. '**Nanum Semperflorens**'), from Japan, is narrow and upright, its small, lacecap flowers appearing on young plants, and continuing, in a small way, to bloom throughout the summer. Advisable to provide shelter; excellent for small gardens. '**Summer Snowflake**' is similar. Both H1.2-1.5m/4-5ft, W60-90cm/2-3ft. F5-8.

V. sargentii '**Onondaga**'. Narrow and upright, its bronze shoots open

Weigela praecox 'Variegata'

to maroon-purple leaves, the flower buds purple, surrounded by white florets. Shoots break freely from the base, given hard pruning in early spring, but flowers will be lost. H1.5-1.8m/5-6ft, W90-120cm/3-4ft. F6-7. Z4-7.

WEIGELA

Ornamental group of easily grown flowering shrubs, include dwarf, coloured-foliage and long-flowering types. Once listed under *Diervilla*, weigelas flower only on last year's stems, the former genus flowering on new season's growth. The trumpet-like flowers, often with prominent stamens, are sometimes so profuse that they weigh down the outer branches. Prune after flowering, thinning congested, old stems to the base and shortening untidy shoots by half, keeping the general habit of the plant. Most are very hardy, though some can be tender and vulnerable to spring frosts. Those offering a longer season of interest than the flowers alone are best value for space. ✿ ✸ ■

W. florida. Parent to many hybrids but rarely grown, it and most hybrids have an upright, arching habit, dark green leaves and rosy-pink flowers, paler inside. H1.5-1.8m/5-6ft, W1.2-1.5m/4-5ft. F5-6. Z5-8. '**Foliis Purpureis**' has purple-green leaves and purplish-pink flowers. The Canadian '**Minuet**', similar in habit and leaf, has clusters of rosy-purple flowers, with prominent, creamy-white stamens. '**Rumba**' is similar again, but with red flowers. '**Tango**' has purplish foliage and red flowers. All H75-90cm/30-36in, W90cm/3ft. F5-6. Z5-8. '**Variegata**', similar to the species, has coarse leaves with creamy-yellow margins, pinkish in autumn, and pink flowers; more erect, with coarser, yellower leaves than *W. praecox* 'Variegata'. H1.5-

Wisteria sinensis

1.8m/5-6ft, W1.2-1.5m/4-5ft. F5-6. Z5-8.

W. praecox '**Variegata**'. White-edged, wavy leaves in sun, golden-yellow in shade, and fragrant, rose-pink flowers with a yellow throat. Can suffer from spring frost; best in shelter. ✿ ✸ H1.2-1.5m/4-5ft, W1.2-1.5m/4-5ft. F5-6. Z6-8.

Hybrids. Most flower from mid-summer. Unless otherwise indicated, all H1.5-2.4m/5-8ft, W1.5-1.8m/5-6ft. F5-6. Z5-8. '**Abel Carrière**', over 100 years old, is still one of the best; red buds opening carmine-rose, large and free-flowering. '**Boskoop Glory**', large, satin-pink flowers. '**Bristol Ruby**', large, deep red flowers, good foliage. '**Candida**', white-flowered. The French '**Carnival**', salmon-pink, white and dark pink. '**Dropmore Pink**', deep pink, very hardy. '**Eva Supreme**', vigorous, profuse, deep red flowers. '**Looymansii Aurea**', open and graceful, golden-yellow leaves and pink flowers all summer; lovely in part shade. '**Mont Blanc**', fragrant, white flowers. '**Rubigold**' (syn. 'Briant Rubidor'), French sport of 'Bristol Ruby', golden-yellow leaves prone to sunscorch, occasional green variegations, deep red flowers. '**Snowflake**', pale foliage, robust

white flowers. '**Victoria**', dwarf, black-purple leaves, rose-pink flowers, often recurring. H90-120cm/3-4ft, W90-120cm/3-4ft. F5-8. Z6-8.

WISTERIA

Small group of ornamental twiners, with pinnate leaves and often spectacular, pendulous racemes of white, blue, purple or pink flowers. Most named forms are grafted and usually flower within two or three years of purchase, but cheaper, seed-raised plants can take several years to flower. Wisterias can be trained and tied against walls and fences and over pergolas. They can also be trained up stakes and carefully pruned to form small trees, or grown as patio specimens in containers, as long as they are regularly fertilized. Plant in a sunny, sheltered spot and well-drained, fertile soil.

In climates with late spring frosts, grow against a west-facing wall, to protect the flower buds. Prune to control size and improve flowering. Train new growth to form a framework for two or three years, longer if necessary. On established plants, prune long shoots in late summer back to about 15cm/6in of the season's new growth, and in mid-winter, prune a few more

centimetres/inches back to two or three flowering buds which should have formed. Once out of reach, wisterias can be allowed to go their own way.

W. floribunda. The Japanese wisteria has stems which twine in a clockwise direction, while the Chinese wisteria, *W. sinensis,* goes anti-clockwise – one of the small wonders of nature! The Japanese wisteria has dark green leaves which unfurl as the 15-25cm/6-10in pendulous racemes of fragrant, bluish-purple flowers appear in succession. Pale yellow autumn leaf colour. '**Alba**' has 60cm/2ft long racemes on established specimens, the white flowers often tinged lilac. '**Macrobotrys**' (syn. 'Multijuga'), impressive, with racemes sometimes reaching 90cm/3ft or more in length; a specimen draped with numerous flowers is, quite breathtaking. '**Rosea**', pale rose-pink and purple. '**Violacea**', violet-blue. '**Violacea Plena**', unusual double, violet-blue. All H5-6m/16-20ft, W5-6m/16-20ft. F5-6. Z4-9.

W. sinensis. The Chinese wisteria is the most widely grown form. It is often sold as a seed-raised plant, liable to have inferior flowers and take up to ten years to flower, so be sure to look for grafted plants. The species has mauve-lilac, fading to pale lilac, fragrant flowers on pendulous racemes to 30cm/1ft long, all opening at once and before the leaves appear. '**Alba**' has white flowers. '**Black Dragon**', double, dark purple, long trusses. '**Peaches and Cream**' (syn. 'Kuchibeni'), pink buds opening creamy-white. '**Pink Ice**' (syn. 'Hond Beni'), rose-pink, long racemes. '**Plena**', lilac double flowers. '**Purple Patches**' (syn. 'Murasaki Naga Fuji'), long trusses, deep violet-purple flowers. '**Snow Showers**' (syn. 'Shiro Naga Fuji'), pure white. All H6-8m/20-26ft, W6-8m/20-26ft. F5. Z5-9.

CONIFERS

Juniperus communis 'Suecica Nana'

Flowers on *Pinus heldreichii*

Though a full conifer directory cannot be included in this book for reasons of space, conifers have a definite part to play in creating summer colour in the garden. Contrary to some views, conifers can and do change quite dramatically with the seasons, as is illustrated in the introductory chapters of this book as well as in its sister publication, *Winter Garden Glory*.

Though conifers tend to have a more supporting role in summer, when there is so much of interest in the garden, their colour and effects can be breathtaking, particularly during the period of new growth in early to mid-summer. The foliage varies according to type, with firs (*Abies*), spruce (*Picea*) and pines (*Pinus*) having needles or leaves which are completely different to those of the junipers (*Juniperus*) or the chamaecyparis. Some, like the larch (*Larix*) or swamp cypress (*Taxodium*) are deciduous.

Conifers come in all shapes and sizes and can be fast or slow-growing. They may be low, bushy or bun-shaped, narrow, upright, prostrate or semi-prostrate, wide-spreading – or indeed any shape in between. Foliage colours vary from silver-blue, deep blue, gold, yellow and, of course, all shades of green as well as variegated. Their colours have the most intensity during the periods of active growth in spring and summer, though the winter colours on some plants are even brighter than in summer.

Most conifers actually have flowers – some a dramatic red – and many have attractive cones. Some, for

Pinus mugo 'Jeddeloh' making new growth in early summer

example the pines, put on only one burst of growth each year, while chamaecyparis will continue to make growth throughout the summer.

As the illustrations from Foggy Bottom earlier in the book will show, conifers act as important background plants, offering colour contrasts to shrubs, perennials, alpines and grasses. They do not have to be grown on their own or with plants like heathers but can be an integral part of garden planting, either as hedges or specimens. What must be remembered is that conifers will not only provide valuable year-round colour but, in the larger types, will give structure to the garden. This book can present only a general view of conifers and their role in the garden but this should be sufficient to promote wider interest.

New growth on *Abies lasiocarpa* 'Compacta'

An association of conifers at Foggy Bottom

PERENNIALS ARE THE PERFECT INGREDIENT to create spring and summer colour in the garden, however large or small. Enormously diverse and adaptable, perennials can be found to fit almost all garden sites and situations. This, the largest single section of the Directory, includes a few bulbs as well as my selection of the most worthwhile of all perennials. Remember that if a particular recommended selection is not available to you, good alternatives can usually be found at either local specialist growers or at garden centres. Local and regional climates will of course have a bearing on what can be grown successfully, flowering times and longevity also varying according to seasonal variations.

H:	Approximate height
W:	Approximate width
F :	Months in flower
Z:	Relevant hardiness zone(s)

Mid-summer grouping: *Acanthus spinosus, Geranium* 'Mavis Simpson'

ACANTHUS Bear's breeches
Stately plants with handsome, divided leaves and striking flower spikes of overlapping bracts, good for drying. Protect young plants with a mulch where winters are cold. The deep, fleshy roots are difficult to eradicate once established. ✿ ■
A spinosus. Large, glossy, divided leaves, tipped with spines, form handsome mounds of deep green foliage. Tall spikes bearing hooded purplish flowers are dramatic and imposing. H1.2m/4ft, W60cm/2ft. F7-9. Z7-10.

ACHILLEA Yarrow, milfoil
Most achilleas have ferny leaves and small, tight clusters of flowers, some excellent for cutting or drying. ✿ ■
A. 'Anthea'. A first class hybrid, with soft and silvery foliage. The flower heads, 8-10cm/3-4in across, are primrose-yellow and fade to creamy-yellow. Cut out faded stems to prolong flowering. H60cm/2ft, W30cm/1ft. F6-8. Z4-8.
'Galaxy Hybrids'. A range of hybrids between *A. millefolium* and *A. sibirica* 'Taygetea'. Colourful, easy to grow, good for cutting. All

W60cm/2ft. F6-9. Z4-8. '**Apple Blossom**' (syn. 'Apfelblüte') light lilac-pink. H40cm/16in. '**Great Expectations**' (syn. 'Hoffnung') buff-primrose flowers. H60cm/2ft. '**Salmon Beauty**' (syn. 'Lachsscönheit') light salmon-pink. H60cm/2ft. '**The Beacon**' (syn. 'Fanal') bright red flowers, with yellow centres. H60cm/2ft.
A. '**Moonshine**'. Showy, flat heads of lemon-yellow above silvery foliage. H60cm/2ft, W45cm/18in. F6-9. Z4-8.

ACONITUM Aconite, monkshood
Distinctive but underrated garden plants. Divide congested clumps every 2 or 3 years. Roots are poisonous if eaten. ✿ ✺ ☆ ✬
A. '**Blue Sceptre**'. A striking cultivar with erect spikes of violet-blue and white flowers. H75cm/30in, W45cm/18in. F7-9. Z4-8.
A. '**Bressingham Spire**' makes a strong-stemmed, perfect narrow pyramid with deeply cut green leaves. Flowers violet-blue. H90-100cm/36-39in, W45cm/18in. F7-9. Z4-8.
A. '**Ivorine**'. Distinctive bushy habit with good foliage; ivory-white flowers on branching spikes. H up to 90cm/3ft, W75cm/30in. F6-8. Z5-8.

AGAPANTHUS African lily
Popular perennials originally from South Africa, some hardier than imagined. Strap-like leaves and rounded stems bearing heads of blue or white flowers. Ideal for containers. In colder areas mulch in late autumn with straw or bracken. All below Z8-10. ✬ ☆
A. '**Bressingham Blue**'. Amethyst-blue, free-flowering. *A.* '**Bressingham White**'. Pure white blooms. Both H90cm/3ft, W45cm/18in. F7-9.
A. companulatus '**Isis**'. A sturdy cultivar with a bright display of deep blue flowers. H60cm/2ft, W45cm/18in. F7-9.
A. '**Lilliput**'. Quite dwarf with small,

Allium schoenoprasum 'Forescate'

rich blue flowers on slender stems. H10cm/12in, W10cm/4in. F7-8.

ALCHEMILLA MOLLIS Lady's mantle
Indispensable, adaptable perennial. Large, grey-green, rounded leaves are slightly hairy and hold raindrops. Good for cutting, sprays of tiny, yellow-green flowers are attractive. Self-seeding so remove heads after flowering if required. H45cm/18in, W60cm/2ft. F6-8. Z4-8. ✿ ✺

ALLIUM Ornamental onion
Strictly bulbs but often grown as perennials. A very wide range of generally easy to grow plants. ✿ ■
A. afflatuense. The Persian Onion fits well with other perennials, pushing up stump-like leaves which soon disappear as large purple flower heads appear in late spring. H60-90cm/ 2-3ft, W45cm/18in. F5-6. Z4-8.
A. schoenoprasum '**Forescate**' has bright purple-crimson blooms. H30cm/1ft, W23 cm/9in. F6-8. Z3-9.
A. senescens. Late-flowering display of flesh-pink flowers from neat-growing, grey-green clumps. H30cm/12in, W15cm/6in. F8-9. Z4-8.

AMSONIA
A. tabernaemontana. Pretty species forms clump with narrow willow-like leaves on arching stems tipped with

small, light blue flowers for many weeks. Graceful, long-lived. H75cm/30in, W45cm/18in. F6-9. Z4-9. ✿ ❋ ☆

ANAPHALIS Pearl everlasting
A. triplinervis 'Summer Snow'. Perhaps the most effective of these grey- and silver-leaved plants. Easy to grow. Flowers white with yellow centres, excellent for cutting, makes a good foil. H30cm/12in, W60cm/2ft. F7-9. Z4-9. ✿ ◢ ❋

ANCHUSA
A group of fleshy rooted perennials. From coarse, hairy leaves emerge branched spikes carrying striking blue flowers in early summer. Cut stems back after flowering. May need staking. ✿ ■
A. 'Royalist'. Perhaps the most reliable, with gentian-blue flowers. H1.5m/5ft, W60cm/2ft. F5-7. 'Opal', light blue. H1.1m/43in, W60cm/2ft. F5-7.

ANEMONE
There are some excellent perennials in this genus, few more so than the **Japanese anemones** (*A.* × *hybrida*) flowering in late summer/autumn.
A. **x** *hybrida*. Classic perennials with leafy foliage, wiry stems and single and double yellow-stamened flowers. ✿ ❋ ☆ (including lime).
'Alba', strong grower, pure white flowers, golden yellow stamens. H75cm/30in, W45cm/18in. F8-10. Z5-8. '**Bressingham Glow**', rich, deep pink, semi-double flowers. H60cm/2ft, W45cm/18in. F8-10. Z5-8. '**Hadspen Abundance**', deep rose-pink, almost semi-double flowers. H60cm/2ft, W30cm/1ft. F8-10. Z5-9. '**Lady Gilmour**', large, double clear pink flowers. H60cm/2ft, W45cm/18in. F7-10. Z5-8.

ANTHEMIS
Easy-to-grow sun lovers for open positions. ✿ ■

Anemone 'Hadspen Abundance'

A. cupaniana. Greyish, aromatic leaves and a spectacular show of white, yellow-centred daisies. H25cm/10in, W75cm/30in. F5-8. Z5-8.
A. tinctoria 'E C Buxton'. Free-flowering daisy, ideal for hot, dry positions. Spreading habit, rich green foliage and a succession of lemon-yellow petalled flowers with a gold centre; provides weeks of summer colour. Cut back hard after flowering to create basal growth which will help over-wintering. H75cm/2ft 6in, W75cm/2ft 6in. F6-8. Z 4-8.

AQUILEGIA Columbine
Popular plants, though few are long-lived and, while freely seeding, they are inclined to cross-breed. Space each group some distance apart. ✿
A. vulgaris. Clustered flowers come in a profusion of white, pink, indigo, violet and crimson. H60cm/2ft, W45cm/18in, F5-7. Z5-9. There are several selections with yellow leaves: '**Granny's Gold**' is distinctive but can have white or lilac-purple flowers; '**Mellow Yellow**' similar, with white flowers. '**Nora Barlow**' is an interesting variation with double rose-pink and cream flowers. H60cm/2ft, W30cm/1ft. F6-7. Z5-9. **McKana Hybrids**. Mixed colours with extra-long spurs. H75cm/30in, W30cm/1ft. F5-7. Z3-9.

ARTEMISA
Primarily used as foliage plants, with flowers of little significance. Woodier types need pruning in spring if becoming unshapely. ✿ ■
A. lactiflora. Fine green, deeply cut leaves and stiff stems carrying creamy-white plumes in late summer. '**Guizhou**', with bronze-purple leaves, is even more effective. H1.5-1.8m/5-6ft, W60cm/2ft. F8-10. Z4-9. ◢
A. ludoviciana 'Silver Queen'. Rapid-spreader with willow-like silvery leaves and leafy stems. '**Valerie Finnis**' has broader leaves and is more vigorous. Both H80cm/32in, W60cm/2ft. Z4-9.
A. stelleriana. Vigorous, spreading habit, deeply cut silver leaves carried on ground-hugging stems. Good evergreen ground cover. '**Mori**' (sometimes called '**Silver Brocade**'), is similar but more compact. H30cm/1ft, W60cm/2ft. Z4-8.

ARUNCUS Goat's beard
Showy plants, closely related to *Spiraea*, are adaptable to moist or dry soils. ❋ ◢
A. dioicus (syn. *A. sylvester*). Imposing, creamy-white plumes are carried above a mass of fern-like foliage. H1.5-2.1m/5-7ft, W1.2m/4ft. F6-7. Z3-8. '**Kneiffii**' is dwarfer, with dark green, deeply cut leaves,

wiry stems and flower plumes. '**Dublin**' has finer creamy-white plumes. H90cm/3ft, W45cm/18in. F6-7. Z3-8.
A. sylvester. See *A. dioicus*.

ASCLEPIAS Butterfly weed, milkweed
A. luberosa. Butterfly weed is the best known species but is not always easy to grow. It prefers a warm, sandy loam to produce its bright heads of burnished deep orange and needs summer warmth to succeed. H45cm/18in, W30cm/1ft. F7-9. Z4-9.

ASPHODELINE
A. lutea. King's spear, or asphodel, forms clumps of narrow, glaucous leaves and strong spikes of bright yellow starry flowers, followed by attractive seedheads. The German cultivar '**Gelbkerze**' has larger, slightly brighter flowers. Both H1m/39in, W30cm/1ft. F6-8. Z6-8.

ASTER
This vast and varied genus has many species of great garden value, varying in height from 10cm/4in to 2.1m/7ft and flowering from mid-spring to late autumn. Most are easy to grow and popular for cutting. ✿ ■
A. amellus. Trouble-free perennials, all single rayed, yellow-centred flowers with no faults or diseases. All

Aruncus dioicus (syn. *A. sylvester*)

Astilbe simplicifolia 'Sprite'

long-lived and long-flowering. For autumn planting, pot-grown plants are best. All F8-10. Z5-8. ☼ ☀
'King George', an old, violet-blue favourite. H60cm/2ft, W45cm/18in. 'Nocturne', rich lilac-lavender. H75cm/30in, W45cm/18in. 'Pink Zenith', the most prolific pink variety. H60cm/2ft, W45cm/18in. 'Violet Queen', masses of deep violet-blue flowers. H60cm/2ft, W45cm/18in. *A. × frikartii* 'Flora's Delight'. Dwarf, free flowering, disease-free. Raised by my father Alan Bloom and named for my stepmother, first class with bluish-lilac flowers for months. H45cm/18in, W40cm/16in. F7-10. Z4-9. 'Mönch' and 'Wunder von Stäfa' are outstanding perennials, long-flowering with soft lavender-blue petals, yellow daisy centres Both H1m/39in. F7-9. Z5-8. ☼ ■
A. laterifolius 'Prince'. Really a foliage plant of stiff, upright habit, bronze-purple from spring onwards. Flowers pink, small. H60cm/2ft, W45cm/18in. F9-11. Z4-8.
A. novae-angliae. The New England asters offers some bright colour late in summer. All trouble-free and easy to grow; some are quite tall. 'Alma Pötschke', striking, warm salmon-rose. H1.5m/5ft, W60cm/2ft. 'Autumn Snow' (syn. 'Herbst-

Astrantia carniolica rubra

schnee'), large white flowers in bushy heads. H1.5m/5ft, W50cm/20in. 'Harrington's Pink', clear pink. 'Rosa Sieger' is similar. H1.5m/5ft, W60cm/2ft. F8-10. Z4-8.
A. thomsonii 'Nanus'. A first class perennial of bushy habit, set with grey-green foliage and rayed, light blue flowers for weeks on end. H40cm/16in, W25cm/10in. F7-10. Z4-9.

ASTILBE
Popular hardy perennials ranging in size from a few centimetres to over a metre, some with attractive foliage. Good for cutting and excellent as container plants given adequate moisture. Divide and replant every few years from late autumn to early spring. The very dwarf ones are shade lovers. All benefit from a spring mulch of enriched peat or leafmould. ☼ ☀ ◪
A. chinensis 'Pumila'. Low spreading foliage and short lilac-pink flower spikes. Good ground cover. H30cm/1ft, W25cm/10in. F7-9. Z4-8.
A. chinensis tacquetii 'Superba'. Tall spikes of purple magenta flowers.

'Purpurlanze' (Purple Lance) is brighter. Both H1.2-1.5m/4-5ft, W45cm/18in. F8-9. Z4-8.
A. simplicifolia. Parent of several good dwarf hybrids. Small leaves, pink flowers. H30cm/1ft, W20cm/8in. F6-8. All Z4-8.
'Bronze Elegans' arching stems, pink flowers, pretty bronze-tinged leaves, compact habit. 'Sprite', dark bronze-green, deeply cut foliage and late display of arching sprays of pink flowers, fading to white. Both H25-30cm/10-12in, W30cm/1ft. F8-9.
Hybrids. The following are sometimes classified as A. × *arendsii* or A. *japonica*. All Z4-8. 'Amethyst', full, lilac-rose spikes. H90cm/3ft, W60cm/2ft. F6-7. 'Bressingham Beauty', fine pink spikes on strong stems above attractive foliage. H1m/39in, W60cm/2ft. F6-8. 'Catherine Deneuve', deep rose-pink spikes, dark foliage. 'Elizabeth Bloom', free-flowering, rich pink spikes, abundant dark green foliage. Both H60cm/2ft, W60cm/2ft. F6-8. 'Fanal', long-flowering, with short, red, dense spikes, striking foliage.

H50cm/20in, W45cm/18in. F6-8. 'Federsee', sturdy, full rosy red plumes. H60cm/2ft, W60cm/2ft. F6-8. 'Ostrich Plume', distinctive, arching, salmon-pink plumes. H80cm/32in, W60cm/2ft. F7-8. 'Sheila Haxton', outstanding, compact, pink with a hint of lilac. H40cm/16in, W30cm/1ft. F6-8. 'Snowdrift', bright green mounds of cut foliage, clear white plumes. H60cm/2ft, W45cm/18in. F6-8.

ASTRANTIA Masterwort
Popular for garden and cut flowers, their curiously shaped blooms each have a dome of tiny florets backed by a collar-like bract. Clump-forming and easy to grow. Some seed freely and can soon become mixed. All Z4-8. ☼ ☀ ◪
A. carniolica rubra. Deep crimson-green flowers above mounds of divided foliage. H45cm/18in, W30cm/1ft. F6-8. ◪ ✶
A. major involucrata 'Shaggy' (syn. 'Margery Fish') has larger bracts and is quite showy. H75cm/2ft 6in, W45cm/18in. F6-8. 'Rosea' has deep rose-red flowers. H75cm/30in, W45cm/18in. F6-8. 'Ruby Wedding', outstanding, glowing ruby-red flowers. H75cm/2ft 6in, W45cm/18in. F6-8. 'Sunningdale Variegated', bright foliage in spring and early summer, the leaves edged white then cream, but fading when greenish-white flowers appear. H75cm/2ft 6in, W45cm/18in. F6-8.

BAPTISIA Wild indigo
B. australis. Long-lived, bushy perennial with abundant blue-green foliage topped by short spikes of indigo-blue, lupin-like flowers, followed by attractive seed pods. Non-invasive. H90-120cm/3-4ft, W60cm/2ft. F6-8. Z3-9. ☼ ◪

BERGENIA
Good foliage in summer, some colouring up well in winter. Flowers

attractive in spring but can get spoilt by frost. Mainly evergreen, shiny leaves up to 25cm/10in across. Spreading habit, good ground cover. ☼ ■ ☀

Hybrids. Crosses between various species have produced some excellent forms. '**Abendglut**' (syn. 'Evening Glow'), small, almost prostrate, with short spikes of crimson flowers and purplish leaves in winter. H25cm/10in, W30cm/1ft. F3-5. Z3-8. '**Baby Doll**', compact spikes of sugar-pink flowers. H20cm/8in, W30cm/1ft. F3-5. Z4-8. '**Bressingham Ruby**', intense, deep red flowers and almost beetroot-red leaves in winter. H30cm/1ft, W30cm/1ft. F3-5. Z3-8. '**Bressingham White**', clean white flowers, handsome rounded leaves. H30cm/1ft, W30cm/1ft. F3-5. Z4-8. '**Morgenröte**', dwarf, bright carmine-pink flowers, often flowering a second time in summer. H30cm/1ft, W30cm/1ft. F3-5. Z3-8.

BRUNNERA
B. macrophylla. Adaptable perennial with large, heart-shaped, deep green leaves, sprays of bright blue forget-me-not flowers in spring. Good ground cover for all but hot, dry

positions. H40cm/16in, W60cm/2ft. F4-6. All Z4-8. '**Hadspen Cream**', vigorous, with wide, creamy-buff-edged leaves. H35cm/14in, W60cm/2ft. F5-6. '**Langtrees**' has small, silvery-white blotches on the leaves. H40cm/16in, W60cm/2ft. F4-6. '**Variegata**' has bright leaf variegation, but needs shelter from sun and some moisture. H40cm/16in, W60cm/2ft. F4-6.

CAMPANULA **Bellflower**
A varied and invaluable genus from dwarf alpine to tall perennials which is easy to grow. ☼ ■ ☀ (*See also* Alpines Directory).
C. '**Burghaltii**'. Distinctive for its large, dangling bells of smokey lavender-blue, hanging from short, leafy stems. H60cm/2ft, W30cm/1ft. F6-8. Z4-8.
C. glomerata. Species with violet-blue flowers, variable and inclined to be invasive. Selections recommended: '**Schneekrone**' (Crown of Snow), sturdy spikes of white bells. '**Purple Pixie**', late, with dark foliage and deep blue flowers on stiff spikes. Both H45cm/18in, W30cm/1ft. F7-9. '**Superba**', large, rich purple-violet flowers, but can be invasive. H80cm/32in, W60cm/2ft. F6-8.
C. '**Kent Belle**'. A striking hybrid with arching stems carrying rich violet-blue bells. H120-150cm/4-5ft, W45cm/18in. F6-8. Z4-8.
C. lactiflora. The milky bellflowers add a considerable presence in the summer garden with their willowy stems and heads of massed flowers. Adaptable to sun or shade; some taller forms may need staking. All Z4-8. '**Alba**' has milky-white flowers. '**Loddon Anna**' is equally imposing, with flesh-pink flowers. Both H1.8m/6ft, W60cm/2ft. F6-8. '**Pouffe**', forms dense mounds of light green foliage, with light lavender-blue flowers. H25cm/10in, W25cm/10in. F6-9. '**Prichard's Variety**', outstanding show of lavender-blue

flowers. H1.2m/4ft, W60cm/2ft. F6-8. '**White Pouffe**', similar to 'Pouffe'; both flower best in sun. H25cm/10in, W25cm/10in. F6-9.
C. persicifolia. Popular bellflower with nodding, cup-shaped flowers varying from white to pale and deep blue. Good for cutting. H70-80cm/28-32in, W30cm/1ft. All F6-8. Z4-8. '**Alba Coronata**', with semi-double pale white flowers. H90-120cm/3-4ft, W30cm/1ft. '**Chettle Charm**', a pretty selection with off-white, blue-tinged cup-shaped bells on wiry stems. Excellent for cutting. H90-120cm/3-4ft, W30cm/1ft.

CATANANCHE CAERULEA
Sun-loving perennial with lavender-blue flowers surrounded by papery bracts, grassy foliage. The white form '**Alba**' is an interesting variation. Good for cutting and drying. H60cm/2ft, W30cm/12in. F7-8. Z3-9.

CENTAUREA **Knapweed**
The perennial cornflowers include some good species, usually with purple, thistle-like flowers, easy to grow in open, sunny positions.
C. hypoleuca '**John Coutts**' has bright, glistening pink flowers above

ample grey foliage. H60cm/2ft, W45cm/18in. F5-7. Z4-8.
C. macrocephala. The globe centre has large mid-green leaves and stout stems topped by large yellow thistles, good for drying. H1.2-1.5m/4-5ft, W60cm/2ft. F6-8. Z3-8.
C. montana. Mountain knapweed has a spreading habit. The lance-shaped leaves are grey and slightly hairy; flowers on single stalks have one row of toothed or lacy petals around a central cone. Colours vary from white to pink, light blue, lilac and violet-blue. A few cultivars are offered. '**Gold Bullion**' is worth special mention for its yellow-gold foliage and blue flowers, giving summer-long appeal. Excellent on chalk and poor soil. All H30cm/1ft, W30cm/1ft. F5-6. Z3-8.
C. '**Pulchra Major**'. Outstandingly handsome, deeply cut, arching grey leaves and rigid stems topped by large, deep pink thistles. H90cm/3ft, W30cm/1ft. F6-8. Z7-8.

CENTRANTHUS **Valerian**
C. ruber. This easily grown plant will colonize almost anywhere from self-sown seed, even in the poorest soil, on walls and rocky banks, especially

Brunnera macrophylla 'Variegata'

Campanula 'Kent Belle'

Centaurea montana 'Gold Bullion'

Chrysanthemum weyrichii

on limestone. The colours are mostly pink to brick-red but **'Albus'** is a good white form. All have fleshy leaves. H80cm/32in, W45cm/18in. F6-9. Z5-8. ✿ ❋

CHELONE Turtle head
C. obliqua. An underrated perennial with erect, leafy stems tipped with a good display of ruby-pink flowers. A reliable plant for sun. The white form **'Alba'** is also worth growing. Both H80cm/32in, W45cm/18in. F7-9. Z4-9.

CHRYSANTHEMUM
There have been so many name changes in this popular genus in recent years that even the genus name itself, *Chrysanthemum,* has disappeared! *C. weyrichii* (syn. *Dendranthema weyrichii*). Early summer-flowering species with low, spreading habit and large, brilliant white yellow-centred flowers, on stems only 10cm/4in high, fading to pink. Flowers again in autumn. H10-15cm/4-6in, W15cm/6in. F6-7. Z4-9.

CIMICIFUGA Bugbane
C. cordifolia. Broad, deep green leaves and tapering spikes of creamy-white on wiry, purplish stems.

H90-120cm/3-4ft, W60cm/2ft. F8-9. Z4-8.
C. ramosa. Large, divided leaves and lofty, tapering, branched spikes, creamy-white, late in the season. H2.1m/7ft, W60cm/2ft. F8-9. Z4-8. **'Atropurpurea'**, outstanding for its purplish leaves and stems, contrasting effectively with the white flowers. H2.1m/7ft, W60cm/2ft. F8-9. Z4-8. **'Brunette'** has even more striking black-purple foliage. H1.8m/6ft, W60cm/2ft. F8-10. Z4-8.

CLEMATIS
This genus includes perennial, non-climbing species of real garden value, reliably hardy and long-lived, needing minimal attention. ✿ ❋ ☆
C. davidiana See *C. heracleifolia.*
C. × eriostemon 'Hendersonii'. Nodding flowers with deep blue, reflexed petals from late spring to mid-summer, followed by attractive seedheads. This, and the similar *C. integrifolia* are inclined to flop. Both H60-70cm/24-28in if supported, otherwise 40cm/16in, W60cm/2ft. F5-7. Z4-9.
C. heracleifolia (syn. *C. davidiana*). Makes a woody-based, leafy bush with hyacinth-like clusters of scented blue flowers for many weeks, followed by attractive seedheads. Though dying down over winter, its lush summer growth needs ample space. **'Alan Bloom'**, a new selection, has an upstanding habit, dark green leaves and deep blue fragrant flowers. **'Crepescule'**, **'Cote D'Azur'** and **'Wyevale'** are all slightly different shades of blue, all worthwhile. All H90cm/3ft, W60cm/2ft. F7-9. Z4-9.

COREOPSIS Tickseed
Yellow daises, with yellow or orange central discs. ✿ ☆
C. auriculata 'Nana'. A splendid dwarf perennial whose deep green mounds produce a summer-long succession of bright yellow flowers. H30cm/1ft, W30cm/1ft. F5-10. Z4-9.

Coreopsis verticillata 'Moonbeam'

C. rosea. Unique for its small, pale pink flowers on narrow-leaved stems. Spreads below ground. A selected form, **'American Dream'**, has deeper pink flowers. Both H30cm/1ft, W30cm/1ft. F8-9. Z3-9.
C. verticillata 'Golden Gain'. Makes a compact bush with finely divided leaves and bright yellow flowers for weeks. H60cm/2ft, W38cm/15in. F7-9. Z4-9. **'Grandiflora'** has larger, deeper yellow flowers. H50cm/20in, W45cm/18in. F7-9. Z4-9. **'Moonbeam'**, light lemon-yellow flowers, scented foliage and spreading growth. H40cm/16in, W30cm/1ft. F7-9. Z3-9. **'Zagreb'** has clear yellow flowers, dwarf bushy growth. H35cm/14in, W30cm/1ft. F7-9. Z3-7.

COSMOS
C. atrosanguineus (syn. *Bidens atrosanguinea*). Long succession of chocolate-scented, rich deep crimson, single dahlia-like flowers above bushy, dark green, divided foliage. Tuberous root. Survives outdoors only if covered to prevent frost penetration; roots may be lifted and stored as for dahlias. H80cm/32in, W38cm/15in. F7-10. Z8-9. ✿ ◢ ■

CORDYALIS FLEXUOSA
A species only recently discovered in China, with finely cut leaves through late winter and into summer and azur-blue flowers for many weeks in spring and early summer. Foliage dies back in summer, shows again in autumn or early spring. ❋ ◢
Several selections, including **'Père David'**, **'China Blue'**, **'Purple Leaf'** and **'Blue Panda'** are all good. Some variations, but generally H30-45cm/12-18in, W20cm/8in. F4-6. Z7-8.

CROCOSMIA
Some of these South African plants create vivid splashes of colour in late summer and autumn. Parentage very mixed: montbretia types (M) are less hardy. Plant in spring and protect by leaves or dig up for winter. ✿ ■
C. 'Bressingham Beacon'. Vigorous flame-orange cultivar, dark stems, good cut flower. H75cm/2ft 6in, W15cm/6in. F7-8. Z5-9.
C. 'Emberglow'. A glowing, burnt red shade with abundant, rush-like foliage. H1.2m/4ft, W15cm/6in. F7-9. Z5-9.
C. 'Jenny Bloom'. This has soft butter-yellow flowers and is strong-growing and prolific. H75cm/2ft 6in, W15cm/6in. F7-9. Z5-9.

Crocosmia 'Spitfire'

C. 'Lucifer'. The flowers on wiry, upstanding spikes are deep flame-red. H1.2-1.5m/4-5ft. F6-8. Z5-9.
C. masonorum. The parent of many hybrids, selected for its hardiness and arching stems revealing wide-petalled, upward-facing, vermilion-orange flowers. Handsome broad foliage. H80cm/32in, W15cm/6in. F7-9. Z7-9. **'Firebird'**, an improved Bressingham selection, is quite outstanding for its large, flame-orange flowers on arching stems. H80cm/32in, W15cm/6in. F7-9.

Delphinium × *belladonna* 'Peace'

Z6-9. **'Rowallane Yellow'**, similar, with large, pure-yellow flowerheads making a striking variation. H90cm/3ft, W15cm/6in. F6-9. Z7-9.
C. 'Spitfire'. Dense foliage, brilliant fiery orange flowers on strong stems. H75cm/2ft 6in, W15cm/6in. F7-9. Z5-9.
C. 'Vulcan'. Bright flame-red flowers with a yellow throat. Compact habit. H60cm/2ft, W15cm/6in. F7-9. Z5-9.

CYNARA **Cardoon**
C. cardunculus. Closely related to the globe artichoke, *C. scolymus*, and, like it, a very ornamental species for the decorative garden. Tall, strong stems carry terminal thistle flowers, with scaly bracts enclosing a large, purple-mauve tuft. The basal foliage has large, silvery, deeply jagged leaves up to 60cm/2ft long. Handsome all summer, attractive to bees. H1.8-2.1m/6-7ft, W60cm/2ft. F7-8. Z7-9. ☼ ■

DELPHINIUM
Magnificent perennials at their best, many grown from seed, the more choice cultivars by cuttings or division. Taller forms will need to have their spikes supported by canes. In warmer climates few will be long lived. ☼ ⚹
D. × belladonna. Perhaps the best perennial delphinium. This type is single-flowered, producing an abundance of graceful, loose racemes of flowers and deeply cut leaves. If cut back after flowering, most flower again. All Z3-8. **'Blue Bees'**, a favourite, with sky-blue flowers. H1m/39in, W60cm/2ft. F6-7. **'Casa Blanca'**, a white which comes true from seed. H90cm/3ft, W60cm/2ft. F6-7. **'Lamartine'**, shapely Oxford-blue spikes. H1.2m/4ft, W60cm/2ft. F6-7. **'Peace'** (syn. 'Volkerfrieden') the finest, brightest mid-blue. H1.2m/4ft, W60cm/2ft. F6-7.
D. grandiflorum (syn. *D. chinensis).* A short-lived dwarf species. **'Blue Butterfly'** is especially popular for its

Dianthus 'Pretty'

brilliant cobalt-blue flowers and finely cut leaves. Good drainage needed. H25-30cm/10-12in, W25cm/10in. F6-8. Z4-9.

DENDRANTHEMA *See* CHRYSANTHEMUM

DIANTHUS **Pink**
The dianthus are a large and highly interbred family for the front of the perennial border or on a scree or rock garden. Most garden favourites, but not all, are grey leaved; many are fragrant. ☼ ■
The border pinks cover taller varieties – single or double flowered, mostly highly fragrant – and dwarfer forms, with often spreading habits; the latter fall under alpine or rock garden types but vary greatly. Most flower late spring to summer. Z3-8.

DIASCIA
These free flowering South African plants are very popular, with new introductions each year. Though not fully hardy they are easy to grow, creating low-growing mats from which a continual display of blooms emerge. Take cuttings in late summer to ensure continuity in the event of cold winters. Most F6-9. Z7-8. ☼ ◢

'Blackthorn Apricot'. Just a suggestion of apricot in the warm pink of this low, floriferous variety. H15cm/6in, W30cm/1ft.
D. rigesens × lilacina. Richer, almost magenta-pink, vigorous spreading habit. H20-25cm/8-10in, W30cm/1ft.
D. barberiae. Deep pink, free flowering spurred shell-like blooms. H30cm/1ft, W45cm/18in.
D. vigilis (syn. *D. elegans).* Slender spikes bear clear pink flowers all summer. H30cm/1ft, W30cm/1ft.

DICENTRA **Bleeding heart**
A group of popular and garden-worthy perennials with flowers like hanging lockets. Finely cut foliage and fleshy roots. ☼ ✾ ⚹ ◢
D. eximia. From the eastern USA, grey-green fine cut leaves, dangling pink flowers and spreading habit. **'Alba'** is an attractive variation with white flowers.
D. formosa. The 'Pacific bleeding heart' is very similar to *D. eximia.* Rose pink flowers. Both H45cm/18in, W45cm/18in. F5-7. Z4-8.
Hybrids between the above. All Z4-8. **'Adrian Bloom'**, profuse crimson-rose flowers, glaucous green leaves. H25cm/10in, W20cm/8in. F5-8. **'Luxuriant'**, deep green leaves,

Digitalis purpurea 'Alba'

crimson flowers. H25cm/10in, W20cm/8in. F5-8. **'Pearl Drops'**, white flowers on arching tips above a mass of bluish-green foliage. H30cm/1ft, W45cm/18in. F5-8. **'Snowflakes'**, long succession of pure white flowers from early spring. H25cm/10in, W25cm/10in. F4-9. *D. macrocapnos* and the similar *D. scandens* are vigorous climbing perennials with yellow flowers and glaucous foliage. H1.8-2.4m/6-8ft, W150cm/5ft. F7-9. Z8-9. *D. spectabilis.* The true bleeding heart, with deep pink and white lockets dangling above light green, delicately cut foliage. The ivory-white **'Alba'** is also charming, with lighter green foliage. Both H60cm/2ft, W45cm/18in. F5-7. Z3-8.

DICTAMNUS **Burning bush**
Named for its volatility when ignited on a hot summer's day as the seedpods ripen. Best raised from seed and must be planted young. ✿ ■ ✭
D. albus (syn. *D. faxinella albus).* Also called dittany or fraxinella, it has strongly aromatic, light green pinnate leaves and stiff spikes of white flowers with prominent stamens. The more commonly seen form, *D. a. purpureus*

has reddish-lilac flowers. H80cm/32in, W60cm/2ft. F6-8. Z3-8.

DIGITALIS **Foxglove**
Many foxgloves are biennial and even the perennials are short-lived, but they are excellent for naturalizing and will colonize shady places. ✿ ❀ ☆
D. grandiflora (syn. *D. ambigua).* Most live for three or four years, with spikes of primrose-yellow flowers on compact plants. H60cm/2ft, W30cm/1ft. F6-8. Z4-8.
D. purpurea. Biennial but some forms are ideal to naturalize in garden. Good in half shade, allow to seed. *D. p.* **'Alba'** (syn. *D. albiflora),* attractive white flowers all held on one side of the stem. Bees continue to hybridize, so remove coloured selection near white early to avoid degeneration to other colours. F5-7. Z4-9.

DISPORUM **Fairy bell**
D. sessile 'Variegatum'. Prettily variegated woodland plant which spreads just below the soil surface, producing creamy-white striped foliage and greenish flowers. Most effective grown in a container where it looks good all summer. H30cm/1ft, W30cm/1ft. F5-6.

DORONICUM **Leopard bane**
These easy to grow, yellow-flowered daisies herald spring. Their toothed, heart-shaped leaves usually die down in hot summers. Clumps need replanting every three years to renew vigour. Good for cutting. ✿ ❀ ◪
D. **'Miss Mason'**. A hybrid, making a fine show for weeks with persistent, clump-forming leaves. H50cm/20in, W60cm/2ft. F4-6. Z4-8.
D. orientale (syn. *D. caucasicum).* Bright green leaves, cheerful yellow daisies 8cm/3in across. Dies down quickly in summer heat. H45cm/18in, W30cm/1ft. F4-5. Z5-8. **'Goldzwerg'** is the best dwarf form. H25cm/10in, W30cm/1ft. F4-6. Z4-8.

Doronicum caucasicum 'Goldzwerg'

Echinacea purpurea 'Magnus'

D. **'Spring Beauty'**. Showy with fully double flowers, but can be unreliable. H30cm/1ft, W30cm/1ft. F4-6. Z4-8.

ECHINACEA **Coneflower**
First class perennials for summer colour, being reliable and easy to grow. Daisy-like flowers with prominent dark centres and radiating, crimson-magenta petals, often with lighter tips. Much loved by bees. ✿ ✭
E. purpurea. The purple coneflower is mostly represented by named cultivars. All Z4-9. **Bressingham**

Hybrids have stout stems and cerise-purple shades. H1m/39in, W45cm/18in. F7-9. **'Magnus'**, outstanding large-flowered selection, the flowers almost 10cm/4in across, a warm purplish-rose, and borne on sturdy stems for a long period. H90cm/3ft, W38cm/15in. F7-10. **'Robert Bloom'**, rich, glowing rose-red flowers and sturdy stems. **'White Lustre'**, a striking variation. Both H90cm/3ft, W38cm/15in. F7-9.

ECHINOPS **Globe thistle**
Distinctive perennials with jagged, mostly greyish, prickly foliage and spherical, metallic blue flowerheads on branching stems. Taller species may need staking. All attractive to bees and butterflies. Drought-resistant. Excellent for cutting and drying. ✿ ☆
E. ritro. The best garden species. Compact with abundant, mid-blue flowers above greyish, thistle-like foliage. **'Veitch's Blue'** is a good selection with smaller, lighter blue heads. Both H1.2m/4ft, W60cm/2ft. F7-8. Z3-9.

EPIMEDIUM **Barrenwort**
Valuable evergreen and deciduous perennials, good foliage effects on new

Erigeron 'Dimity'

growth. Many new species being introduced from Asia. ☼ ✳ (in cooler climates) ☆

E. grandiflorum. '**Album**', pretty white starry flowers on long stems. '**Crimson Beauty**', outstanding deep crimson red flowers. '**Lilafee**', free flowering, deep lilac purple, dark new leaves. All H20cm/8in, W20cm/8in. F3-5. Z5-8.

E . × perralchicum. '**Fröhnleiten**', a neat evergreen form, with yellow flowers and marbled new foliage. H25cm/10in, W25cm/10in. F4-5. Z5-9.

E. × rubrum. Compact clumps of rounded foliage, attractively coloured when young, and deep pink, white-spurred, starry flowers. H20cm/8in, W20cm/8in. F3-5. Z4-9.

ERIGERON Fleabane

A useful genus with daisy-like flowers and lance-shaped leaves. Most are hybrids with bright colours and semi-double flowers, easy to grow and tolerant of maritime conditions. Almost all are good for cutting. Best divided in spring. ☼ ■

Hybrids. A selection of some of the best: '**Amity**', single, lilac-pink flowers. H70cm/28in, W45cm/18in.

F6-8. Z5-8. '**Dimity**', light green leaves, obliquely held sprays of pink flowers, orange-tinted buds. H25cm/10in, W25cm/10in. F6-8. Z4-8. '**Foerster's Liebling**', still popular for its deep pink, semi-double flowers. H40cm/16in, W45cm/18in. F6-8. Z5-8. '**Prosperity**', dwarf and spreading, near double, light blue flowers. H35cm/14in, W45cm/18in. F6-8. Z5-8. '**Rotes Meer**', near red, finely rayed petals. '**Schwarzes Meer**', deep violet with prominent yellow disc. Both H60cm/2ft, W45cm/18in. F6-8. Z5-8.

Eryngium alpinum 'Superbum'

ERYNGIUM Sea holly

These distinctive thistle-like sun lovers have attractive foliage as well as long-lasting, rounded, teazle-like flowers, or bracts, excellent for cutting and drying. Bees love them. ☼ ■

E. alpinum. This has rounded green basal leaves and smooth, branching, blue stems with large steely-blue bracts, each with a decorative calyx 'ruff'. There are several named selections. H75cm/2ft 6in, W45cm/18in. F6-8. Z5-8.

E. bourgati. Striking silver, jagged basal leaves veined white; wiry, much branched stems carry blue ruffled flowers with the upper stems also blue. H60cm/2ft, W30cm/1ft. F6-9. Z5-9.

E. giganteum. Though a biennial, included for its large showy flowers which are surrounded by silvery ruffled bracts. Free seeding on well-drained soil. H60-75cm/2ft-2ft 6in, W45cm/18in. F6-8. Z4-8.

E. '**Jos Eijking**'. Striking hybrid with upright stems, the cones of blue flowers surrounded by silver-blue bracts; as flowering develops, stems turn a deep blue. H70cm/28in, W45cm/18in. F6-8. Z5-8.

EUPATORIUM

Easily grown perennials, some tall with large flower heads, becoming fluffy in autumn. ◢

E. purpureum. American Joe Pye weed. Stately, late-flowering background plant. Stiff stems with whorls of pointed leaves carry wide, flat, rose-purple flower heads. '**Atropurpureum**', deep purple heads. '**Album**', white flowers. H1.8-2.1m/6-7ft, W90cm/3ft. F8-10. Z3-9. Some new selections of dwarfer habit are worth noting, particularly '**Glutball**', large heads of intense purple-red. H1.5m/5ft, W60cm/2ft. F8-10. Z3-9.

EUPHORBIA Spurge

Popular deciduous and evergreen plants for foliage and flower, mostly

Euphorbia amygdaloides 'Rubra'

spring and summer flowering in the form of bracts, generally in shades of yellow. When trimming or taking cuttings, use gloves as the milky sap can irritate skin. Many types.

E. amygdaloides '**Rubra**'. Excellent foliage plant with purple, semi-evergreen leaves, contrasting with yellow flowers. Will seed itself. H30cm/1ft, W45cm/18in. F4-5. Z7-9. ☼ ✳ ■

E. characias. There is much confusion between this and the sub-species *wulfenii*, especially as there now exist innumerable selections. Both have evergreen, glaucous leaves, except in the variegated forms. *E. characias* has dark brown centres to greenish-yellow flowers while *E.* **subsp.** *wulfenii* and hybrids have yellow-centered flowers. From the western Mediterranean, all prefer sun and good drainage. Flower heads begin to form in late winter, opening into full flower in mid- to late spring. In summer, cut back dying flower heads to allow new foliage to develop. Free seeding. *E.c.* '**Humpty Dumpty**', compact bushy form. H75cm/2ft 6in, W90cm/3ft. F3-5. Z8-9. *E.c.* '**Burrow's Silver**' has brightly variegated leaves but lacks

Euphorbia characias 'Burrow's Silver'

vigour. H60cm/2ft, W45cm/18in. F3-5. Z8-9. *E.c.* subsp. *wulfenii* 'Lambrook Gold' and 'Spring Splendour', large heads on tall stems. H1.5m/5ft, W1.2m/4ft. F3-5. Z7-10. *E. griffithii* 'Fireglow'. This striking, slow-spreading plant emerges in spring with reddish-purple shoots that develop into a bushy mass of greenery, carrying fiery orange flowers. 'Dixter' has a slightly darker hue. Revels in moisture. H1m/39in,

Fragaria 'Pink Panda'

W60cm/2ft. F4-6. Z4-9. ☼ ☆
E. myrsinites. Attractive, blue-grey fleshy leaves closely set along the trailing stems which carry heads of sulphur-yellow flowers. Evergreen. H15cm/6in, W30cm/1ft. E5-7. Z5-8.
E. palustris. Vigorous, clump-forming and deep-rooted species, its huge, greenish-yellow flowerheads make a spectacular late spring display, the foliage orange and yellow in autumn. H1m/39in, W1m/39in. F5-6. Z5-8. ◧

E. polychroma (syn. *E. epithymoides*). Compact and clump-forming, its outstanding yellowish flowers appear before the foliage. As the flowers fade to green, the whole plant become a neat, leafy bush. 'Purpurea' has purple-tinged foliage. 'Sonnengold' has showy yellow bracts. All H50cm/20in, W50cm/20in. F4-5. Z4-9.
E. schillingii. Soft green leaves, bushy habit and yellow-green flowers make this a useful late-flowering spurge. H90cm/3ft, W60cm/2ft. F7-9. Z6-9. *E. longifolia* and *E. wallichii* have similar foliage attractions and yellow summer flowers.

FILIPENDULA Meadowsweet
Closley related and often confused with the astilbes, the meadowsweets used to be called *Spiraea*. ☼ ❁ ☆
F. kakome. A cultivar from Japan of great garden merit. Compact habit and a succession of miniature rosy red plumes over green leaves. H30cm/1ft, W30cm/1ft. F7-9. Z3-9.
F. ulmaria. Queen of the Meadows. The species is seldom grown except as a wildflower, with its creamy white fragrant flowers held above the leaves. 'Aurea' is first class as a foliage plant for shade, with golden-yellow cut leaves which can scorch. 'Variegata', brightly variegated leaves, dark green splashed with yellow. Cut away flowers as soon as finished on larger two varieties as any seedlings will come up green. All H60-120cm/2-4ft, W45cm/18in. F6-8. Z3-9.
F. purpurea. Outstanding for its display of cerise-red flowers over leafy, bushy foliage. H90cm/3ft, W60cm/2ft. F6-7. Z4-9. ❁ ◧

FRAGARIA Strawberry
F. 'Pink Panda'. A large pink-flowered hybrid crossing *Potentilla palustris*, the marsh cinquefoil, with the domestic fruiting strawberry. Excellent for ground cover, containers and hanging baskets, it flowers from early summer to late autumn, less in extreme heat. Fruits occur in hotter climates. 'Red Ruby' and 'Serenata' are other selections with deeper coloured flowers. H30cm/1ft, W45cm/18in. F5-10. Z5-9.

GAILLARDIA Blanket flower
Colourful perennials and annuals, the former mostly represented by selected cultivars. Daisy-like flowers have a reddish brown or burgundy centre and yellow or red petals, sometimes both, creating colour at the expense of subtlety! Some strains come from seed; selected cultivars are propagated by root cuttings. ☼ ■
G x *grandiflora* 'Goblin', an eye-

Galega officinalis 'His Majesty'

catching dwarf form, petals deep crimson, tipped yellow. H30cm/1ft, W30cm/1ft. F6-8. Z2-10. 'Croftway Yellow', pure yellow. 'Mandarin', deep flame orange, mahogany centre. Both H60cm/2ft, W30cm/1ft. F6-8. Z2-10.

GALEGA Goat's rue
Vigorous members of the pea family, useful for their long-flowering period and abundant fresh green foliage. ☼ ■
G. officinalis 'Alba'. The species can be variable, with light blue or white flowers, but this selection holds its own in any garden, with showy white-flowered racemes over a long period. A closely related hybrid 'His Majesty', often misnamed 'Her Majesty', is of a similar status, with blue and white flowers. May need staking. H1.5m/5ft, W60cm/2ft. F6-8. Z3-8.

GAURA
G. lindheimeri. A free-flowering perennial with insignificant foliage but the small flowers which cling to willowy stems provide a mass of white-petalled blooms all summer. 'Whirling Butterflies' is a well-named selected form. 'Corrie's Gold' offers golden variegated leaves as an added attraction. All 75-90cm/2ft 6in-3ft, W45cm/18in. F6-10. Z5-9. ☼ ■

GERANIUM Cranesbill

One of the indispensable perennials, now available in an increasingly wide range. Species exist for sun or shade, with selected varieties useful to cover the flowering period from late spring to late autumn. Dwarfer types are listed in the Alpine Directory (see page 137). The forms listed below represent a limited selection. ☼ ❋ ☆

G. 'Ann Folkard'. Wide-spreading, with magenta-purple, saucer-shaped flowers. Yellow-tinged leaves early in the year. Excellent if allowed to scramble among other plants. H30cm/1ft, W30cm/1ft. F6-9. Z5-8.

G. × cantabrigiense. Two outstanding forms of this hybrid, like a dwarf *G. macrorrhizum*, are the semi-evergreen 'Cambridge', with glossy leaves and rose-pink flowers, and 'Biokovo', which makes a spreading carpet topped by white flowers with pink centres. Both 20-30cm/8-12in, W30cm/1ft. F6-8. Z3-8.

G. himalayense. Good ground cover forming low, leafy carpets, with finely cut leaves and blue flowers with a fine red veining and reddish-purple centre. 'Gravetye' (formerly *G. h. alpinium*) is

slightly more reddish veined and centred. 'Plenum' is vigorous and quite distinct, with masses of fully double purplish-blue flowers. All easy and trouble-free. H30cm/1ft, W60cm/2ft. F6-7. Z4-8. ☼ ❋

G. 'Johnson's Blue'. Perhaps the most popular hardy geranium ever. Finely cut leaves and a glorious display of clear blue, darker-veined flowers in mid-summer, with some re-blooming. H30cm/1ft, W60cm/2ft. F6-7. Z4-8.

G. macrorrhizum. Semi-evergreen sweet briar-scented leaves, colouring well in autumn, somewhat woody stems and short sprays of magenta flowers, 4cm/1.5in across. The form *album* is white, 'Ingwersen's Variety' is soft pink, 'Bevan's Variety' deep rose-pink. Good, quick-spreading, weed-proof ground cover for sun or shade. All H25cm/10in, W60cm/2ft. F6-7, Z4-8.

G. × magnificum. Striking deep violet blue flowers held above hairy leaves. Vigorous and upright but can flop. ☼ ■

G. × oxonianum. Under this hybrid come many first class free-flowering

Geranium pratense 'Mrs Kendall Clark'

selections; all have light green, semi-evergreen leaves and make leafy mounds of foliage, varying in vigour and colour. All Z4-8. 'A.T. Johnson' is one of the oldest selections, good ground cover with silvery pink flowers. H40cm/16in, W60cm/2ft. F6-8. Z4-8. 'Bressingham's Delight' was selected for its light pink veined flowers which continue for months.

G. phaeum. The mourning widow. Named for its small, nodding purple-black flowers, excellent for shade, but a trifle dull. 'Album' is brighter, with an erect habit and masses of white flowers. Both H60cm/2ft, W45cm/18in. F5-7. Z4-8.

G. pratense. The meadow cranesbill. Finely cut leaves, good autumn tints. Somewhat floppy stems bear sprays with flowers in shades of violet-blue, freely seeding as do most of the singles. 'Album' is good but the erect-flowered white 'Galactic' is outstanding. 'Mrs Kendall Clark' is an old favourite with pale blue flowers marked with lilac. Doubles include white 'Plenum Album', light blue 'Plenum Caeruleum' and deep violet-blue 'Plenum Violaceum'. 'Summer Skies' has masses of small double flowers with shades of blue, pink and white all on the same plants. All 60-75cm/2-2ft 6in, W60cm/2ft. F6-7. Z5-8.

G. psilostemon (syn. *G. armenum).* Large, deeply cut leaves make this an attractive foliage form above which bright magenta flowers with black centres make an arresting display. 'Bressingham Flair', slightly lower-growing, flowers more carmine. Full sun; some seeding may occur. Both H90cm/3ft, W90cm/3ft. F6-8. Z4-8.

G. × riversleianum 'Mavis Simpson'. A superb long flowering plant with grey-green leaves and wide spreading foliage, giving a succession of pale pink flowers from mid-summer until autumn. Equally garden worthy is 'Russell Prichard', an older variety with vivid magenta-rose flowers for a similar period. Both H30cm/12in, W60cm/2ft. F6-9. Z6-8. ☼ ■

G. sanguineum. The bloody cranesbill. Most forms have sharply divided leaves, forming mounds studded with flowers from mid-summer for several weeks. 'Alan Bloom' makes low hummocks with bright magenta-pink flowers, *G. s. album*, a taller white, 'John Elsley' deep magenta pink, 'Shepherd's Warning', lower spreading, lighter pink, *G. s. striatum* 'Splendens' (syn. *G. lancastrense* 'Splendens'), outstanding and distinct, pale pink flowers veined crimson. All approx. H30cm/12in, W45cm/18in. F6-8. Z4-8.

G. sylvaticum. Early flowering European species, forming clumps of green-fingered leaves and mostly blue or lilac-white centres. Seeds freely. ☼ ❋ 'Album' lights up a shady corner. 'Mayflower' is a fine deep blue selection. All 60cm/2ft, W45cm/18in. F5-7. Z4-8.

G. wallichianum 'Buxton's Variety'. Splendid spreading leafy plant with dark green foliage and a succession of light blue saucer-shaped flowers with white centres, the blue turning to lilac in heat. Ideal for a frontal position in a border or on a bank or a wall. H30cm/1ft, W75cm/2ft 6in. F6-10. Z4-8.

Geranium phaeum 'Album'

Gypsophila repens 'Rosa Schonheit'

GEUM Avens

Colourful clump-forming perennials, best if divided every few years. ✿ ✷
G. 'Borisii'. Popular and reliable, the low clumps of green leaves bear bright orange or scarlet flowers in late spring and occasionally, later coppertone sprays of coppery orange flowers. 'Georgenberg', dwarfer, with pale yellow flowers. All approx. H30cm/1ft, W30cm/1ft. F5-7. Z5-8.

GYPSOPHILA Baby's breath

Sun loving, drought-resistant perennials. They resent disturbance once established. Good for cut flowers. ✿ ☆ ⊙ ■
G. paniculata. The single-flowered perennial baby's breath has deep, fleshy roots, much branched, airy stems, small greyish leaves and masses of tiny white flowers. This and its cultivars are much used for cutting and flower arranging. H90cm/3ft, W90cm/3ft. F6-8. All Z4-9. The double white 'Bristol Fairy' is a little less robust but the flowers are larger. H90cm/3ft, W90cm/3ft. F6-8. 'Compacta Plena' is a very reliable double white. H50cm/20in, W45cm/18in. F6-9. 'Rosenschleier' ('Rosy Veil'), taller with airy stems and clear pink flowers. H30cm/1ft, W45cm/18in. F5-7. Z3-8.

G. repens 'Rosa Schonheit'. Outstanding for its free-flowering pink flowers and mounded grey-green foliage. H15cm/6in, W30cm/1ft. F5-7. Z3-8.

HELENIUM Sneezewort

Most of these well-loved plants bloom in late summer, producing daisy flowers in bright shades of yellow, orange and brownish-crimson with a central conical disc. Lift and divide regularly. All Z4-8. ✿ ☆
'Bressingham Gold', deep yellow, crimson-streaked flowers, long, spear-shaped stem leaves. H1.1m/43in, W45cm/18in. F7-8. 'Bruno', late-flowering crimson-mahogany. H1.2m/4ft, W45cm/18in. F8-9. 'Butterpat', pure yellow, late-flowering. H1.1m/43in, W45cm/18in. F8-9. 'Coppelia', warm coppery orange, sturdy growth. H1m/39in, W45cm/18in. F8-9. 'Morheim Beauty', bronze-red flowers and a sturdy habit. H1.1m/43in, W45cm/18in. F7-8. 'Wyndley', compact, leafy, orange-brown flecked flowers for a long period. H70cm/28in, W45cm/18in. F6-8.

HELIANTHELLA

H. quinquinervis. A pleasing plant for the back of the border. Leafy clumps produce a mass of small, lemon-yellow flowers. H1.5-1.8m/5-6ft, W90cm/3ft. F8-9. Z4-8.

HELIANTHUS Perennial sunflower

Though some species are invasive, those below make compact clumps and strong stems topped by single, double or semi-double yellow flowers in late summer: a good, trouble-free display.
H. decapetalus (syn. *H. multiflorus*). 'Capenoch Star' has single lemon yellow flowers; 'Lemon Queen' is similar and both fit better into colour schemes than brighter yellows. Both H1.5-1.8m/5-6ft, W60cm/2ft. F8-9. Z4-8. 'Loddon Gold', a sturdy plant

Helenium 'Butterpat'

with fully double bright yellow flowers in late summer. H1.5-1.8m/5-6ft, W60cm/2ft. F8-9. Z4-8.

HELIOPSIS

H. scabra. Related to the sunflowers, these are brash, colourful perennials for sunny spots which thrive in any reasonable soil. All F6-9. Z4-9.
'Ballerina', very free-flowering, single yellow. H1m/39in, W60cm/2ft. 'Gold Green Heart', semi-double, lemon-yellow flowers with greenish centre. H1.1m/43in, W60cm/2ft. 'Golden Plume', almost double, bushy habit. H1.1m/43in, W60cm/2ft. 'Bressingham Doubloon' large, semi-double blooms make a impressive display. H1.2m/4ft, W40cm/18in.

HEMEROCALLIS Day lily

These tough perenials with fresh green, arching leaves and lily-like, often fragrant, flowers, are immensely popular. The blooms last for only one day but open in succession. All are reliable and adaptable and, though preferring good soil, will do well on most. ✿ ✷ ✸
H. dumortieri. This has early, deep yellow, fragrant flowers, dark brown in bud. H70cm/28in, W45cm/18in. F5-7. Z3-9.

Hybrids. Recent hybridizing, particularly in the USA, has created innumerable hybrids, including some with large flowers, ruffled flowers, brightly and subtly coloured, miniatures and re-blooming types. The selections made below have all succeeded well at Bressingham. All Z4-9. 'Anzac' is as near to true red as you are likely to find. H75cm/30in, W45cm/18in. F6-8. 'Children's Festival', compact habit, ruffled peach, apricot-throated trumpets. H60cm/2ft, W45cm/18in. F6-7. 'Burning Daylight', deep glowing orange. H90cm/3ft, W60cm/2ft. F7-

Hemerocallis Children's Festival'

9. **'Catherine Woodbury'**, deep pink flowers. H80cm/32in, W60cm/2ft. F6-8. **'Cherry Cheeks'** has extra large, cherry-pink flowers. H80cm/32in, W60cm/2ft. F6-8. **'Corky'**, free flowering pale yellow, backed brown gold, dark brown, stems, grassy foliage. H75cm/ 2ft 6in, W45cm/18in. F6-8. **'Golden Chimes'**, fairly dwarf and very free to flower. H70cm/28in, W45cm/18in. F6-8. **'Hyperion'**, long a favourite, with scented, pure yellow flowers. H90cm/3ft, W45cm/ 18in. F6-8. **'Lark Song'**, light canary-yellow. H90cm/3ft, W45cm/18 in. F6-8. **'Luxury Lace'**, light satiny pink, with ruffled edges to the petals. H80cm/32in, W60cm/2ft. F6-8. **'Cream Drop'**, scented miniature creamy yellow blooms held above the foliage. H45cm/18in, W45cm/18in. F6-7. **'Stafford'**, rich red with a deep yellow throat. H90cm/3ft, W90cm/3ft. F7-9. **'Stella de Oro'**, distinctive for its dwarf, dense clumps of leaves and long season of pale gold flowers. Divide regularly. H50cm/20in, W45cm/18in. F6-10. **'Varsity'**, large peach flowers, maroon in the centre. H75cm/30in, W45cm/18in. F6-8.

HEUCHERA Coral bells

This distinctive plant group has had much attention from hybridists in recent years, particularly in the development of coloured or marbled foliage leading to a longer appeal than the flowering season alone. Older plants become woody and younger side shoots should be used for replanting. ✷ ■

H. × *brizoides.* Hybrids with large leaves and large sprays of flowers good for cutting. **'Charles Bloom'** has large purplish, crinkled leaves and sprays of light pink flowers; **'Pearl Drops'** is white. Both H60-70cm/24-28in, W30cm/1ft. F6-8. Z3-8. *H. cyclindrica.* A species with greenish-white bells and clumps of deep green silver-marbled leaves.

Heuchera micrantha 'Bressingham Bronze'

'Green Ivory' and **'Greenfinch'** are distinct improvements, much used by flower arrangers. All H60-70cm/24-18in, W30cm/1ft. F6-8. Z4-8. *H. micrantha* **'Palace Purple'** is variable from seed but at its best an excellent garden-worthy form whose leaves are large, glossy and richly coloured, almost beetroot-red. **'Bressingham Bronze'** is an outstanding selection with large, crinkled bronze leaves, bright purple beneath. The tiny flowers have a hint of white. Both H70cm/28in, W30cm/1ft. F6-8. Z4-8. *H.* **'Pewter Moon'** Forms a low hummock of silver marbled leaves on a deep maroon reverse. Pretty, light pink flowers. H30cm/1ft, W30cm/1ft. F6-8. Z4-8.
Hybrids. As a mixed strain **Bressingham hybrids** have an international reputation. Those below are named cultivars which have *H sanguinea* **'Coral Bells'** as their dominant parent, a great many introduced by my father Alan Bloom over the years. All approximately W30cm/1ft, F5-7 or F5-8 where suited in fertile soil. **'Bressingham Blaze'**, bright coral-red bells. H50cm/20in. Z3-8. **'Pretty Polly'**, compact but with large, pure pink

flowers. H35cm/14in. Z4-8. **'Red Spangles'**, intensely blood-red flowers. H50cm/20in. Z3-8. **'Rosemary Bloom'**, bright coral pink bells, with light pink centre, for many weeks. H45-60cm/18-24in. F6-8. Z4-8. **'Scintillation'**, red tipped, deep pink flowers. H50cm/20in. Z3-8. **'Snowstorm'**, notable for its white and green leaves, which contrast with the cerise flowers. H40cm/16in. Z4-8.

× HEUCHERELLA

Hybrids between *Heuchera* and *Tiarella.*
× *H.* **'Bridget Bloom'**. The first inter-generic hybrid raised by Alan Bloom in 1950 and named after my sister. It makes compact mounds of pretty evergreen foliage and stems of starry pink flowers which will often bloom a second time in late summer. H35cm/14in, W30cm/1ft. F5-7. Z4-8. ✷ □

HOSTA Plantain lily

Deservedly popular plants for their hardiness, adaptability and, in the best foliage types, long period of interest. Since the first species arrived from Asia, much breeding and selection has given us a bewildering choice, from miniatures to giants, some with astonishing blue or variegated leaves and many with fragrant flowers. Their only drawback is that slugs like them too! All Z3-9. ✷ ✷ ◢
H. **'August Moon'**. This has bright golden-green leaves in summer and pale mauve flowers. H60cm/2ft, W45cm/18in. F8-9.
H. **'Big Daddy'**. Large, puckered leaves, decidedly bluish, make a fine specimen plant in semi or full shade. H90cm/3ft, W60cm/2ft. F8-9.
H. **'Blue Moon'**. Small round, intensely blue ribbed leaves and profuse light mauve flowers. H30cm/12in, W30cm/12in. F7-8.
H. fortunei **'Albo-marginata'**. Striking, with large leaves margined creamy white. H80cm/32in, W60cm/2ft. F6-8. **'Aureo-marginata'**,

Hosta fluctuans 'Variegated'

similar, but with a yellow leaf margin. The vigorous **'Francee'** is outstanding with wide, oval, white-edged leaves making a splendid clump. H60cm/2ft, W50cm/20in. F8-9.
H. **'Frances Williams'**. Deservedly popular with its huge, glaucous ribbed leaves and buff variegations. H1m/39in, W60cm/2ft. F6-8.
H. fluctuans **'Variegated'**. A most impressive variegated Japanese hosta whose large, wavy green-edged, creamy yellow leaves and open habit give it a sculptural quality. H75cm/2ft 6in, W75cm/2ft 6in. F6-8.
H. **'Gold Standard'**. This strong-growing, free-flowering form has leaves with green outer edges and colourful golden centres. H60cm/2ft, W50cm/20in. F7-8.
H. **'Ground Master'**. Dense spread of green and white variegated foliage for sun or shade, giving a good display of purple flowers. H30cm/1ft, W45cm/18in. F6-7.
H. **'Halcyon'**. Very glaucous blue foliage and a good show of mauve flowers make this English variety especially garden-worthy. H45cm/18in, W45cm/18in. F7-8.
H. **'Krossa Regal'**. Strong-growing, erect and glaucous-leaved, with purple flowers. H80cm/32in, W60cm/2ft. F6-8.

H. 'Montana Aurea Margianata'. The large soft-textured leaves are bright green, edged golden yellow, and very striking. H60cm/2ft, W60cm/2ft. F6-7.

H. 'Sum and Substance'. Considered to have the largest leaves of any hosta, and slug resistant. Impressive ribbed leaves light green to soft green, golden green in summer. Lavender flowers. H60cm/2ft, W60cm/2ft. F7-8.

H. 'Shade Fanfare'. Light green leaves with a broad creamy margin, mauve flowers and a rapid spread. H40cm/16in, W45cm/18in. F7-8.

H. sieboldiana. Large glaucous leaves with mauve flowers. H80cm/32in; 'Elegans', even larger, with grey-blue ribbed leaves up to 50cm/20in across and 1m/39in high flower spikes. 'Bressingham Blue', equally robust but the leaves have a distinctive bluish tinge. All H90cm/3ft. W60cm/2ft. F7-8.

H. ventricosa. The species has deep green leaves and upstanding deep lavender-blue flowers. 'Aureo-Maculata' has glossy leaves with a central greenish-gold splash. 'Variegata' (syn. *H.v.* 'Aureo Marginata') whose ribbed foliage is

margined creamy yellow. All are free flowering. H75cm/2ft 6in, W60cm/2ft. F7-8.

H. 'Wide Brim'. Dense overlapping leaves are green, broadly edged cream to golden yellow, and finely ribbed. Lavender flowers. H40cm/16in, W60cm/2ft. F7-8.

HOUTTUYNIA

H. cordata 'Chameleon'. A spreading plant, particularly in moist soils and hot climates, but undoubtedly colourful. Leaves appear late in the season and vary in intensity and colour, usually mixing green, yellow, cream and red. The small flowers are white and the plant has a distinctive aroma. Striking and safe in a container! H15cm/6in, W30cm/1ft. F6-8. Z5-9.

INCARVILLEA

Tap-rooted plants which appear above ground in mid-spring and within a few weeks show their quite large, trumpet-shaped flowers, followed by deeply cut leaves. ☼ ■ ☆

I. delavayi. Rosy-red trumpets borne on spikes which expand from a few centimetres (inches) to nearly

60cm/2ft, by the time flowering ends. 'Alba', a recent selection of merit, with striking white trumpets. Both H60cm/2ft, W30cm/1ft. F5-7. Z6-8.

IRIS

The iris are a large and varied family, mostly easy to grow and often providing spectacular flowers. Though there are several notable exceptions, most flower in spring or summer.

I. ensata (syn. *I. kaempferi*). Large-flowered and popular, but not always easy, the Japanese iris dislikes lime, heavy clay and excessive winter wet, but needs moisture in summer. Its single or double, often velvety flowers, up to 20cm/8in across, can be quite spectacular. A huge variety of shapes, colours and sizes is now available, in seed mixtures and named varieties.

I. germanica. Flag, bearded or June-flowering iris are colourful, often spectacular perennials which are not fussy about soil, but need good drainage and like lime. The following are good colour representatives. They need to be placed carefully in the garden since, once flowers are finished, there is little to recommend them. Grow among or through low spreading plants. 'Berkeley Gold', deep yellow. 'Black Swan', nearly black. 'Braithwaite', lavender and purple. 'Edward Windsor', pastel pink. 'Frost and Flame', snow-white with tangerine beard. 'Jane Phillips', light blue. 'Kent Pride', chestnut-brown, with yellow and white markings. 'Party Dress', peach-pink and tangerine-yellow. 'Tall Chief', purple and maroon. 'Wabash', white and violet. All H60-90cm/2-3ft, W30cm/1ft. F6. Z4-9. ☼

I. kaempferi. See *I. ensata*.

I. pallida 'Argentea' (formerly *I.p.* 'Variegata'), with white and grey striped leaves, and 'Variegata' (formerly *I.p.* 'Aurea Variegata'), with golden-yellow stripes, deserve a place

in any garden. Both have clear blue flowers. All H60-75cm/2ft-2ft 6in, W30cm/1ft. F6-7. Z4-8. ☼ ✳

I. sibirica. These are easy to grow in sun and moist soil, especially as waterside subjects. They form clumps of upright, grassy foliage. Erect stems carry graceful flowers. 'Butter and Sugar', large flowers, deep yellow outer petals, creamy white inner. H60cm/2ft, W30cm/1ft. F6-7. 'Ego', bright blue, deepening towards the centre. H80cm/32in, W25cm/10in. 'Flight of Butterflies', relatively small flowers, blue with white veining. H90cm/3ft, W30cm/1ft. 'Persimmon', mid-blue. H90cm/3ft, W25cm/10in. 'Silver Edge', outstanding: large flowers, lilac-blue with yellow markings and a clear silver edge to the petals. H75cm/2ft 6in, W45cm/18in. 'White Swirl', pure white. H90cm/3ft, W25cm/ 10in. All F6-7. Z3-9.

KNIPHOFIA Red hot poker

A wide range is now available of these plants indispensable for summer colour, some flowering well into autumn. They vary from 35cm/14in

Iris sibirica 'Silver Edge'

Kniphofia 'Percy's Pride'

Lamium maculatum 'Pink Pewter'

Ligularia przewalskii 'Sungold'

to over 1.8m/6ft in height, some needing considerable space. Best planted in spring, though pot grown plants can be planted in early autumn if protected in their first winter. Generally easy. ☼ ■

K. 'Atlanta' (syn. *K. tuckii*). Early-flowering, with heavy spikes of yellow and red above broad glaucous foliage. H90cm/3ft, W60cm/2ft. F5-7. Z6-9. 'Bressingham Comet', bright orange, red-tipped spikes and grassy leaves. H60cm/2ft, W45cm/18in. F8-10. Z6-9. 'Fiery Fred', striking orange-red flowers and green leaves. H90cm/3ft, W60cm/2ft. F6-8. Z6-9. 'Little Maid', a charmer with narrow leaves and profuse, ivory-white spikes. H60cm/2ft, W45cm/18in. F7-9. Z5-9. 'Percy's Pride', robust, with sulphur-yellow flowers. H1.1m/43in, W60cm/2ft. F8-10. Z6-9. 'Shining Sceptre', glowing, orange-gold spikes. H90cm/3ft, W60cm/2ft. F7-9. Z6-9. 'Samuel's Sensation', truly red hot with fiery orange-flame heads. H1.2m/4ft, W45cm/18in. F7-9. Z6-9.

LAMIUM Deadnettle
This genus includes useful ground-cover plants for shade and a few of greater garden value both as foliage and flowering plants.

Leucanthemum maximum 'Snowcap'

L. *galeobdolon* 'Hermann's Pride', with silvery leaves; compact, with free-flowering yellow blooms. H15cm/6in, W20cm/8in. F4-7. Z4-8.
L. *maculatum*. There are some attractive and garden worthy selections of this species, ideal to create eye-catching plant associations. 'Aureum', bright golden-yellow leaves and pink flowers. 'Beacon Silver', one of the best for leaf colour, with leaves silvered with green margins, and 15cm/6in high red to pink flowers in early summer. 'Beedham's White', flowers freely, from golden carpets. 'Pink Pewter',

silver leaves and soft pink flowers. 'White Nancy', silvered foliage with green margins and pure white flowers. All H30cm/1ft, W60cm/2ft. F4-7. Z4-8.

LAVANDULA. *See under* Shrubs (p.84)

LEUCANTHEMUM
(syn. *Chrysanthemum leucanthemum*, L. *vulgare*). H50-70cm/20-28in, W30cm/1ft. F5-7. Z4-9.
L. *maximum*. The shasta daisy includes single and double flowers, such as the well-known doubles, 'Esther Read' and 'Wirral Supreme'. Both H50-75cm/20-30in, W30cm/1ft. Forms with lacy-edged petals include 'Aglaia' and 'Thomas Killin'. H75cm/30in, W30cm/1ft. 'Snowcap', single white flowers massed on stems only 35cm/14in tall, W30cm/1ft. 'Summer Snowball', outstanding pure white, fully double. H75cm/30in, W30cm/1ft. Support may be needed. All F6-8. Z4-8.

LIATRIS Gayfeather, Blazing star
These spike-forming plants are unusual in opening from the tip down, and make a bright display with narrow leaves and mostly light purple, fluffy pokers. The plants are

fleshy but not deep-rooted and any reasonable soil in sun suits them.
L. *spicata* (syn. *L. callilepis*). This has stiff spikes of bright lilac-purple flowers. H60cm/2ft, W25cm/10in. F6-8. Z4-9. 'Floristan White' is an attractive variation. H60cm/2ft, W25cm/10in. F6-8. Z4-9. 'Kobold' (syn. 'Gnome'). Lilac mauve with shorter, sturdy spikes. H45cm/18in, W23cm/9in. F6-8. Z4-9.

LIGULARIA
All the species below are partial to moisture but most thrive in any good soil and sun. Almost all have yellow, daisy-type flowers.
L. *dentata* (syn. *L. clivorum*) 'Desdemona'. This striking plant has very large, leathery, heart-shaped, brownish-green leaves, purple when young and later purplish beneath, and branching stems of orange daisy flowers. H1.2m/4ft, W60cm/2ft. F7-8. Z4-8.
L. *przewalskii*. Outstanding for its deeply cut, elegant foliage, black slender stems and small yellow flowers. H1.8m/6ft, W45cm/18in. F7-8. Z4-8. 'The Rocket' is a striking variation, showier and with leaves more rounded and toothed. H2.1m/7ft, W60cm/2ft. F7-8. Z4-8.

L. 'Sungold'. A first-class plant, adaptable, bushy and with a fine display of deep golden-yellow flowers on branching stems. H1.5m/5ft, W60cm/2ft. F7-8. Z4-8.

LIMONIUM

L. platyphyllum (syn. *L. latifolium*). This needs a warm, dry place to produce its sprays of tiny blue flowers in late summer. These are a deeper shade in 'Violetta'. Both H80cm/32in, W60cm/2ft. F7-9. Z4-9.

LOBELIA

Somewhat flashy perennials with bright colours in foliage and flower. Well worth growing as border plants. Cultivars are best covered by litter over winter if left *in situ*.

L. fulgens. The main parent of many hybrids, this has downy purple stems, purple leaves and bright red flowers. H75cm/2ft 6in, W30cm/1ft. F8-10. Z8-9. The following are some of the hybrids: 'Bees Flame', large, very bright scarlet flowers and beetroot-red foliage. H80cm/32in, W30cm/1ft. F7-10. Z4-8. 'Dark Crusader', similar leaves and deep crimson-purple flowers. H80cm/32in, W30cm/ 1ft. F7-10. Z4-8. 'Eulalia Berridge' , a tall cerise pink, H1.2,/4ft, W30cm/1ft. F7-10. Z4-8. 'Queen Victoria', an old favourite, with purple foliage and bright red flowers. H80cm/32in, W30cm/1ft. F7-10. Z4-8. 'Will Scarlet', green-leaved with red flowers. H80cm/32in, W30cm/1ft. F7-10. Z4-8.

LUPINUS Lupin

Popular and colourful perennials which are now mostly represented by seed strains originating from *L. polyphyllus* which come true to colour. They are relatively short lived but add much vibrancy to the early summer garden, coming in a wide range of colours, single as well as bicolored on the same plant, from white, pink, yellow, red, blue, purple

Lychnis flos-jovis 'Hort's Variety'

and orange. Seed strains and selected varieties come in varying heights from 45cm/18in to 1.2m/4ft, their spikes carrying multitudes of small flowers which open from the base to the top. Cut the spikes back immediately after flowering to prevent unwanted seedlings. H(see above), W30-45cm/12-18in. F6-7. Z3-6. ✿ ⊖

LYCHNIS

Brightly flowered perennials which are easy to grow. ✿ ■

L. × arkwrightii. Intense vermilion-scarlet open flowers, 2.5cm/1in or more across, above purple-bronze foliage; can be short-lived. H30cm/1ft, W25cm/10in. F6-8. Z6-8.

L. chalcedonica. The Maltese cross, or Jerusalem cross, has green leaves and stems crowned by cross-shaped scarlet-vermilion flowers, 1.5cm/½in across, in heads up to 13cm/5in wide. H1.1m/43in, W30cm/1ft. F6-8. Z4-8. ◢

L. coronaria. The rose campion or mullein pink has rosettes of hairy, silver leaves and branching stems carrying many open-petalled, magenta flowers for several weeks. A colour difficult to fit with other plants. 'Abbotswood Rose' (syn. *L. ×*

walkeri 'Abbotswood Rose'), intensely bright carmine; 'Alba' is white; 'Atrosanguinea' is purple-red. 'Gardeners World' covers a purple-red double flowered form. 'Oculata' has red-eyed, white flowers. All H60-80cm/24-32in, W45cm/18in. F6-8. Z4-8.

L. flos-jovis. The flower of Jove has felty grey foliage, a dense, tufty habit, and sprays of purple-red flowers for several weeks. 'Hort's Variety' has clear bright pink flowers. Both H45cm/18in, W30cm/1ft. F6-8. Z5-9.

L. viscaria. 'Plena' is a rare double red form. H90cm/3ft, W30cm/1ft. F6-8. Z4-8.

LYSIMACHIA

This genus includes such diverse species as yellow loosestrife and creeping Jenny. Some are inclined to become invasive. ✿ ✿ ◢

L. ciliata 'Firecracker'. Has reddish-purple leaves which offer a striking foliage contrast to yellow flowers. H90cm/3ft, W60cm/2ft. F6-8. Z3-9.

L. punctata. The vigorous yellow loosestrife is showy but invasive, making a splendid display of yellow flowers on leafy stems. H90cm/3ft, W60cm/2ft. F6-8. Z4-8.

LYTHRUM Purple loosestrife

Adaptable and long-lived perennials. Though happiest in moist soil, tolerating even boggy conditions, they still flower where quite dry. Dead-head to prevent self-seeding. Hybrids of both species below are the only ones in circulation, with richer colours than the species. ✿ ✳ ◢

L. salicaria 'Blush'. A colour breakthrough in soft blush-pink. H75cm/2ft 6in, W45cm/18in. Z4-9. 'Firecandle' has graceful, tapering spikes of small but intense rosy-red flowers. H1.2m/4ft, W45cm/18in. F7-9. Z4-9. 'Robert' has a bushier, leafier habit and clear pink flowers. H60cm/2ft, W45cm/18in. F7-9. Z4-9. 'The Beacon' is also bushy, with strong stems and full spikes of rosy red. H1.2m/4ft, W45cm/18in. F7-9. Z4-9.

MERTENSIA

These are valued for their clear blue flowers in spring and early summer. ✿ ■ ✿

M. asiatica. Prostrate, brilliant silver-blue, striking foliage with small, sky-blue flowers. H15in/6in, W30cm/1ft. F6-9. Z4-9. ✿ ✳ ★

M. pulmonarioides (syn. *M. virginica*). A shade lover for cool woodland conditions, fleshy roots produce purplish-blue shoots in spring, unfurling to fragile branching stems from which dangle sky-blue, bell-shaped flowers. The plant dies down in mid-summer. H45cm/18in, W30cm/1ft. F4-5. Z4-9

MIMULUS Monkey flower

Colourful lipped flowers, often blotched or spotted with contrasting colours. Most are not fussy, though mat-forming kinds need replanting every year or two. ✿ ◢

M. cardinalis. The scarlet monkey flower has greener stems and leaves, and orange-scarlet to cerise flowers. H70cm/28in, W45cm/18in. F6-9. Z7-10.

M. guttatus and *M. luteus*, together with *M. cupreus*, have produced several sturdy hybrids and cultivars, listed below, with fascinating bright colours. All F6-8. Z8-10. '**A. T. Johnson**' has large yellow flowers with brown blotches. H30cm/1ft, W30cm/1ft. '**Firedragon**' has flame-orange, dark-spotted flowers. H25cm/10in, W30cm/1ft. '**Puck**' is a vigorous, mound-forming hybrid, covered in butter-yellow flowers, tinged orange. H15cm/6in, W25cm/10in.

MONARDA Bee balm, Sweet bergamot

These showy perennials are back in fashion, with many new selections available. Erect, square stems have aromatic leaves and are topped by brightly coloured heads of hooded flowers. Their mat-like roots are best if divided every year or two. All W45cm/18in. F6-8. Z4-9. ☼ ◢
Hybrids. '**Adam**', bright red, H1.2m/4ft. '**Aquarius**', violet, H1.35m/4ft 6in. '**Balance**', pink, H1.2m/4ft. '**Blue Stocking**', lavender blue, H1.2m/4ft. '**Cambridge Scarlet**', an old favourite introduced prior to 1914, H1.2m/4ft. '**Croftway Pink**', pure rose-pink, H1.2m/4ft. '**Fishes**',

light pink, H1m/39in. '**Gardenview Scarlet**', bright green leaves, brillant, scarlet flowers. H1.35cm/4ft 6in. '**Marshalls Delight**', shining pink, H1.2m/4ft. '**Prairie Night**', close to purple, H1.2m/4ft. '**Scorpion**', deep violet, H1.35m/4ft 6in. '**Snow Queen**', one of several whites, H1.35m/ 4ft 6in. All W45cm/18in. F6-8. Z4-9.

MYOSOTIS Forget-me-not

M. scorpioides (syn. *M. palustris*). '**Maytime**' is an eye-catching forget-me-not with a vigorous habit and leaves brightly margined with white. Flowers bright blue but relatively sparse. H20cm/8in, W45cm/18in. F6-8. Z4-10. ☼ ✳ ◢
'**Mermaid**' makes green mats of foliage and sprays of sky-blue flowers. Hardy, best divided regularly. H15cm/6in, W30cm/1ft. F6-8. Z4-10.

NEPETA Catmint

Mostly good garden plants, easy to grow and with a long season of small flowered spikes and aromatic leaves. ☼ ■
N. racemosa (syn. *N. mussinii*). This is the favourite catmint for bedding and edging, with a succession of bright blue flowers all summer.

Oenothera 'Sonnenwende'

H30cm/1ft, W30cm/1ft. F6-9. Z3-8.
N. nervosa. A neat growing, showy species, with long display of short, violet-blue spikes. Distinct and worthwhile. H25cm/10in, W30cm/ 1ft. F6-8. Z5-8.

OENOTHERA Evening primrose

Several perennials in this family are garden-worthy, with large, saucer-shaped flowers for a long period. ☼ ■
O. fruticosa (syn. *O. tetragona*). Under this species belong some of the brightest and most reliable of all perennials. '**Fireworks**' (syn. 'Fyrverkeri'). Rosette-forming hybrid with multi-coloured leaves in spring, followed by sprays of sizeable yellow flowers. H35cm/14in, W30cm/1ft. F6-8. Z5-9.
O. '**Macrocarpa**' (syn. *O. missouriensis*). Large, light yellow flowers last for weeks on end, followed by huge seedpods, useful in dried flower displays. Its sprawling habit lends itself to sloping ground, but as a deep-rooting hardy plant it is invaluable. H23cm/9in, W60cm/2ft. F6-9. Z5-8.
O. '**Sonnenwende**' (syn. 'Solstice'). Neat and free-flowering with maroon young leaves and flower buds. H60cm/2ft. W30cm/1ft. F6-8. Z5-9.

OMPHALODES Navelwort

These pretty, long-lived plants have forget-me-not-type flowers and lush, oval-shaped foliage.
O. cappadocica. In cool shade this slowly makes a clump of near-evergreen leaves and short sprays of bright blue flowers. '**Starry Eyes**' is a pretty variant with blue flowers edged mauve-white. H13cm/5in, W30cm/1ft. F4-5. Z6-9.
O. luciliae. A choice species for a rock crevice or alpine house, this has blue-grey leaves and sprays of sky-blue flowers. H15cm/6in, W45cm/18in. F4-5. Z6-7. ☼

OPHIOPOGON

O. planiscapus nigrescens. Also known as 'Black Dragon', this is one of the most striking plants for year-round colour. A member of the lily family, it makes a low-spreading, striking hummock of arching black leaves. Slender spikes bear lilac flowers, later black fruits. Best where not too dry; add a mulch. H20cm/ 8in, W20cm/8in. F7-8. Z6-10. ☼ ✳

ORIGANUM Marjoram

Sun-loving herbs, which make first class flowering and foliage plants.

Mimulus guttatus 'Puck'

O. 'Herrenhausen'. This hybrid is mauve-pink, flowering continuously all summer. 'Rosenkuppel' is even brighter. Both H60cm/2ft, W30cm/1ft. F7-10. Z5-8.

O. laevigatum. Dense, twiggy sprays of tiny, deep purple-violet flowers in late summer, with small, rounded, glaucous leaves. 'Hopleys' has brighter, deep mauve blue flowers. H45cm/18in, W30cm/1ft. F8-10. Z5-9.

O. vulgare. The culinary marjoram has a more or less evergreen, golden-leaved form, 'Aureum'. The flowers are insignificant but plants make good ground cover. 'Thumble's Variety' has larger leaves and deeper golden-yellow leaves. Both H15cm/6in, W30cm/1ft. Z4-8.

PAEONIA Peony

These long-lived perennials are a favourite among many gardeners, loved for their often exotic, richly coloured flowers and their foliage. Flowering of some species begins in late spring, but large-flowered types are at their best in early summer. Plant in autumn in well-prepared, enriched, deep soil with buds about 2.5cm/1in below the surface: deeper planting inhibits flowering. Allow ample spacing. Tree peonies (*P. suffruticosa*) are covered under Shrubs.

P. lactiflora. The majority of the early-summer flowering varieties originate from this Chinese species. A small selection is listed below but a wider range can be sought from specialists. All H75-100cm/30-39in, W60cm/2ft. F6. Z3-9. 'Bowl of Beauty', large semi-double flowers of glowing deep pink with a cream centre. 'Duchesse de Nemours', a favourite double white. 'Edulis Superba', fully double soft pink and scented. 'Felix Crousse', free-flowering, carmine-red double. 'Festiva Maxima', large double white, flecked crimson. 'Le Cygne', purest

Origanum 'Rosenkuppel'

white, large-flowered double. 'Sarah Bernhardt', still the most popular double, soft pink. 'Shirley Temple', large, deep rose double. 'Solange', pale salmon double, with a hint of orange. 'Coral Supreme', salmon-coral cup-shaped blooms. 'Miss America', semi-double, snow white, yellow anthers.

P. mlokosewitschii. A superb early-flowering species with light green foliage and soft yellow cups.

P. officinalis. The old-fashioned peony rose flowers a little earlier than *P. lactiflora* varieties. All are strong-growing, usually H80-90cm/32-36in, W60cm/2ft. F5-6. Z3-9. 'Alba Plena', a large double-white; 'Lize van Veen', a double blush-pink; 'Rosea Superba' a bright pink, large double; 'Rubra Plena' deep crimson-red double.

PAPAVER Poppy

These showy, sun-loving plants prefer ordinary or poor, deep soil, dryish rather than moist.

P. 'Fireball'. This resembles a miniature *P. orientale,* except for its spreading habit and shallower roots. The flowers, 5cm/2in or so across, are early and fully double orange-scarlet. H30cm/1ft, W30cm/1ft. F5-

Papaver orientale 'Glowing Embers'

7. Z4-9.

P. orientale. Oriental poppies are quite outstanding for size and brillance, though some flowers are so huge that they are top-heavy and difficult to support. Cut back after flowering. All F5-7. Z4-9. ☼ ▪ 'Beauty of Livermere' (syn. 'Goliath'), one of the most reliable poppies, a fine, upright blood-red single. H1.1m/43in, W60cm/2ft. 'Black and White', striking with its white petals and black centre. H75cm/30in, W60cm/2ft. 'Glowing Embers', fairly erect with glowing orange-red ruffled petals, H1m/39in, W60cm/2ft. 'Harvest Moon', deep orange, semi-double flowers, effective

until they begin to fade. H1m/39in, W60cm/2ft. 'Picotée', frilly white petals suffused scarlet. H70cm/28in, W60cm/2ft. 'Turkish Delight', glowing flesh-pink. H75cm/30in, W60cm/2ft.

PENSTEMON

A large and diverse genus which includes some species with vivid colours, and low-growing, semi-shrubby alpines. Though some are only reliably hardy in milder climates, the hybrid garden cultivars are showy, flowering for months in summer and early autumn if cut back. Most hybrids need winter protection in cold regions. Take cuttings in early autumn and overwinter them under glass, to replace possible losses. ☼ ⚹ ◪ ▪

P. digitalis. Erect stems bear pale lilac foxglove-like flowers, with plenty of basal foliage. 'Huskers Red' is similar in flower but has striking red-purple leaves and stems. Both H60cm/2ft, W38cm/15in. F6-8. Z3-9.

Hybrids. These floriferous semi-shrubby perennials have occured through crossing of *P. hartwegii*, *P. companulatus* and *P. gloxinioides*. The selections arising have then been crossed and selected again. All fill the need for summer colour for the

Penstemon 'King George'

garden or for pots and containers. All F6-10 unless otherwise noted. All Z9-10. **'Apple Blossom'**, blush-pink trumpet flowers. H45cm/18in, W30cm/1ft. **'Blackbird'**, deep purple. H60cm/2ft, W45cm/18in. **'Evelyn'**, pale pink. H45cm/18in, W30cm/1ft. **'Garnet'**, wine-red. H50cm/ 20in, W45cm/18in. **'Hidcote Pink'**, outstandingly free-flowering. H60cm/2ft, W45cm/18in. **'King George'**, salmon-red with a white throat. H60cm/2ft, W45cm/ 18in. **'Purple Passion'**, deep glowing purple, white throat. H60cm/2ft, W45cm/18in. **'Rubicunda'**, large, warm red. H60cm/2ft, W45cm/18in. **'Sour Grapes'**, large, pale purple flowers, strong-growing. H70cm/ 28in, W45cm/18in. F6-9. **'Snowstorm'**, distinctive white flowers. H70cm/28in, W45cm/18in.

PERSICARIA Knotweed

Formerly listed under *Polygonum*, all below now fall under *Persicaria*, a genus which includes some first rate and choice plants as well as easier and spreading types. Most have a long season of flowering. ✷ ◢

P. affine. Long-flowering species for ground cover. Narrow leaves and poker-like flowers. H15-23cm/6-9in, W38cm/15in. F6-7. Z3-9. **'Dimity'** has fuller, long-lasting pink spikes and is more reliable, with good autumn colour. Excellent for containers. H15cm/6in, W45cm/18in. F6-7. Z3-9.

P. amplexicaule. An abundant, leafy perennial with a long succession of red flowers. H1.2m/4ft, W75cm/2ft 6in. F6-9. Z5-9. **'Atrosanguineum'** is a deep crimson; **'Firetail'** is an outstanding bright red. Both H1.2m/ 4ft, W1.2m/4ft. F6-10. Z5-9. **'Taurus'**, perhaps the best to date: bright green leaves set off the succession of crimson bottlebrush flowers from mid-summer to autumn frosts. H75cm/2ft 6in, W1.2m/4ft. F6-10. Z5-9.

Persicaria amplexicaule 'Taurus'

P. bistorta **'Superbum'**. Handsome, finger-sized, light pink pokers on erect stems. Vigorous. H80cm/32in, W60cm/2ft. F5-7 but may repeat. Z4-8. ◢

P. macrophyllum. Deep green leaves and distinct, clear, light pink pokers on erect stems. A choice and beautiful plant. H45cm/18in, W45cm/18in. F7-9. Z4-9.

P. milletii. Choice for good, moist, deep soil, this has clumps of narrow leaves and crimson-red pokers on and off all summer. H30cm/1ft, W30cm/ 1ft. Mainly F6-8. Z5-9. ✷ ✷

PHLOMIS

See also under Shrubs

P. russeliana (syn. *P. samia*). A sturdy plant with large, basal woolly ever-green leaves and whorls of hooded yellow flowers on strong stems. H90cm/3ft, W60cm/2ft. F6-8. Z4-9. ✷ ◢

P. tuberosa **'Amazone'**. An imposing plant with deep green foliage and spikes with rose-pink hooded flowers. H1.5m/5ft, W45cm/18in. F6-8. Z6-8.

PHLOX

Included in this family of spring- and summer-flowering perennials are the indispensable border phlox, mostly

listed under *P. paniculata*. They come in a wide range of colours, the majority being scented.

P. carolina **'Bill Baker'**. Trouble-free selection with a long display of bright pink flowers. H45cm/18in, W30cm/1ft. F6-7. Z5-8. ✷ ✷

P. divaricata. Attractive heads of fragrant blue flowers from creeping basal growth. H25cm/10in, W25cm/10in. F5-6. Z3-9. Two excellent selections include **'Blue Dreams'**, mid-blue, and **'May Breeze'**, lilac-white. Both H40cm/16in. ✷ ✷

P. maculata. Narrow-leaved, slender stems, crowned with cylindrical flower trusses. Grown in light soil, they make a fine show and, like most larger hybrids, are pleasantly fragrant. **'Alpha'** is pink, **'Delta'** is white with a lilac centre and **'Omega'** is white with a red eye. All H90cm/3ft, W30cm/1ft. F7-9. Z4-8.

P. paniculata. Some well-tried selections are listed. All H75-90cm/2ft 6in-3ft, W30cm/1ft. F7-9. Z4-8. **'Bright Eyes'**, neat clusters, pink with crimson centre. **'Caroline van den Berg'**, as near a blue as can be. **'Eva Cullum'**, strong and leafy, warm pink, red eye. **'Franz Schubert'**, lilac, long-flowering and

Persicaria bistorta 'Superbum'

reliable. **'Harlequin'**, golden yellow variegated leaves and violet-purple flowers. H80cm/32in, W30cm/1ft. **'Marlborough'**, violet-purple with dark foliage. H90cm/3ft, W30cm/ 1ft. **'Mother of Pearl'**, white suffused pink. **'Norah Leigh'**, bright, creamy variegated leaves with pale lilac-purple flowers. **'Prince of Orange'**, outstanding salmon-orange. **'Prospero'**, strong-growing light lilac. **'Sandringham'**, cyclamen-pink, with a darker centre; an old but still worthwhile cultivar. **'Skylight'**, lavender-bue, with dark foliage. **'Starfire'**, unsurpassed bright, deep red. **'Windsor'**, deep carmine with a magenta eye.

Phlox paniculata 'Franz Schubert'

PHYSOSTEGIA Obedient plant

Easy plants of spreading habit, which need to be divided and replanted regularly. ☼ ☆ ◪

P. virginiana. Produces an abundance of erect spikes of mauve-pink, snapdragon-like flowers. H1.1m/43in, W60cm/2ft. F7-9. Z4-8. Cultivars include: '**Rose Bouquet**', rosy lilac. H80cm/32in, W60cm/2ft. F7-9. '**Summer Snow**', white. H70cm/28in, W60cm/2ft. F7-9. '**Variegata**', lilac-pink flowers and striking, variegated leaves. H50cm/20in, W45cm/18in. F8-10. '**Vivid**', much dwarfer and later, deep pink. H50cm/20in, W45cm/18in. F8-10.

PLATYCODON Balloon flower

Buds that swell into little 'balloons' before they fully open into saucer-shaped flowers have given this plant its common name. Easily grown, long-lived plants, preferring sun but adaptable to partial shade. ☼ ◪ ✲

P. grandiflorus. The parent species of several forms, incuding the white **alba**, the dwarf, deep blue **apoyama**, **mariesii** in shades of light blue, and the pale pink '**Mother of Pearl**'. All H40-50cm/16-20in, W45cm/18in.

POLEMONIUM Jacob's ladder

Popular perennials, mostly with blue or white flowers with rich yellow stamens and basal clumps of ferny foliage. They are easy to grow, preferring a sunny position.

P. caeruleum. The best known, but not the most reliable, and apt to seed itself. It has heads of lavender-blue, saucer-shaped flowers. H60cm/2ft, W60cm/2ft. F5-7. Z4-8. '**Brise d'Anjou**', an attractive form which makes a mound of finely cut variegated leaves, hardly needing the addition of its blue flowers. Good in a container. H60cm/2ft, W45cm/18in. F6-7. Z4-8. '**Dawn Flight**' is reliably perennial, with light green, ferny foliage and a fine display of white flowers. H70cm/28in,

Polemonium caeruleum 'Brise d'Anjou'

W60cm/2ft. F5-7. Z4-8.

P. carneum. Lilac-pink flowers dangle above low, clumpy growth. H25cm/10in, W30cm/1ft. F6-7. Z4-9.

POLYGONATUM Solomon's seal

Early summer-flowering shade lovers with spreading, fleshy roots. Most have attractive foliage with little white bell-shaped flowers, which dangle from strong, leafy stems, arching in the taller species. ☼ ✲

P. falcatum (syn. *P. japonicum*). A dwarf species with dense, leafy, arching stems and tiny, dangling white flowers. '**Variegatum**' has white-edged leaves. H60cm/2ft, W30cm/1ft. F5-6. Z4-9.

P. biflorum (syn. *P. giganteum*). The tallest, strong-growing species, the giant Solomon's seal. H1m/39in (or more in good soil), W60cm/2ft. F5-7. Z4-9.

P. × hybridum (syn. *P. multiflorum*). A somewhat variable species. It has a striking variegated form '**Striatum**' (syn. 'Variegatum'). H50-60cm/20-24in, W30cm/1ft. F5-7. Z3-9.

POLYGONUM See PERSICARIA

POTENTILLA Cinquefoil

Sun lovers for well-drained soil, with strawberry-like leaves and brightly coloured, saucer-shaped flowers.

P. atrosanguinea. Clumps of silvery lobed leaves and dark red flowers. **P. a. argyrophylla,** similar foliage but sprays of clear yellow flowers. Both H40cm/16in, W60cm/2ft. F-7. Z6-9.

P. argyrophylla hybrids. '**Blazeaway**', suffused orange-red, with greyish leaves. H30cm/1ft, W45cm/18in. F6-8. '**Flamenco**', robust, early, blood-red. H50cm/20in, W60cm/2ft. F5-7. '**Gibson's Scarlet**', popular, glowing red, long season. H60cm/2ft, W60cm/2ft. F6-9. '**William Rollison**', intensely bright flame-orange, semi-double. H40cm/16in, W45cm/18in. F6-8. '**Yellow Queen**', silvery leaves, shining yellow flowers. H25cm/10in, W45cm/18in. F5-7.

P. nepalensis. '**Helen Jane**', bright pink flowers on branching stems. '**Miss Willmott**', a favourite, with strawberry flowers of warm carmine pink. Both H45cm/18in, W40cm/16in. F6-9. Z5-8.

P. recta '**Warrenii**'. Erect-growing, showy, with branching heads of small yellow flowers above dissected greenery. H70cm/28in, W30cm/1ft. F6-8. Z4-8.

PRIMULA

This large and varied genus has many beautiful forms for summer colour, many quite easy to grow. Others require moist soil and some shade to succeed, according to climate. Those below are described under distinct categories.

Candelabra primulas

These include most tall kinds and moisture lovers for sun or part shade. Flowers are carried in whorls up tall stems. Heights vary according to soil fertility and moisture content. Some may be short-lived, others will self-seed in suitable conditions. Besides those listed below, there are several mixed, mostly long-lived candelabra strains, such as '**Bressingham Strain**' and '**Inshriach Hybrids**'.

P. × bulleesiana. A strain of mixed colours, in shades of cream, yellow, apricot, pink, orange, red and purple. Also known as '**Asthore Hybrids**'. H50-60cm/20-24in, W30cm/1ft. F5-7. Z5-8.

P. bulleyana. A popular plant, with dark green leaves and warm, deep orange flowers. H60-80cm/24-32in, W45cm/18in. F5-7. Z6-8.

P. burmanica. Purple-red, yellow-eyed flowers and long, whitish, dusty leaves. H60-70cm/24-28in, W45cm/18in. F5-7. Z5-8.

P. japonica. The Japanese primrose has leafy growth resembling young cabbages, and pink flowers, near red

Primula 'Bressingham Strain'

with a black eye in '**Miller's Crimson**' and white with a yellow eye in '**Postford White**'. All H60-80cm/24-32in, W45cm/18in. F5-7. Z6-8.

P. pulverulenta. Brilliant rosy-red flowers are carried profusely above crinkled leaves. H40-50cm/16-20in, W45cm/18in. F5-6. Z6-8.

P. sieboldii **group**
This charming group produce loose umbels of white-eyed flowers above soft green, lobed and toothed foliage. Hardy, easy and not invasive. Often sold as mixtures but good named selections include: '**Cherubim**', light lavender-blue, '**Geisha Girl**', clear light pink, '**Mikado**', reddish-pink, '**Seraphim**', deep pink, '**Snowflake**', pure white. All H15-25cm/6-10in, W10-20cm/4-8in. F4-5. Z4-8.

☼ ■ ◢ ★

P. vialii. A distinct species with red hot poker-type, lavender-blue flower spikes on smooth stalks above a small and rather sparsely leaved rootstock. Spectacular in some shade in well-drained but moist, humus-rich soil, flowering later than most primulas. Short-lived but worth the effort. H30-50cm/12-20in, W23cm/9in. F6-8. Z6-8.

Primula vialii

PRUNELLA **Self-heal**
These easily grown, mat-forming plants, closely related to *Stachys,* are useful for front-of-the-border groups. *P. grandiflora.* This has dense spikes of tubular, purple-violet flowers. It is best in '**Blue Loveliness**', '**Pink Loveliness**' and '**White Loveliness**'. All H20cm/8in, W45cm/18in. F6-8. Z5-8. '**Little Red Riding Hood**' makes a fine show of rosy red. H15cm/6in, W25cm/10in. F6-8. Z5-8.

PULMONARIA **Lungwort**
Though these are invaluable early spring flowering plants, some flowers last into late spring. The selections listed here offer attractive summer foliage to equal that of any hosta. ☼
☀ ◢

P. longifolia. Conspicuously spotted leaves, 15cm/6in long, blue flowers on terminal sprays; white in the form *alba.* '**Bertram Anderson**', deep violet-blue flowers. '**Roy Davidson**', lighter blue flowers. All H25cm/10in, W45cm/18in. F4-5/. Z5-8.

P. officinalis '**Sissinghurst White**'. White sprays, white-spotted leaves. H25cm/10in, W60cm/2ft. F3-5.

P. rubra '**David Ward.**' A selection with light green leaves and broad white

Ranunculus gramineus

markings, coral-red blooms. H3cm/1ft, W60cm/2ft. F3-4. Z5-8. ☀

P. saccharata Bethlehem sage. Widest range of choice, with overlapping evergreen leaves. Almost all have pink flowers which fade to blue on short sprays. All Z4-8. '**Argentea**', almost entirely silver-leaved. '**Highdown**' (syn. '**Lewis Palmer**'), outstanding for its deep blue flowers, vigour and attractive foliage. '**Leopard**', spotted silver leaves, deep rose-pink spring flowers. All H25cm/10in, W60cm/2ft. F3-5.

PYRETHRUM See *TANACETUM*

RANUNCULUS **Buttercup**
Though generally moisture-loving, any good, well-drained soil and a sunny spot will suit those below. *R. aconitifolius* '**Flore Pleno**'. A choice and lovely form with dazzling, fully double white flowers. H40-70cm/16-28in, W60cm/2ft. F5-6. Z5-9. ■

R. gramineus. A first class perennial with glaucous grassy leaves and sprays of clear yellow flowers. H60cm/2ft, W45cm/18in. F5-7. Z4-8. ☆

RODGERSIA
Long-lived perennials with handsome leaves and imposing flower spikes in

summer. Most species have creamy-white plumes, similar to astilbes. Though adaptable for sun or shade, or as marginal plants, they are not suitable for places where it is both dry and sunny. Early growth can be hit by spring frosts.

R. aesculifolia. '**Chestnut-leaved**' describes the crinkled bronzed foliage, and it has conical creamy-white flower spikes. '**Irish Bronze**' has purple-tinted leaves and stems, and white flowers. Both H1.2m/4ft, W60cm/2ft. F6-8. Z5-8.

R. pinnata. This has paired, fingered, deeply divided leaves, pink or white flowers. The form '**Elegans**' is freer to flower with imposing creamy spikes. H1.2m/4ft, W60cm/2ft. F6-8. Z5-8. '**Superba**' lives up to its name; not only is the foliage tinted purple, but the flowers are a glistening rose-pink. H1.2m/4ft, W50cm/20in. F6-7. Z5-8.

ROMNEYA **California tree poppy**
Glaucous-leaved and semi-shrubby, these perennials have white, scented, poppy-like flowers carried over a long period. Although the roots have a tendency to spread, their beauty outweighs such a disadvantage. They are difficult to divide, so pot-grown plants are best. ☼ ■

R. coulteri. This has large, yellow-centred white flowers and is the species most likely to be available. H2.1m/7ft, W90cm/3ft. F7-10. Z8-10.

ROSCOEA
Fleshy-rooted, distinctive perennials, easy to grow. They are late to break the surface in spring but soon produce light green, sheath-like leaves and spikes of orchid-like flowers on erect stems. ☼ ☀

R. cautleoides. Early and of a more open, slender habit than the above two species, the flowers are soft primrose-yellow. '**Kew Beauty**', later to flower than the species, its leafy stalks sheathe large, primrose-yellow flowers. Both H35cm/14in, W15cm/6in. F6-8. Z7-9.

R. procera. The finest blue-flowered species, this has large, deep violet-blue flowers above abundant greenery. H35cm/14in, W15cm/6in. F6-8. Z6-9.

R. purpurea. Also violet-blue, this has smaller flowers and leaves. H35cm/14in, W15cm/6in. F6-8. Z6-9.

RUDBECKIA Coneflower, Black-eyed Susan

These are some of the showiest and easiest of late-flowering perennials. All come from North America and have daisy-like flowers. ✿ ☆

R. fulgida. There are several selections of this species, somewhat similar to each other, all with a central black cone and golden-yellow rayed petals. They prefer moist to dry soils but are generally quite adaptable. All tend to seed freely. F7-10, Z4-9. *R. f.* var. *deamii* has light green leaves, tall at 90cm/3ft, W45cm/18in. *R. f.* var. *sulllivantii* 'Goldsturm', one of the best plants ever raised, with shining dark green foliage, black-centred gold flowers. H45-60cm/18-24in, W45cm/18in. *R. f.* 'Viette's Little Suzy'. Diminutive selection, smaller flowers and leaves. H30cm/1ft, W30cm/1ft.

Rudbeckia 'Goldquelle'

Salvia × *superba*

R. 'Herbststonne' (syn. 'Autumn Sun'). Garden-worthy, though tall, with long stems of bright green leaves topped with greenish-yellow cone. H2.1m/7ft, W60cm/2ft. F7-9. Z5-9.

R. 'Goldquelle'. A distinctive, very beautiful plant with leafy, deep green bushy growth covered in fully double, chrome-yellow flowers, 8cm/3in across. H1m/39in, W60cm/2ft. F7-9. Z3-9.

SALVIA

A vast genus which includes some good garden plants, though some of the brightest colours are not hardy. Many are aromatic and most have hairy leaves; colourful bracts are also common. They enjoy sun and well-drained soil.

S. nemerosa 'Ost Friesland' (syn. 'East Friesland'). Outstanding free flowering cultivar, bushy habit, numerous spikes bearing violet-blue flowers. 'Lubecca' is similar but twice the height. H45cm/18in, W45cm/18in. F6-8. Z5-9.

S. pratensis 'Rosea'. A pretty form with long brached spikes of pale lilac-pink flowers. H60cm/2ft, W45cm/18in. F6-8. Z5-9.

S. × *superba*. A popular hybrid with fine violet-blue upstanding spikes with crimson-purple bracts, making an excellent contrast to yellow, daisy-flowered subjects. H1.2m/4ft, W60cm/2ft. F6-8. Z5-9.

S. × *sylvestris* 'Blauhügel' ('Blue Hills'). Closest to blue of any of this type, providing a succession of flowers on compact bushes throughout the summer. There is also a white form 'Weisshugel' ('White Hills'). Both 45cm/18in, W30cm/1ft. F6-9. Z5-9. 'Mainacht' ('May Night'), earliest to flower with striking violet-blue flowers on erect spikes. H45cm/18in, W30cm/1ft. F5-7. Z5-9.

S. verticillata 'Purple Rain'. Leafy, hairy foliage and spikes with whorls of rich purple flowers for weeks on end. H45cm/18in, W45cm/18 in. F7-9. Z5-9.

SANGUISORBA Burnet

Strong-growing leafy perennials with elegant, pinnate foliage and bottlebrush flowers. Hardy and long-lived. ✿ ☆

S. magnifica alba. A robust plant with nodding white pokers above abundant foliage. H80cm/32in, W60cm/2ft. F6-8. Z4-8.

SCABIOSA Scabious, pincushion flower

Popular perennials with a long flowering season. ✿ ■

S. 'Butterfly Blue'. Lavender-blue flowers all summer. Similar in habit but with lilac pink flowers is 'Pink Mist'. Both H30cm/1ft, W30cm/1ft. F5-9. Z5-8.

S. caucasica. Valuable perennials for garden and cutting, these prefer sun and well-drained soil, ideally with lime. Deadhead to prolong flowering. All H60-80cm/24-32in, W45-60cm/18-24in. F6-9. Z4-9. 'Blausiegel' ('Blue Seal'), a strong constitution and a succession of rich blue flowers. 'Bressingham White' and 'Miss Willmott' are both good whites, the latter more ivory. 'Clive Greaves', is a prolific mid-blue and 'Moonlight' a fairly tall light blue.

S. graminifolia. One of the finest plants for frontal groups, it makes dense mats of narrow, silver-grey leaves with a long show of light blue flowers. H30cm/1ft, W30cm/1ft. F6-9. Z7-9. 'Pink Cushion', from Bressingham, is light pink and less robust. H25cm/10in, W25cm/10in. F6-9. Z7-9. ✿ Light soil

SEDUM Stonecrop

Indispensable and easy perennials whose flat or domed heads of starry flowers also attract butterflies. ✿ ■ ☆

S. aizoon 'Aurantiacum'. Striking for its bronzy stems and leaves and its deep yellow, almost orange, flowers. H30cm/1ft, W30cm/1ft. F6-8. Z4-9.

S. 'Autumn Joy' ('Herbstfreude'). Spring growth of glaucous, fleshy stem and leaves remaining attractive all summer. Glistening pink flowerheads widen to 25cm/10in across, turning a deep bronze, then coppery red. Divide and replant regularly. H50cm/20in, W50cm/20in. F8-10. Z3-10.

S. 'Mörchen'. Erect habit and deep purple-bronze leaves, smallish yellow flowers but foliage effect impressive. H45cm/18in, W30cm/1ft. F8-9. Z4-9.

S. floriferum 'Weihenstephaner Gold'. For the front of a border, this makes spreading, dark green mats and a long succession of orange-gold heads. H15-18cm/6-7in, W45cm/18in. F6-9. Z4-8.

S. 'Ruby Glow'. Hybrid with greyish-purple foliage and a good display of ruby-red flowers. H20cm/8in, W20cm/8in. F7-9. Z4-8.

S. spectabile. Sometimes called ice plants, their fleshy glaucous foliage is effective infill all summer before the wide heads of chalky pink flowers appear. Not much variation in the varieties offered. 'Brilliant', 'Indian Chief', 'Meteor' and 'September Glow' all have more vivid flowers. H30-40cm/12-16in, W30-40cm/12-16in. F8-10. Z4-9.

S. telephium maximum. 'Atropurpureum' has handsome purple-red leaves and heads of glistening rosy-red flowers. H50cm/20in, W30cm/1ft. F7-8. Z5-9.

S. 'Vera Jameson'. Dwarf form with bluish-purple leaves and loose heads of warm pink flowers. H25cm/10in, W25cm/10in. F7-9. Z4-9.

SIDALCEA
Useful for their spiky habit and mallow flowers which add to the structure of the perennial bed or

Sidalcea candida 'Elsie Heugh'

border. All are easy to grow and have silky, hollyhock-like flowers, graceful divided foliage and a clumpy, ground-covering base.

S. candida. Small pretty white flowers on narrow spikes make an attractive variation. Some may need staking. H90cm/3ft, W30cm/1ft. All F6-9. Z5-8. 'Croftway Red', deep rose. H1m/39in, W45cm/18in. 'Elsie Heugh', upstanding clear pink, fringed petals. H1.2m/4ft, W45cm/18in. 'Loveliness', warm pink, compact. H80cm/32in, W45cm/18in. 'Mrs Alderson', deep pink, heavy foliage. H1.2m/4ft, W45cm/18in. 'Oberon', shell-pink, erect, self-supporting. H80cm/32in, W45cm/18in. 'William Smith', salmon-pink, H1.2m/4ft, W45cm/18in.

SISYRINCHIUM
Resembling the iris, most are classed as alpines. ☼ ■

S. striatum. Broad, light green evergreen leaves and light yellow flowers. Tolerates light shade. Not long-lived but self-seeding. Of considerable merit is the creamy-yellow variegated form 'Aunt May', which has summer-long interest. H60cm/2ft, W23cm/9in. F6-8. Z7-8.

SOLIDAGO Goldenrod
Considered weeds by some and certainly a few of the taller self-seeding or spreading species fit that description. However there are many hybrids which offer attractive foliage and flower to add to the summer palette, all variations of yellow. All Z4-9. ☼ ☀ ☆

'Cloth of Gold', dwarf, abundant foliage, wide heads. H40cm/16in, W30cm/1ft. F6-8. 'Crown of Rays' ('Strahlenkrone'), similar, but a little taller. H45cm/18in, W30cm/1ft. F7-8. 'Golden Shower', attractive splayed plumes. H70cm/28in, W45cm/18in. F7-8. 'Lemore', soft primrose-yellow. H70cm/28in, W45cm/18in. F7-8.

Solidago 'Queenie'

'Mimosa', the best tall form, golden yellow. H1.2m/4ft, W60cm/2ft. F8-9. 'Queenie' (syn. 'Golden Thumb'), neat, small, light-leaved bush, short yellow flower spikes. H25cm/10in, W25cm/10in. F8-9.

STACHYS
These woolly-leaved plants are all easy to grow. ☼ ■

S. byzantina (syn. *S. lanata* and *S. olympica)*. Lamb's tongue, or lamb's ear, is vigorous but shallow-rooting, with lilac flowers above mats of downy leaves. H45cm/18in, W30cm/1ft. F5-6. Z4-9. 'Primrose Heron', new felted leaves emerge golden in spring and last for many weeks. H45cm/18in, W30cm/1ft. F5-6. Z4-9. 'Silver Carpet' is a non-flowering, excellent carpeter. H20cm/8in, W30cm/1ft. Z4-9

S. macrantha. A showy plant with dark green, downy foliage and spikes of dep lilac. 'Robusta', the best form, has stiff growth, crinkly, bright green leaves and deep pink spikes. Both H40cm/16in, W23cm/9in. F6-8. Z4-8.

STOKESIA Stoke's aster, cornflower aster
S. laevis. Formerly *S. cyanea,* this has leathery, broad, strap-like basal leaves

and large, solitary, cornflower-like flowers on short stems for many weeks. These are wide-petalled, in shades of blue and, less commonly, white, with fluffy centres. Ideal for the front of a sunny border. 'Blue Star' has light blue flowers, 'Wyoming', a deeper purple blue. Both H25-30cm/10-12in, W30cm/1ft. F6-9. Z5-8. ■

SYMPHYTUM Comfrey
Most comfreys have coarse, hairy leaves and drooping, tubular flowers. Place with care in the garden due to their invasive nature. Adaptable and not fussy about soil, though cool, moist soil is ideal. ☼ ☀ ☀ ◢ ☆

S. 'Hidcote Blue'. Strong growing ground cover with red buds turning to blue and white bells, making often dark green leafy carpets. 'Hidcote Pink' has deep rose-pink and white flowers. Pretty in flower, useful under trees but both need controlling. Both H45cm/18in, W60cm/2ft. F4-6. Z5-9.

S. ibericum (syn. *S. grandiflorum)*. A vigorous, low-growing spreader with mid-green leaves and creamy-yellow flowers. 'Goldsmith' (syn. 'Variegata'), makes a bright show with green leaves, irregularly edged gold.

Can revert if roots are damaged. Both species and this H20cm/8in, W45cm/18in. F4-6. Z5-9.

TANACETUM

T. coccineum (syn. *Pyrethrum coccineum, Chrysanthemum pyrethrum*). The pyrethrums are showy perennials with carrot-like foliage and early summer daisy-like flowers of red, pink and white, some double, excellent for cutting. Cut back after flowering. Best planted in spring, pot grown plants only in autumn. All F5-7. Z5-9. ☼ ■ ⊙ 'Avalanche', robust, single white. 'Brenda', strong-growing deep pink, single. Both H80cm/32in, W45cm/18in. 'Bressingham Red', blood-red, single-rayed flowers. 'Eileen May Robinson', still supreme as a single clear pink. Both H70cm/28in, W45cm/18in. 'Philippa', double, glowing deep carmine. The following dwarf cultivars are all vigorous: 'Laurin', single pink. H38cm/15in, W30cm/1ft. 'Peter Pan', almost double carmine-red. H30cm/1ft, W20cm/8in. 'Pink Petite', clear pink. H38cm/15in, W25cm/10in. 'Red Dwarf' (syn. 'Rote Zwerg'), compact with yellow centres and bright crimson petals. H30cm/1ft, W20cm/8in. *T. parthenium* (syn. *Pyrethrum parthenium, Chrysanthemum parthenium*) 'Aureum'. Feverfew, a free-seeding perennial of great charm. Bright golden-leaved bushes are covered with tiny single daisy flowers in mid-summer. H45cm/18in, W45cm/18in. F6-7. Z4-8.

TELLIMA Fringecup

T. grandiflora This relative of *Heuchera* has the same mounded, evergreen foliage, but the flowers, on hairy-stemmed sprays, are creamy-green. The purplish-leaved 'Rubra' (syn. 'Purpurea') is more effective. Both H50cm/20in, W50cm/20in. F5-6. Z4-9. ☼ ✳ ▢

THALICTRUM Meadow rue

Tall and robust, small and delicate, both are represented in this variable genus. ☼ ✳ ☆

T. aquilegiifolium. A clump-forming species making an early display of columbine-like leaves and small, fluffy flowers in terminal clusters. The rounded flowers are purplish, except in 'Album' where they are white. H1m/39in, W30cm/1ft. F5-7. Z5-9. 'Purpureum' is purple-lilac, but shades and heights vary greatly since they are often offered from seed-raised plants. H80-120cm/32-48in, W30cm/1ft. F5-7. Z5-9.

T. delavayi (syn. *T. dipterocarpum*). Small mauve-blue flowers with yellow centres appear in great profusion on widely branching stems, apt to tangle. H1.2m/4ft, W45cm/18in. F7-9. Z5-9. 'Hewitt's Double' is a choice and beautiful plant. H90cm/3ft, W30cm/1ft. F7-9. Z5-9. ✳ ▰

T. flavum. Yellow meadow rue is green-leaved, with yellow flowers in terminal clusters on strong stems. H1.5m/5ft, W45cm/18in. F6-8. Z6-9.

THERMOPSIS False lupin

Lupin-like in appearance, with palmate leaves and racemes of yellow

Thalictrum flavum

Tiarella polyphylla 'Moorgrün'

flowers in early summer. All are easy, given sun and well-drained soil. ■

T. angustifolia, T. caroliniana and *T. mollis* are clump-forming, sun-loving plants, giving a good display from leafy bushes. All H80-100cm/32-39in, W60cm/2ft. F5-7. Z3-9.

T. montana. Bright yellow, pea-like flower spikes on smooth stems. H75cm/2ft 6in, W60cm/2ft. F6-7. Z3-8.

TIARELLA Foam flower

Dwarf, shade-loving plants allied to *Heuchera,* these are shallow-rooting and like sandy, cool, moist soil. New breeding work is bringing forward some valuable new forms. ✳ ■ ★

T. cordifolia. This carpets shady places with pretty evergreen leaves, bronzy in winter, and gives a charming summer display with racemes of starry small white flowers. Spreads by runners. H15cm/6in, W45cm/18in. F5-6. Z3-8.

T. polyphylla. This forms low green hummocks of lobed, toothed leaves and tiny, pearl-like, white or pink-tinged flowers. 'Moorgrün' makes effective ground cover, with a mass of pure white flowers. Both H20cm/8in, W30cm/1ft. F5-7. Z5-8.

T. wherryi (syn. *T. collina*). This species varies in the wild, but all the selections are clump-forming, not

spreading or invasive, many with attractive bronze foliage and spikes of dainty star-like flowers, white or pink. 'Bronze Beauty' is outstanding, with maple-like leaves with bronze markings and narrow spikes, whose pink buds open to delicate blush-pink flowers. 'Green Velvet' has white flowers. Both H25cm/10in, W30cm/1ft. F5-6. Z-8.

TRADESCANTIA

Free-flowering hardy perennials, mostly represented in cultivation by hybrids. Easy to grow and long-flowering. Bright, three-petalled flowers are carried amid copious narrow foliage. Apt to become untidy with lolling stalks, but worthwhile. ☼

T. × andersoniana 'Carmine Glow' (syn. 'Karminglut'). Crimson flowers, neat habit. 'Iris Prichard', white flowers stained azure-blue. 'Innocence', large-flowered white. 'Isis', warm Oxford blue. 'Osprey', white, lilac-centred flowers. 'Pauline', light lilac-pink flowers. 'Purple Dome' rich velvety purple flowers. 'Zwanenburg Blue'. Another good deep blue. All approx. H50cm/20in, W50cm/20in. F6-9. Z5-9.

TRICYRTIS Toad lily

A wider range now exists of these charming and distinctive plants. Most have spotted, bell-shaped flowers and grow reliably in good, deep soil. Besides those listed, there are several other more recently introduced species. ☼ ✳ ☆

T. formosana. This makes a clumpy plant, best in sun, with erect leafy stems carrying open heads of mauve, yellow-throated flowers with a hint of brown. H75cm/2ft 6in, W45cm/18in. F8-10. Z5-9.

T. hirta. The flowers along the stems are near-white, heavily spotted lilac; the leaves are hairy. H90cm/3ft, W60cm/2ft. F8-10. Z4-9. 'Miyazaki', arching stems have leaves edged with yellow, flowers white with prominent lilac spots. H75cm/2ft 6in, W45cm/18in. F8-10. Z6-9.

TRILLIUM **Wood lily, Wake robin**
Bulbous perennials for a late spring display. The flowers have three petals and three calyces; three leaves form a ruff-like whorl beneath each flower. All are woodland subjects and respond to humus-rich, moist, but well-drained soil and light shade. Slow-growing, and once they settle satisfactorily they can be left alone for years, expanding into clumps producing more and more flowers. ☼ ☼ ■

T. erectum. This has rich maroon nodding flowers with recurving petals, among large deep green leaves. The white form, *T. e. albiflorum*, with yellow anthers and reddish centres, is even more striking. Both H30cm/1ft, W30cm/1ft. F4-6. Z4-9. *T. grandiflorum.* The wake robin has large, beautiful, pure white flowers, but most prized of all is the sumptuous double white, '**Flore Pleno**' which remains lovely for a long time. So does the rare, single, clear pink '**Roseum**'. All H30cm/1ft, W30cm/1ft. F4-6. Z4-9. *T. sessile.* The maroon flowers have

narrow, slightly twisted petals and stand erectly above the beautifully marbled, grey and dark green leaves. Forms with yellow and white flowers exist. H45cm/18in, W30cm/1ft. F4-6. Z5-9.

TROLLIUS **Globe flower**
These make a fine display in early summer of mainly globe- or bowl-shaped, buttercup-like flowers. They thrive in deep soil which does not dry out. Flowers vary from pale primrose to yellow and orange and are carried above deeply divided leaves. ☼ ■
T. chinensis (syn. *T. ledebourii*). '**Golden Queen**' and '**Imperial Orange**' are distinctive in having open, deep yellow flowers with a central tuft of fiery orange, petal-like stamens. Later than most to flower. H90cm/3ft, W45cm/18in. F6-7. Z4-8. *T. × cultorum.* These hybrids between *T. chinensis*, *T. europaeus* and *T. asiaticus* provide a good colour range. All F5-7. Z4-8. '**Bressingham Sunshine**', pure, glistening yellow, vigorous. H75cm/2ft 6in, W45cm/18in. '**Commander in Chief**', extra-large flowers, warm orange-gold. H70cm/28in, W45cm/18in. '**Cressida**', a more vigorous creamy-

Trollius europaeus 'Superbus'

yellow. H60cm/2ft, W45cm/18in. '**Orange Princess**', deep yellow. H75cm/2ft 6in, W45cm/18in. *T. europaeus.* Compact habit, making clumps of bright green leaves and a fine show of lemon-yellow globe flowers. '**Superbus**' is a select form worth looking for. H60cm/2ft, W45cm/18in. F5-7. Z4-8.

TROPAEOLUM
T. speciosum. From Chile. this climber thrives in cool, moist climates. Its fast-growing, slender stems grow up and into plants to surprise in late summer with small, bright scarlet trumpet flowers, making a striking contrast to almost any tree, conifer or shrub to which it attaches itself. H1.5-3m/5-10ft, W60cm/2ft. F7-9. Z8-9.

VERBASCUM **Mullein**
Spiky perennials with fleshy roots thrive in quite poor soil. All Z5-9. ☼ ■
V. chaixii. This has imposing, very erect spikes of rather small flowers, yellow with mauve eyes, rising from a leafy base. '**Album**' has mauve-centred white flowers; both forms are inclined to self-seed. Both H1.1m/43in, W45cm/18in. F6-8. **Hybrids.** Three are very similar – '**Cotswold Beauty**', '**Gem**' and

'**Queen**' – all with branching stems and flowers of varying buff-yellow shades with purple or mauve centres. All H1m/39in, W45cm/18in. F6-8. '**Gainsborough**', woolly grey foliage, light yellow spikes. H1.1m/43in, W45cm/18in. F6-8. '**Helen Johnson**', a unique and striking plant with well branched spikes with grey felted stems and leaves, the flowers a warm coppery beige. H60-75cm/2ft-2ft 6in, W45cm/18in. F6-9. '**Mont Blanc**', the finest white, felty grey leaves, short-lived. H1.1m/43in, W45cm/18in. F6-8. '**Pink Domino**',

Trillium grandiflorum

Verbascum 'Helen Johnson'

deep green leaves, full, deep rosy pink
flowers. H1 1m/39in, W45cm/18in.
F6-8.

VERBENA
A genus of colourful plants which
includes several non-hardy species,
suitable for bedding. ☼ ■
V. bonariensis. This has little heads of
lavender-blue, fragrant flowers above
slender, sparsely leaved, branching
stems. Long-flowering and pretty as a
group. Excellent for late flower. Not
very long-lived, but self-seeds freely.
H1.5m/5ft, W60cm/2ft. F6-9. Z7-10.
V. 'Homestead Purple'. A vigorous
spreading selection found in a
homestead garden in Georgia, U.S.A.
Bright purple flowers last all summer.
Hardy at least to minus 10°C (12°F).
H30cm/1ft, W60cm/2ft. F6-10.
Z8-10.

VERONICA Speedwell
This widely varying genus provides
some good, reliable perennials as well
as alpines. The spike-forming kinds
are especially useful and almost all are
hardy and easy to grow in mainly
sunny positions.
V. austriaca teucrium (syn. *V.
teucrium*). Reliable, clump-forming
plants with fresh green, deciduous
foliage and profuse spikes of tiny
flowers. All have bright mid- to deep
blue flowers, but vary in height. All
Z5-8. 'Blue Fountain', rich blue.
H50cm/20in, W30cm/1ft. F6-8.
'Crater Lake Blue', dark blue.
H30cm/1ft, W30cm/1ft. F6-8.
'Kapitan', light blue. H25cm/10in,
W30cm/1ft. F5-7.
V. gentianoides. This forms basal,
light green, rosette-type foliage with
ample spread and pleasing early
spikes of light blue. 'Variegata' has
creamy variegated leaves. All 35cm/
14in, W35cm/14in. F5-6. Z5-8.
V. longifolia 'Blauriesin' (syn.
'Foerster's Blue') and 'Schneeriesin'
are outstanding forms with abundant
spikes bearing deep blue and white

Veronica peduncularis 'Georgia Blue'

flowers respectively. Moist soils will
produce taller plants. Both H50-
90cm/20-36in, W38cm/15in. F7-9.
Z4-8.
V. peduncularis 'Georgia Blue'. Dark
green hummocks of foliage covered
with masses of deep blue flowers.
H15cm/6in, W30cm/1ft. F4-6. Z6-8.
V. spicata. Mat-forming, deciduous
perennials, many with greyish foliage.
All Z4-8. ☼ ■ 'Barcarolle', deep rosy-
pink spikes, green foliage. H30cm/1ft,
W45cm/18in. F7-9. 'Blue Fox',
lavender-blue spikes, green-leaved.
H30cm/1ft, W45cm/18in. F7-9.
'Heidekind', short, rosy red, not
vigorous. H20cm/8in, W30cm/1ft.
F4-5.

VIOLA
Popular plants which add early colour
in the garden. Those mentioned are
hardy and should be cut back after
spring flowering. ☼ ❋ ✳
V. cornuta. Masses of small, violet-
purple flowers for many weeks, and
clumps of rich green leaves, making
effective ground cover. H15-25cm/6-
10in, W30cm/1ft. F5-7. Z5-8. 'Alba'
has white flowers. H15cm/6in,
W3cm/1ft. F4-7. Z5-8.
V. cucullata. The marsh violet has
white flowers on erect stems and
tolerates damp soil. H8-15cm/3-6in,

W15cm/6in. F4-5. Z4-9. 'Freckles'
has palest blue flowers with purple
spots. H15cm/6in, W15cm/6in. F4-
5. Z4-9.
Hybrids. All Z5-7. 'Ardross Gem',
light blue flowers, flushed with gold.
H13cm/5in, W30cm/1ft. F4-7.
'Boughton Blue', charming ethereal
blue. H15cm/6in, W30cm/1ft. F4-7.
'Bullion', the most reliable pure
yellow. H15cm/6in, W30cm/1ft. F5-
8. 'Clementina' large violet flowers,
vigorous. H15cm/6in, W30cm/1ft.
F4-9. 'Columbine'. Lilac white petals
streaked with blue. H15cm/6in,
W30cm/1ft. F4-9. 'Irish Molly'
softly suffused colours. H15cm/6in,

Viola 'Columbine'

W30cm/1ft. F5-8. 'Maggie Mott',
light blue and scented. H13cm/5in,
W30cm/1ft. F5-8. 'Norah Leigh',
mid-blue. H13cm/5in, W30cm/1ft.
F4-7. 'Molly Sanderson', nearly
black. H8-15cm/3-6in, W15-25cm/
6-10in. F4-7. Z5-7.

YUCCA
These evergreen plants, often classed
as shrubs, display sword-like foliage
throughout the year and, though
long-lived, some flower irregularly. It
is worth the wait for the spectacular
ivory-white or pink-tinged, lily-like
flowers on stiff spikes. ☼ ■
Y. filamentosa. Adam's needle is
almost stemless and has greyish
foliage with hair-like fibres along the
edges and ivory-white, bell-shaped
flowers most years. H1. 5m/5ft,
W1.5m/5ft. F7-8. Z5-10. 'Bright
Edge', gold, and 'Variegata' have
brightly variegated leaves. Both
H90cm/3ft, W60cm/2ft. F7-8. Z5-9.
Y. flaccida. Notable for flowering
most seasons, it is similar to the
above, but with narrower, less rigid
leaves. 'Golden Sword' has irregular
central golden stripes on the leaves.
H1.5m/5ft, W1.5m/5ft. F7-8. Z5-10.
Y. gloriosa. The Spanish dagger
grows large and is spectacular in
flower. 'Variegata' has brightly striped
leaves. H2.1-3m/7-10ft, W1.5m/5ft.
F8-9. Z7-10.

ZANTEDESCHIA Arum lily, Calla lily
Z. aethiopica. Hardy given ample
covering from mid-autumn to mid-
spring in cold districts. 'Crowborough',
widely accepted as the most reliable
form, with handsome white spathes
above large, shiny green leaves.
Although moisture-loving and able to
grow in mud in 15-30cm/6-12in
deep water, it is surprisingly
adaptable to any fertile soil. 'Green
Goddess', with greenish flower
spathes, scarcely different in colour
from the lush foliage. H1.2m/4ft,
W60cm/2ft. F7-9. Z8-10.

HARDY FERNS DIRECTORY

HARDY FERNS ARE A GROUP OF PLANTS which have many uses in the summer garden, their bright green foliage a wonderful foil to summer-flowering subjects. but they are still under-used. Their names are confusing, and their parentage too. Not all ferns need shade and damp soil but those that do fit in well with moisture-loving plants such as hostas or astilbes or will thrive in woodland conditions.

H:	Approximate height after 2 years
W:	Approximate width after 2 years
Z:	Relevant hardiness zone(s)

ADIANTUM **Maidenhair fern**
Deciduous, delicate looking ferns with new growth appearing in spring and lasting until winter. ✳ ★
A. pedatum. The American or northern maidenhair has branching fronds made up of many toothed lobes on slender black stems. H45cm/18in, W30cm/1ft. Z3-8.

ASPLENIUM
This genus of evergreen lime lovers now includes what were formerly *Phyllitis* and *Scolopendrium*.
A. scolopendrium. The hart's tongue, a British native, is well known for its long, leathery leaves. Given shade it is easy to grow, in crevices or on walls. H up to 35cm/14in, W40cm/16in. Z4-8. 'Cristatum' has curiously dissected crests on the light green fronds. H35cm/14in, W40cm/16in. Z4-8. 'Undulatum' has narrow fronds with attractive wavy edges. H30-40cm/12-16in, W30-45cm/12-18in. Z4-8.

ATHYRIUM
A. filix-femina. The lady fern has lacy, light green, deciduous fronds. Damp shade is best. H60-100cm/24-39in, W60cm/2ft. Z4-9. There are many variations.
'Plumosum'. Plumosum Group covers variations with elegant, leathery, golden-green fronds. H90cm/3ft, W60cm/2ft. Z4-9.
A. nipponicum 'Pictum' (syn. 'Metallicum') the Japanese painted fern is low-spreading, with dark red, arching stems and silvery fronds. It needs shelter. H30-60cm/1-2ft, W45cm/18in. Z3-8.
A. otophorum var. *okanum.* Outstanding foliage form whose spring fronds emerge daubed with silver-white, remaining silvery all summer. H30cm/1ft, W30cm/1ft. Z5-9.

BLECHNUM **Hard fern**
Most have a moderately spreading habit and deep green, fairly narrow, leathery evergreen fronds. They dislike lime, but tolerate a dry atmosphere.
B. spicant. The common hard fern, or deer fern, is clump-forming and produces two types of pinnate frond: arching, spreading, sterile ones and erect, spore-bearing, deciduous ones. H30-60cm/1-2ft, W45cm/18in. Z4-8. ★

Athyrium filix-femina

Polystichum setiferum 'Plumosum'

DRYOPTERIS **Buckler fern**
This genus is widely variable but most species are long-lived, vigorous, hardy and deciduous and form stout clumps which rise above soil level.
D. affinis (syn. *D. borreri* and *D. pseudomas*). 'Crispa', a group form with usually arching, deep green, crisped fronds. The form 'Cristata The King', a selection of the golden-scaled male fern, has evenly crested, arching fronds from a symmetrical central crown. Tolerates dry soil. Both H80-90cm/32-36in, W80-90cm/32-36in. Z4-8.
D. erythrosora. The Japanese shield fern has unusual pink or bronze-tinged young fronds that mature to light green. Deciduous, but the leaves remain until mid-winter. H60cm/2ft, W30cm/1ft. Z5-9. ✳ ★
D. filix-mas. The common male fern is adaptable to almost any but parched places. H90cm/3ft, W90cm/3ft. Z4-8. There are many varieties.
D. wallichiana. A beautiful fern whose unfolding golden green shoots in spring, deepen to rich green fronds, erectly held, in summer. H1.2m/4ft, W90cm/3ft. Z7-9.

MATTEUCCIA **Ostrich fern, Shuttlecock fern**
M. struthiopteris. This is quite spectacular, with large, shapely fronds forming shuttlecock-like rosettes from stout stocks and spreading runners which are likely to colonize in rich, moist soil. H1m/39in, W60-90cm/2-3ft. Z2-8.

OSMUNDA **Royal fern**
O. regalis. A majestic specimen, forming a massive crown above ground from which sprout deciduous fronds, coppery when young, then fresh green and, finally, yellow-brown in autumn. H up to 1.8m/6ft, W1.8m/6ft. Z3-9. ✿ ✳ ★ ◪ ⊕

POLYSTICHUM **Shield fern, holly fern**
These attractive evergreen ferns have large, broad fronds. Most are fully hardy and adaptable even where soil is poor, dry or limy if they are given a good start. ✳
P. setiferum. The soft shield fern. The several forms differ in the pattern of the broad, deeply cleft fronds, arching from a stout central crown. H up to 90cm/3ft, W90-120cm/3-4ft. Z5-8. **Divisilobum Group** has finely divided fronds and tolerates fairly dry conditions. 'Herrenhausen', dense clumps of spreading fronds of finely feathered, mid-green foliage. H45cm/18in, W75cm/2ft 6in. Z5-8. 'Plumosum' has soft, semi-prostrate, densely clothed, evergreen fronds. H30cm/1ft, W50cm/20in. Z5-8.

Matteuccia struthiopteris

GRASSES DIRECTORY

ORNAMENTAL GRASSES ARE FINALLY BEING RECOGNIZED for the colour, grace and movement they can bring to the garden. More than that, they have a long period of interest which, for many, lasts throughout autumn and winter. They can be planted with many different groups of plants, but they associate particularly well with perennials, conifers, heathers and shrubs, softening harsh or bright colours and adding their own in summer, in both foliage and flowers. Grasses provide the perfect plant associations to colourful perennials such as crocosmias, kniphofias and phlox . Many are effective used in pots and other containers for patios and terraces. Container-grown plants can be planted out at any time of year in free-draining soil, but most field-grown plants, and those divided from garden clumps, are best planted in mid-spring. Because of their winter interest, it is best to leave most grasses until early or mid-spring to be cut back, just before the new growth starts. Though there are variations according to species, most ornamental grasses prefer well-drained, if not dry, soil.

H: Approximate height
W: Approximate width
F :   Months in flower
Z: Relevant hardiness zone(s)

Stipa tenuissima in the volcano bed at Foggy Bottom

Carex hachijoensis

ACORUS
A. gramineus '**Ogon**'. Not strictly a grass but looks like one with rush-like foliage. Narrow, gold and green leaves arching in fan-like sprays are almost brighter in winter than summer. '**Variegatus**', less showy with white-edged leaves. ☼ ❅ ◢

ARUNDO **Giant reed**
A. donax. This is a giant among grasses, having strong stems with floppy, wide, somewhat sheathed glaucous leaves. It does not flower in cool temperate climates but is still worthwhile where space allows, in any reasonable or moist soil and sun. H3m/10ft, W1.2m/4ft. Z7-10. '**Versicolor**' (syn. 'Variegata') is less vigorous but has very effective brightly variegated leaves, and is particularly suited to patio containers. Hardier than often supposed. H1.8-2.4m/6-8ft, W90cm/3ft. Z7-10.

BOUTELOUA **Mosquito grass**
B. gracilis (syn. *B. oligostachya*). Short sprays of curious, brownish flower spikes, at right angles to the stems, resemble hovering mosquitoes, above a tufty, semi-evergreen, deep green base. Attractive in winter frost. H25cm/10in, W20cm/8in. F6-8. Z5-9.

CALAMAGROSTIS
C. × acutiflora '**Karl Foerster**'. This is an attractive hybrid with an erect habit, its foliage a rich green followed by plum-brown spikes which remain until spring growth is renewed. '**Overdam**', a striking plant whose early growth is striped with white flushed pink, then forming erect green stems prior to a late summer display of feathery plumes. Both H1.5m/5ft, W60cm/2ft. F7-8. Z5-9.

CAREX **Sedge**
Though members of the *Cyperaceae* family, these are grass-like in appearance and are identifiable by their stems, triangular in section. *C. buchananii.* Leatherleaf sedge. Evergreen, erect tufts of unusual coppery-brown, thin, needle-like blades, reddish towards the base. H60cm/2ft, W20cm/8in. Z6-9. *C. comans.* More mounded, wide-spreading habit. The thin, dense growth has a decidedly light brownish hue, held all year round. Flowers are not conspicuous. There are various forms of the species. '**Bronze**', deep bronze-green foliage. Very similar in form but classed as a hybrid is '**Frosted Curls**' which looks, even in summer, as though its

narrow foliage is frosted with creamy white. All H45cm/18in, W60cm/2ft. F6-8. Z6-9.

C. elata (syn. *C. stricta*) **'Aurea'**. Bright golden yellow leaves during spring and summer and deep brown flowers in mid-summer. H50cm/ 20in, W45cm/18in. F6-8. Z5-9. ☼ ◢

C. hachijoensis **'Evergold'** (syn. *C. morrowii* 'Evergold') is one of the brightest year-round plants, forming large clumps with narrow, shiny, dark green leaves, striped golden-yellow. H25cm/10in, W60cm/2ft. Z7-9.

C. morrowii (syn. *C. oshimensis*). The Japanese sedge has dark evergreen foliage in long-lived clumps, but rarely flowers. **'Fisher's Form'** and **Variegata'** are both good foliage plants with golden-edged leaves. Both 30cm/1ft, W30cm/1ft. Z7-9.

C. pendula. A plant for woodland or wild garden. Clumps of broad green leaves and long arching stems terminate in long grass tassels. H1.2m/4ft, W1.2m/4ft. F6-7. Z7-9.

CHIONOCHLOA

C. rubra. Finely spaced, arching leaves rounded and graceful in habit, olive-green in summer, bronzed in winter. H60cm/2ft, W60cm/2ft. F7-8. Z7-9.

CORTADERIA Pampas grass

Often spectacular flowering grasses, most of which are not suitable for the smaller garden. The variegated forms offer year round interest in milder climates, but foliage dies back in colder ones.

C. selloana. Several variations, from 1.5m/5ft to 3m/10ft high, making large clumps and silvery white plumes in autumn. In **'Pumila'** and others in sheltered situations, these last until spring. **'Gold Band'**, narrow, golden-green striped leaves and silvery plumes. H1.8m/6ft, W1.2m/4ft. F9-10. Z8-10. **'Silver Comet'**, leaves margined white and a good display of flowers but needs a

warm, sheltered spot. H1.5m/5ft, W90cm/3ft. F9-10. Z8-10.

DESCHAMPSIA **Tufted hair grass**
D. caespitosa. Large tufts of narrow, deep green leaves and sheaves of very graceful spikes, valuable for autumn and winter interest. Self-seeds freely. **'Bronze Veil'** (syn. 'Bronzeschleier'), effective bronze plumes. **'Gold Veil'** (syn. 'Goldschleier'), strong, clumpy evergreen with plumes of green stems and flowers which turn a warm golden-yellow. H90cm/3ft, W90cm/3ft. F6-8. Z4-9. **'Golden Dew'** (syn. 'Goldtau'), similar growth with fountains of green stems and flowers which mature to a rich golden-brown. Good, compact form. H70cm/28in, W50cm/20in. F6-9. Z4-9.

ELYMUS

E. magellanicus (syn. *E. pubiflorum*). One of the brightest blue grasses with narrow sword-like leaves of silvered blue. H60cm/2ft, W45cm/18in. Z5-8.

FESTUCA Fescue

F. glauca. Blue fescue. Neat, bluish evergreen tufts, useful as edging,

Festuca glauca 'Blue Glow'

ground cover or frontal groups. Several selections worth looking for: **'Blue Glow'** (syn. 'Blauglut'), striking silver-blue leaves and a good show of flowers; **'Elijah Blue'**, compact, silver-blue. Colour good into winter. Best divided every two or three years. Average H25cm/10in, W25cm/10in. F6-7. Z4-8. **'Golden Toupee'**, an unflattering name for a pleasing, brightly coloured grass. It makes hummocks of silver gold, light brown plumes in summer.

Hakonechloa macra 'Alboaurea'

HAKONECHLOA

H. macra Seldom offered species with wavy bright green leaves and slowly spreading habit. **'Alboaurea'** is one of the best of all ornamental grasses, with bright green and yellow striped leaves in spring and summer, ageing to reddish brown then light brown into late autumn. Appreciates friable, well drained but not too dry soil. In a container it is magnificent. H25cm/ 10in, W39cm/15in. F8-9. Z7-9. ☼ ✳ ■

IMPERATA CYLINDRICA **'Rubra'** Known as **'Japanese Blood Grass'** for good reason: the soft erect leaves become ruby crimson from base to tip, stunning when light shines through. H45cm/18in, W30cm/1ft. ☼ ■

MILIUM

M. effusum **'Aureum'** Bowles Golden Grass. A self-seeding plant with soft, bright golden, arching leaves. A cheery sight in light shade, the golden flower plumes are an added bonus. H45cm/18in, W30cm/1ft. Z5-8.

MISCANTHUS Silver grass

This genus includes some very good grasses, mostly fairly tall and clump-

Imperata cylindrica 'Rubra'

forming, with an annual crop of strong stems with bladed leaves. Taller forms are good as windbreaks and for specimen planting. Though none is evergreen, the foliage remains attractive over winter, and is then cut down in spring. They flower best in hot summers. Some selections have been introduced which flower regularly in cooler, northerly climates. A number are quite dwarf and many variegated, so excellent for the smaller garden.
M. sacchariflorus. Much like a bamboo in appearance with a wealth of long blades, Amur silver grass makes an effective screen from early summer until the following early spring. Does not flower in cooler climates. H3m/10ft, W90cm/3ft. F9-10. Z5-10.
M. sinensis. Chinese silver grass. Ample green and silver-striped foliage but seldom planted. H1.8m/6ft, W90cm/3ft. F7-9. Z5-10. Its many erect-growing and non-invasive cultivars are more garden-worthy. All Z5-10. **'Cascade'** (syn. 'Kaskade'), pendulous, silvery white flowers. H1.2-1.5m/4-5ft, W60cm/12ft. F8-10. **'Flamingo'**, deep crimson flowers fading to white. H1.2-1.5m/4-5ft, W60cm/2ft. F8-10. **'Gracillimus'**, elegant narrow leaves and a shapely habit; seldom flowers in cooler climates. H1.5m/5ft, W45cm/18in. **'Purpureus'**, bronze-purple leaves in late summer. 1.2m/4ft, W90cm/3ft. F8-9. **'Strictus'**, a stiff columnar habit and green leaves, horizontally striped yellow, brighter than **'Zebrinus'**. H90cm/3ft, W50-60cm/20-24in. **'Variegatus'** is stately and brightly variegated with vertical white stripes. H1.5m/5ft, W90cm/3ft. **'Zebrinus'**, or zebra grass, is distinctive for having lateral bands of gold across green leaves. H1.5m/5ft, W90cm/3ft. **'Kleine Fontane'**, tall, free flowering with pendulous silver heads. H1.5cm/5ft,

W90cm/3ft. F7-10. **'Malepartus'**, vigorous, broad, silver-striped leaves, crimson flowers fading pink then light brown. H1.8m/6ft, W90cm/3ft. F8-10. **'Morning Light'** outstanding variegated Japanese selection: compact, densely foliage, silver and white. Needs heat to flower. H1.2m/4ft, W60cm/2ft. F9-10.

MOLINIA **Moor grass**
M. caerulea subsp. *altissima* (syn. *M. litoralis*). Strong-growing, free-flowering, good autumn colour as stems fade. The terminal flower sprays are greenish purple, turning brown in autumn. Some good selections: **'Fontane'**, pendulous heads; **'Transparent'**, slender stems, wispy flower heads; **'Windspiel'**, smaller heads, all turning to golden brown autumn colours. All 1.5-1.8m/5-6ft, W45cm/18in. F8-10. Z5-9.
M. caerulea subsp. *caerulea.* Purple moor grass. British native for damp, acid soils. **'Moorehexe'** a good green-leaved selection with purplish flower heads, brown in autumn. H40cm/16in, W40cm/16in. F8-9. Z5-9. **'Variegata'**, stout clumps of soft, deciduous, creamy yellow-green leaves and long-lasting, small, purplish buff flowers. Prefers a light, deep soil and sun. H60cm/2ft, W60cm/2ft. F7-10. Z5-9.

PANICUM **Switch grass**
P. virgatum **'Rubrum'**. A pretty grass with red-tinted leaves in summer, crimson in autumn. A haze of brown seedheads complement the airy feel. H90-120cm/3-4ft, W60cm/2ft. F8-9. Z5-9.

PENNISETUM
Large, deciduous tussocks, but not all produce their bottlebrush flowers freely. Long, arching and narrow grey-green leaves.
P. alopecuroides (syn. *P. compressum*). Shy to flower in cool temperate zones but **'Hameln'** and **'Woodside'** are

Miscanthus sinensis 'Variegatus'

much freer, their flowers attractive well into winter. All H60-90cm/2-3ft, W60cm/2ft. F8-10. Z5-10.
P. orientale. Hairy leaves, tufty growth. Its bottlebrush, silvery pink flowers are long-lasting and reliable, fading to grey. H45cm/18in, W30cm/1ft. F7-9. Z6-9.

PHALARIS **Gardener's garters**
P. arundinacea var. *picta.* This variegated leaved grass, its creamy green and white stripes brightest in spring, should be planted only where its invasive habit can do no harm. Less invasive and more striking in its white intensity is *P.a.* var. *picta.* Both H90cm/3ft, W60cm/2ft. Z4-9.

STIPA **Feather grass, Needle grass**
S. arundinacea. Compact clump of narrow-leaved, arching, bronze-green stems and diffuse, brownish flowers. Foliage tinged red, bronze, yellow and orange in winter. H45cm/18in, W60cm/2ft. F7-9. Z7-9.
S. calamagrostis. Clump-forming species which flowers freely with dense, buff-white, gracefully arching plumes. H1.2m/4ft, W60cm/2ft.

F7-9. Z5-10.
S. gigantea. Imposing specimen clumps. Narrow green leaves above which tall, erect stems carry oat-like flowers for months which are still attractive in winter. H1.8-2m/6-8ft, W60-75cm/2ft-2ft 6in. F6-10. Z5-10.
S. tenuissima. Beautiful ornamental grass forming a dense, grassy, deep green clump, topped in mid-summer by fluffy plumes which turn from

Stipa gigantea

ALPINES DIRECTORY

USUALLY REFERRED TO AS ALPINES OR SOMETIMES AS ROCK PLANTS, this group of plants is a diverse one that can be confusing to beginner and expert alike. Many of the plants offered by garden centres in this category are not necessarily native to mountainous regions, but are usually of dwarf or compact stature and are in fact simply dwarf perennials. Late spring and early summer is the peak flowering time for most plants classed as alpines but many flower later too. They lend themselves to associating with other dwarf and slow-growing plants such as conifers or shrubs, or can be used as frontal groups to perennial borders. The smaller ones can be used on scree gardens, raised bed, sinks and troughs and spreading types among paving or gravel. A gravel mulch makes a good surface, retaining moisture but allowing good surface drainage. The range described here is limited to a few major groups of generally easy cultivation and to those with a flowering period or foliage attraction in late spring to late summer.

H: Approximate height after 2 years
W: Approximate width after 2 years
F: Months in flower
Z: Relevant hardiness zone(s)

A collection of alpines on the scree garden

Campanula carpatica var. *turbinata* 'Karl Foerster'

ACHILLEA
The alpine dwarf yarrows make modestly spreading mats of soft filigree or divided foliage. All are easy to grow in poor soil. ☼ ■
A. × lewisii 'King Edward'. A form with primrose-yellow flowers and grey green mats of foliage. H10cm/4in, W20cm/8in. F5-8. Z4-8.
A. tomentosa. Woolly yarrow has grey-green, filigree mats and dense golden-yellow heads. H15cm/6in, W30cm/1ft. F5-7. Z3-7.

AJUGA Bugle
Creeping, semi-evergreen, flowering plants and colourful ground cover.
A. reptans. Carpet or common bugle is mat-forming. Its many colourful varieties do best in some sun. All H15cm/6in, W30-45cm/12-18in. F5-6. 'Braunherz', shiny purple-bronze leaves and blue flowers. 'Burgundy Glow', light blue flowers and wine-red, bronze and cream leaves. 'Pink Surprise', lilac-pink, purplish leaves. 'Variegata' grey-green and cream leaves.

ARABIS Rock cress
This genus flowers for several weeks in spring. All prefer light soil. ☼
A. ferdinandi-coburgii. The green-leaved species has dainty sprays of flowers. 'All Gold' shows up boldly on its evergreen mat, and the slightly less variegated, green and cream

evergreen 'Variegata' (syn. *A. procurrens* 'Variegata'), both have white flowers. Remove any reversion to green. All H10cm/4in, W20cm/8in. F4-6. Z5-7.

CAMPANULA Bellflower
Among the dwarf companulas are some choice as well as more vigorous and spreading types, several of which are suitable for use among other dwarf perennials. ☼ ❋ ■
C. carpatica Carpathian bellflower. Long-lived, and makes shapely summer growth, with wide open, cup-and-saucer shaped, upturned flowers on thin stems. All W20cm/8in. F6-8. Z4-7. 'Blue Moonlight' has large, china-blue blooms. H10cm/4in. 'Bressingham White' is one of several whites. H20cm/8in. 'Chewton Joy' has small, smoky blue bells later than most. H13cm/5in. 'Maureen Haddon' masses of pale lavender-blue flowers. H8-10cm/3-4in. *C. carpatica* var. *turbinata.* 'Isabel' has rich blue, saucer flowers. H23cm/9in. 'Karl Foerster' has deep cobalt-blue prolific blooms. H23cm/9in. 'Snowsprite' is the purest white and very free flowering. H20cm/8in. 'Wheatley Violet' is a charming miniature. H10cm/4in.
C. garganica Adriatic bellflower. Forms compact, leafy tufts and lax sprays of starry flowers, good in

crevices and walls. H8cm/3in, W15-30cm/6-12in. F6-8. Z6-8.
'**Dickson's Gold**' has golden-green, almost evergreen leaves and sprays of mid-blue flowers. H13cm/5in, W15-30cm/6-12in. F6-8. Z6-8.
C. portenschlagiana (syn. *C. muralis*). An adaptable plant with its long display of violet, bell-shaped flowers. '**Resholt's Variety**' is the best form. Both H15cm/6in, W60cm/2ft. F6-9. Z4-8.
C. poscharskyana. Sprays of pale lavender, starry flowers make a fine show. A good wall plant. H30cm/1ft, W60-90cm/2-3ft. F6-9. Z4-7.

DIANTHUS Rock pink
Most have mats or tufts of silvery- or bluish-green, evergreen foliage. ☼ ■ ☉
D. deltoides. Maiden pinks are distinctive trailing types with green or purplish foliage and masses of flowers in summer. Named varieties include '**Albus**', white, **Brilliant**, carmine, '**Leuchtfunk**', crimson. Good for walls. H15-23cm/6-9in, W40cm/16in. F5-7. Z3-7.
Hybrids. The following are just a few well-tried selections. All F6-8. Z4-8.

Dianthus 'Pike's Pink'

'**Bombardier**', red. H13cm/5in, W30cm/1ft. '**Dubarry**', double pink, crimson-centred. H10cm/4in, W20cm/8in. '**Garland**', pure pink. H10cm/4in, W20cm/8in. '**La Bourboule**', pink and white. H8cm/3in, W15cm/6in. '**Nyewood's Cream**', dwarf, cream flowers. H8cm/3in, W15cm/6in. '**Oakington**', a soft double pink. H10cm/4in, W25cm/10in. '**Pike's Pink**', double, showy pink. H10cm/4in, W20cm/8in.

GENTIANA Gentian
These classic alpine plants fall into three fairly distinct groups of spring, summer and autumn flowering species. The first prefer some lime, the second are lime-tolerant and the third need an acid soil. Only late spring and summer types are covered.
G. acaulis. The trumpet, or stemless, gentian has large, upstanding, blue trumpets from low, slow-spreading mats. H10cm/4in, W30-45cm/12-18in. F4-5. Z4-7. ☼ ◢ ■
G. septemfida. A popular and easy to grow gentian, forming clumps whose many leafy stems produce a mass of

deep blue flowers for most of the summer. H15-20cm/6-8in, W30cm/1ft. F6-9. Z4-8.

GERANIUM Cranesbill
The ever popular hardy geraniums have several dwarf varieties which make good alpines. ☼ ■
G. cinereum '**Ballerina**'. Popular for its adaptability and long display of lilac-pink flowers, charmingly flecked and veined with crimson. H13cm/5in, W25cm/10in. F5-9. Z5-8.
'**Laurence Flatman**' has sprays of larger flowers with heavy crimson markings, deeper than '**Ballerina**'. H15cm/6in, W30cm/1ft. F5-9. Z5-8.
G. cinereum subcaulescens (syn. *G. subcaulescens*). Mounds of green leaves set off bright magenta-red flowers. '**Guiseppii**' is a vigorous selection with similarly strong but magenta-purple blooms. '**Splendens**', less vigorous but arguably one of the most striking of all geraniums with magenta-rose flowers. All 15cm/6in, W30cm/1ft. F6-8. Z5-8.
G. × *lindavicum* '**Apple Blossom**'. Pretty hybrid, close to *G. cinereum* with grey-green leaves and soft, pale pink flowers. H15cm/6in, W23cm/9in. F5-8. Z5-8.
G. '**Sea Spray**'. An outstanding hybrid making low spreading hummocks of soft purplish-green leaves and masses of small pink flowers fading to white. H10cm/4in, W30cm/1ft. F6-10. Z-9.

HELIANTHEMUM Sun rose
Indispensable for a bright summer display, though strictly speaking deciduous shrubs. Trim with shears after flowering to keep them neat and tidy. All are sun lovers and can withstand, dry and even starved soil.
Hybrids. The following are some of the best: '**Annabel**', soft pink, double. '**Cerise Queen**', cherry-red, double. '**Fireball**', deep red, double. '**Firedragon**' (syn. '**Miss Clay**'), silvery grey leaves, orange-flame

Geranium × *lindavicum* 'Apple Blossom'

flowers, single. '**Henfield Brilliant**', deep orange, single. '**Jubilee**', clear yellow, double. '**Raspberry Ripple**', crimson centre, petals edged white, single. '**Red Orient**', deep crimson, yellow stamens, single. '**Wisley Pink**', pale pink, grey foliage, single. '**Wisley Primrose**', pale yellow, single. '**Wisley White**', white, single. All H15-30cm/6-12in, W60-90cm/2-3ft. F5-7. Z5-7.

HYPERICUM St John's wort
A reliable source of summer colour, some are excellent in hot, dry walls. A few are tender. ☼ ■
H. olympicum (syn. *H. polyphyllum*). This and its forms are especially good in sunny crevices or on walls. Foliage is blue-grey and yellow flowers have prominent stamens. Variations include the larger-flowered *uniflorum* (syn. *H. olympicum* 'Grandiflorum') and '**Citrinum**', with pale yellow flowers. All H15-20cm/6-8in, W30cm/1ft. F6-8. Z6-8.

LYSIMACHIA Loosestrife
L. nummularia '**Aurea**'. The golden-leaved creeping Jenny is useful as ground cover or crevice planting in shade, or sun where not dry. Excellent for a container or hanging basket. Yellow, buttercup flowers. H5cm/2in, W60cm/2ft. F6-7. Z3-8.

PHLOX

The dwarf species make a fine show to follow early spring subjects. Most are easy in light soil and sun.
P. procumbens (syn. *P. amoena*). Mat-forming species with small heads of purplish-pink flowers. The vigorous '**Millstream**' has round leaves and lilac-pink flowers. '**Variegata**', leaves margined white and at times pink. All H15cm/6in, W30cm/1ft. F5-6. Z7-8.
P. douglasii. Popular for its fine spring display, this creeping evergreen is covered with almost stemless flowers. Good forms include the blue-mauve '**Eva**' and '**Kelly's Eye**', pink with a red eye, '**Lilac Cloud**' and '**Lilac Queen**', '**Red Admiral**' and '**Waterloo**', an intense crimson-red. All H2.5cm/1in, W15-45cm/6-18in. F4-6. Z5-8.
P. subulata. Like *P. douglasii* but a little less compact, moss phlox, or moss pink, carries its flowers well above the mat. '**Alexander's Surprise**' is salmon-pink. '**Benita**' is lavender-blue with a purple eye. '**MacDaniel's Cushion**' is rose pink. '**May Snow**' is white. '**Nettleton**', an attractive variegated-leaf form with pink-flushed flowers. '**Oakington Blue Eyes**' is an excellent light blue; '**Red Wings**' is crimson. "**Scarlet Flame**' is

scarlet. '**Tamaongalei**' has white flowers splashed pink. '**Temiskaming**' is rosy red. '**White Delight**' is self-descriptive. All H8-13cm/3-5in, W45cm/18in. F4-6. Z2-9.

POTENTILLA Cinquefoil

See also Perennials and Shrubs. ☼ ■
P. aurea '**Aurantiaca**'. Uunusual, orange-buff flowers. H2.5cm/1in, W15cm/6in. F4-7. Z4-8. The form '**Chrysocraspeda**' (syn. *P. ternata*) has bright yellow flowers. '**Plena**' is a double, yellow form. Both H5cm/2in, W13cm/5in. Z5-8.
P. × *tonguei*. A striking, quite vigorous hybrid, it forms a bronzy-green clump, sending out branching, prostrate sprays of apricot-yellow flowers, suffused crimson, for weeks on end. H10cm/4in, W45cm/18in. F6-10. Z5-7.

SEDUM. Stonecrop

This vast genus includes good, late-flowering alpines. ☼ ■
S. cauticolum. This has arching stems of profuse, rosy crimson flowers above bluish, deciduous foliage. '**Lidakense**' is a selection with rose-red heads. Both H10cm/4in, W30cm/1ft. F6-7. Z3-8.
S. kamtschaticum. A trouble-free deciduous species, this has dark green, spatula-shaped leaves and golden flowers. '**Variegatum**' is equally attractive. Both H15cm/6in, W20cm/8in. F6-8. Z3-8.
S. spathulifolium. Powdery, bluish, fleshy leaves and yellow flowers. '**Cape Blanco**' is more compact, with low mounds of near-white leaves, and '**Purpureum**' has larger, purplish leaves. All H5cm/2in, W25cm/10in. F6-7. Z4-7.
S. spurium. A rapid growing nearly evergreen mat-former, this has red leaves and pale pink flowers on red stems. '**Erdblut**' has bright carmine-red flowers. '**Purple Carpet**' has reddish leaves and flowers. All H8cm/3in, W40cm/16in. F6-7. Z3-8.

SEMPERVIVUM Houseleek

Rosette-forming succulents offering a wide range of size and colour. Flowers curious and sometimes spectacular. Gritty soil. Hundreds of species and cultivars exist; the following are a few outstanding choices. Plants may vary in size but all F6-7. Z5-9. ☼ ■
S. arachnoideum '**Laggeri**'. One of the best silvered, 'cobwebby' types. H3-8cm/1-3in, W20-30cm/8-12in.
S. '**Blood Tip**', compact rosettes with upturned red tips. *S.* '**Engle's Rubrum**', soft grey-green rosettes, edged with red. *S.* '**Jubilee**', compact and free-flowering, with green and maroon foliage. *S.* '**Lavender and Old Lace**', pinkish-lavender rosettes, covered in silvery hairs. *S.* '**Othello**', large rosettes of deep crimson, tall spikes topped by pink flowers. *S.* '**Patrician**', green, bronze-tipped rosettes, red-centred in winter. *S.* '**Royal Ruby**', rich ruby-red. *S.* '**Snowberger**', jade-green rosettes have a silvery sheen. *S.* '**Wollcotts Variety**', greenish-grey foliage with silvery overtones.

THYMUS Thyme

Sun-loving aromatic plants.
T. × *citriodorus*. Makes lemon-scented little bushes, showier in the variegated form such as '**Archer's

Gold**' and golden-leaved '**Bertram Anderson**' (syn. '**Anderson's Gold**'), a bushy evergreen, good golden ground cover though seldom flowers. '**Silver Queen**' with creamy-white margins is colourful but may revert in parts to green. All H15cm/6in, W30cm/1ft. F5-6. Z4-8.
T. doefleri '**Bressingham Pink**'. Forms grey-green mats and gives a bright display of clear pink flowers. H2.5cm/1in, W15cm/6in. F5-6. Z4-7.
T. '**Doone Valley**'. Deep green foliage, speckled with gold. Lavender flowers are sparse. H15cm/6in, W30cm/1ft. F5-6. Z4-8.

VERONICA Speedwell

A large genus, generally hardy and easy to grow in mainly sunny positions. Their saucer-shaped flowers are carried in spikes.
V. prostrata (syn. *V. rupestris*). Sturdy mat-former with little, upright spikes of rich blue. '**Blauspiegel**' ('Blue Mirror') is a brilliant blue. '**Blue Sheen**' is a very profuse pale blue. '**Mrs Holt**' is a deep pink, '**Rosea**' lighter pink. '**Spode Blue**' is china-blue. The golden-leaved '**Trehane**' prefers some shade. All H8-10cm/3-4in, W30-40cm/12-16in. F5-7. Z5-8.
V. teucrium. *See under* Perennials (p.110).

Sempervivum arachnoideum '**Laggeri**'

INDEX

Note: *italic* page numbers refer to illustrations.

Abies 20
  koreana 'Aurea' *23*
  lasiocarpa 'Arizonica Compacta' *109*
Acanthus 110
  spinosus 110
Acer 30, 64–5, 81, 84
  japonicum 'Aureum' *7, 29, 32, 64, 65*
  negundo 'Flamingo' *30*, 70, *71, 77*
  palmatum
    'Aureum' *84*
    'Dissectum Garnet' *14, 29, 64*
  platanoides 'Princeton Gold' *81*
Achillea 110, 139
  'Anthea' *47*
Aconitum 110
Acorus gramineus 136
  'Ogon' *63*, 65
Actinidia kolomikta 84
Adiantum 135
Aegopodium podograria 'Variegata' 67
Aesculus paniflora 84
Agapanthus 110
  'Bressingham Blue' *75, 110*
  'Bressingham White' *76*
  'Isis' *76*
Ajuga 139
  reptans 'Braunherz' *54, 68*
Akebia quinata 84
Alchemilla mollis *32*, 110
Allium 110
  schoenoprasum 'Forescate' *110*
  senescens 'Glaucum' *39*
alpines 22–3, 36, 46–7, 139–41
Amsonia tabernaemontana 110–11
Anaphalis triplinervis 'Summer Snow' *111*
Anchusa 111
Anenome 111
  'Hadspen Abundance' *111*
  hybrida 'Alba' *77*
Anthemis 111
  tinctoria 'E.C. Buxton' *76*
Aquilegia 111
Arabis 139
Arbutus unedo 75
Artemisia 85, 111
  nutans 71
  'Powis Castle' *75*
Aruncus 111
  dioicus 111
Arundinaria viridistriata 67
Arundo 136
Asclepias luberosa 111

Asphodeline lutea 111
Asplenium 135
Aster 36, 111–12
  × *frikartii* 54, *55, 76*
  × *thompsonii* 'Nana' 54, *73*
Astilbe 112
  'Ostrich Plume' *112*
  'Sprite' *74*
Astrantia 112
  carniolica rubra 112
Athyrium 135
  filix-femina 135
Aurelia 84
azalea see Rhododendron
Azara 43

Baptisia australis 112
bees 38–9, 53
Berberis 85
  temolaica 84
  thunbergii
    'Bagatelle' *69*, 85
    'Dart's Red Lady' 62, *73*
Bergenia 62–3, 112–13
  'Bressingham Ruby' *65, 73*
Betula 'Trosts Dwarf' *60*
Blechnum 135
Bouteloua gracilis 136
Brunnera macrophylla 113
  'Variegata' *113*
Buddleia 85
  davidii 'Pink Delight' *13, 36, 45, 56*
  globosa 85
bulbs 22, 36
butterflies 38–9
Buxus 85

Calamagrostis
  × *acutiflora* 136
    'Overdam' *51, 76*
Calluna vulgaris 62, 91
  'Allegro' *62*
  'Dark Beauty' *91*
Campanula 113, 139–40
  carpatica 69, 70
    'Forester's Blue' *71*
    turbinata 'Karl Foerster' *139*
  'Kent Belle' *113*
  persicifolia 'Chettle Charm' *40, 77*
  pusilla 47
  'Stella' *30*
Campsis 31
Carex 136–7
  comans 'Bronze' *76*, 136
Carpenteria californica 85–6
Caryopteris 86
  × *clandonensis* 86
Catananche Caerulea 113

Ceanothus 86
  'Blue Mound' *86*
Centaurea 113
  macrocephela 39
  montana 'Gold Bullion' *113*
Centranthus ruber 113–14
Ceratostigma 86
Cercis 86
  canadensis 86
    'Forest Pansy' *77*
Chamaecyparis
  lawsoniana 30
    'Stewartii' *42*
Chelone obliqua 114
Chionochloa rubra 137
Choisya 86
  'Aztec Pearl' *86*
Chrysanthemum 114
  leucanthemum see Leucanthemum
  weyrichii (*Dendranthema weyrichii*) 46, 114
Cimicifuga 114
Cistus 86
Clematis 31, 36, 87, 114
  'Dr Ruppel' *30*
  heracleifolia davidiana 'Wyevale' *36*
  'Jackmanii Superba' *87*
  tangutica 87
Clethra 87
climbers 31, 36
colour
  planting associations 72–7
  year-round 64–5, 68–9, 73
Colutea arborescens 87
conifers 6–7, *13*, 22–3, *29, 63*, 108–9
containers 66–7
Coreopsis 114
  verticillata
    'Golden Gain' *69, 77*
    'Moonbeam' *75, 114*
Cornus 43, 60, 87–8
  alba 'Aurea' *43*, 87
  controversa 'Variegata' *81*, 81
Cortaderia 137
Corydalis
  flexuosa 114
    'China Blue' *16*
    'Purple Leaf' *61*
Corylus 88
Cosmos 114
  atrosanguinea 75
Cotinus 88
  coggygria 'Purpureus' *77*
  'Grace' *88*
Cotoneaster 88
Crataegus 29
Crocosmia 114–15
  'Bressingham Beacon' *76*

  'Lucifer' *7*, 34
  'Spitfire' *34, 115*
cross-fertilization 38
Cynara cardunculus 115
Cytisus 19, 88–9
  ardoinii 18
  battandieri 88

Daboecia 91–2
  cantabrica 'Rosea' *91*
Daphne 89
  × *burkwoodii* 89
Delphinium 115
  × *belladonna 115*
    'Peace' *38*, 115
Dendranthema see Chrysanthemum
Deschampsia 51
  caespitosa 137
    'Golden Dew' *74*, 137
Deutzia 89
  × *hybrida*
    'Pink Pompon' *28*
    'Rosea Plena' *28*
    'Strawberry fields' *89*
Dianthus 115, 140
  'Pike's Pink' *140*
  'Pretty' *115*
Diascia 40–1, 115
  'Blackthorn Apricot' *41*
  elegans 71
  rigescens × *lilacina 73*
  vigilis 76
Dicentra 16, 31, 115–16
  'Pearl Drops' *7, 61*
  'Snowflakes' *74*
  spectabilis 'Alba' *16*
Dictamnus 116
Digitalis 116
  purpurea
    'Alba' *116*
    albiflora 39
Disporum sessile 116
  'Variegatum' *67*
Dodecatheon pulchellum 'Red Wings' *25*
Doronicum 116
  caucasicum 'Goldzwerg' *116*
Dryopteris 135
  affinis 'Crista' *135*
  erythrosora 74

early summer 14–25
Echinacea 116
  purpurea 'Magnus' *116*
Echinops 116
Elymus magellanicus 137
Epimedium 116–17
  × *perralchicum* 'Frohnleiten' *15*
Erica 62, 92–3

arborea 'Alpina' *93*
cinerea 'Rock Pool' *92*
erigena 'Irish Dusk' *92*
Erigeron 117
   'Dimity' *117*
   'Vanity' *39*
Eryngium 117
   alpinum 'Superbum' *39, 117*
   giganteum *41*
   'Jos Eijking' *39*
Escallonia 89
   'Apple Blossom' *89*
Eucalyptus niphophila 43, 75, *81*, 81
Euonymus 31, 57, 90
Eupatorium 55, 117
Euphorbia 117–18
   amygdaloides 'Rubra' *117*
   characias
      'Burrows Silver' *118*
      wulfenii *42*, 43, 75
   griffithii 'Fireglow' *32*
   myrsinites *73*
Exochorda 90
   macrantha 'The Bride' *90*

Fagus sylvatica 81–2
   'Dawyck Gold' *83*
ferns 135
Festuca glauca 137
   'Blueglow' *50, 73, 76, 137*
   'Elijah Blue' *77*
Filipendula 118
Foggy Bottom, history 11
Fothergilla 90
Fragaria 118
   'Pink Panda' *118*
fragrant plants 36
Fremontodendron 31
   californicum *90*, 90
Fuschia 90

Gaillardia 118
   'Goblin' *39*
Galega 118
   officinalis 'His Majesty' *118*
Gaura 118
   lindheimeri *75*
Genista 19, 91
   aetnensis *75*
   pilosa 'Lemon Spreader' *90*
Gentiana 140
Geranium 23, 24, 31, 36, 63, 119, 140
   'Ann Folkard' *23, 31, 62, 71*
   cinereum 'Laurence Flatman' *43, 68*
   himalayense *24, 74*
   'Lancastriase Splendens' *63*
   × lindavicum 'Apple Blossom' *140*
   × oxonianum 'Bressingham's Delight'

46, 65, 77
   phaeum 'Album' *119*
   pratense 'Mrs Kendall Clark' *77, 119*
   × riversleaianum 23
      'Mavis Simpson' *73*
      'Russell Prichard' *71*
   sanguineum
      'Alan Bloom' *75*
      'John Elsley' *77*
   subcaulescens 'Splendens' *46*
   sylvaticum 'Mayflower' *12*, 20, 22, 24
Geum 120
Gleditsia Triacanthos 'Sunburst' *82*, 82
grasses, ornamental 32–3, *34*, 50–2, 54, 60, 63, 76
   directory 136–8
Gypsophila 120
   repens 'Rosa Schonheit' *120*

Hakonechloa
   macra 137
      'Alboaurea' *51, 137*
Halimiocistus see Cistus
Halimium see Cistus
Hamamelis mollis 'Pallida' *7*
hardiness zones 80
heaths and heathers 56, 62, 91–3
Hebe 28, 56, 62, 93
Hedera 31, 93
Helenium 120
   'Butterpat' *120*
   'Coppelia' *46*
   'Waltraud' *39*
Helianthella quinquinervis 120
Helianthemum 140
Helianthus 120
Heliopsis scabra 120
Hemerocallis 34–5, 36, 120–1
   'Children's Festival' *120*
   'Holiday Mood' *46*
   'Stella d'Oro' *35, 73*
   'Whichford' *35*
Heuchera 121
   micrantha 'Bressingham Bronze' *121*
   'Rosemary Bloom' *39*
× Heucherella 121
   'Bridget Bloom' *7, 74*
Hibiscus syriacus 93
   'Pink Giant' *93*
Hosta 7, 23, 36, 63, 66, 121–2
   fluctuans 'Variegated' *14, 121*
   'Francee' *15, 74*
   'Krossa Regal' *74*
Houttuynia cordata 'Chameleon' *67*, 122
Humulus lupulus 'Aureus' *93*
Hydrangea 31, 56–7, 93–5

arborescens 'Annabelle' *57, 94*
   paniculata 'Pink Diamond' *94*
Hypericum 56, 95, 140

Imperata cylindrica 137
Incarvillea 122
Indigofera 95
   heterantha 95
Iris 122
   germanica 'Patterdale' *36*
   pallida 'Argentea' *73*
   sibirica 'Silver Edge' *122*

Jasminum 31, 36, 95
Juniperus
   chinensis 'Blue Alps' 34
   communis 'Sieben Nana' *108*
   horizontalis 'Blue Chip' *77*
   × media 'Gold Sovereign' *68*

Kalimeris yomena 'Shogun' *67*
Kalmia 95
   latifolia 'Ostbo Red' *95*
Kerria japonica 95
Kniphofia 53, 54, 122–3
   'Bressingham Comet' *53*, 54
   'Little Maid' *76*
   'Percy's Pride' *122*
Kolkwitzia amabilis *96*, 96

Lamium 123
   maculatum
      'Pink Pewter' *123*
      'White Nancy' *73*
late summer 44–57
Lavandula 96
   'Blue Cushion' *28, 77, 96*
   'Hidcote' *69*
Lavatera 40, 96
   'Candy Floss' *96*
   'Pink Frills' *40*
   thuringiaca 'Barnsley' *75*
Leucanthemum 123
   maximum 'Snowdrop' *123*
Liatris 123
Ligularia 123–4
   przewalskii 'The Rocket' *123*
Ligustrum 96–7
Limonium 124
Lobelia 124
Lonicera 31, 36, 97
   periclymenum 97
Lupinus 124
   'Russel Hybrids' *47*
Lychnis 124
   flos-jovis 'Hort's Variety' *124*
Lysimachia 124
   nummularia 'Aurea' *74*, 140

Lythrum 124
   salicaria 'Blush' 34, *35*

Magnolia 97
   × liliflora x stellata 'Jane' *97*
Malus 82
   'Liset' *82*
Matteuccia struthiopteris 16, *135*, 135
Melianthus major 41–2
Mertensia 124
Microbiota decussata 69
mid-summer 27–43
Milium effusum 'Aureum' 137
Mimulus 124–5
   'Puck' *47, 125*
Miscanthus 51–2, 137–8
   sinensis
      'Flamingo' *76*
      'Klein Silberspinne' *76*
      'Morning Light' *52, 77*
      'Variegatus' *34*, 51, *76*, 138
mixed borders 77
Molinia
   altissima 'Windspiel' *51*
   caerulea 138
      'Varigata' *75*
Monarda 54, 125
mulches 70
Myosotis scorpioides 125

Nepeta 125

Oenothera 125
   'Sonnenverde' *125*
Olearia 97–8
   'Waikariensis' *98*
Omphalodes 125
   cappadocica 'Starry Eyes' *25*
Ophiopogon planiscapus 'Nigrescens' 62, 65, 125
Origanum 125–6
   'Rosenkuppel' *126*
Osmanthus 98
   heterophyllus 'Tricolor' *98*
Osmunda regalis 135
Oxydendrum 98

Paeonia 98, 126
   delavayi 98
Panicum virgatum 138
Papaver 126
   orientale 'Glowing Embers' *126*
Parthenocissus 31
Passiflora 98–9
Peltiphyllum peltatum 48
Pennisetum 138
   alopecuroides 'Hameln' *76*
   orientale 63

Penstemon 54, 126–7
  'Blackbird' *40*
  digitalis 'Husker's Red' *36*
  'Hidcote Pink' *40*, *75*
  'King George' *126*
  'Mother of Pearl' *40*
perennials 36, 46–7, 62–3, 76
  directory 110–34
  flowering periods 15, 32–4, 53
Perovskia 99
  'Blue Spire' *75*
Persicaria 127
  affinis 'Dimity' *43*, *73*
  amplexicaule 'Taurus' *53*, *76*, *127*
  bistorta 'Superbum' *127*
  miletti 74
Phalaris arundinacea var. *picta* 'Feesey'
  67, 138
Philadelphus 99
  'Beauclerk' *99*
Phlomis 99, 127
  'Edward Bowles' *99*
  fruticosa 75
Phlox 127, 141
  divaricata 'Blue Dreams' *7*, *16*, *46*,
   64
  paniculata
   'Eva Cullum' *37*
   'Flamingo' *47*
   'Franz Schubert' *10*, *37*, *51*, *55*,
    76, *127*
   'Mother of Pearl' *55*
Phormium 99–100
Photinia 100
Phyllitis see *Asplenium*
Physocarpus opulifolius 100
  'Dart's Gold' *100*
Physostegia 128
Picea
  glauca 'Laurin' *18*
  pungens
   'Globosa' *29*, *30*, 64
   'Hoopsii' *77*
Pieris 27, 100
  'Forest Flame' 19, *100*
  japonica 'Flaming Silver' *19*
Pinus
  heldreichii 108
  mugo 'Jeddeloh' *109*
Piptanthus 100–1
Pittosporum 101
Plactycodon 128
planning 10–13
planting 45, 48, 80
  associations 72–7
  containers 66–7
  year-round colour 64–5, 68–9, 73
Polemonium 128

  caeruleum
   'Brise d'Anjou' *16*, 19, *74*, *128*
   'Dawn Flight' *77*
Polygonatum 128
Polygonum see *Persicaria*
Polystichum 135
Populus Alba 'Richardii' 82, *83*
Potentilla 28, 56, 61, 101, 128, 141
  'Goldfinger' *101*
Primula 128–9
  'Bressingham Strain' *128*
  vialii 129
Prunella 129
Prunus 82–3, 101
  'Accolade' *82*
  'Amanogowa' *18*
  laurocerasus 'Otto Luyken' *101*
Pulmonaria 62, 129
  augustifolia 'Azurea' *65*
  'Highdown' *77*
  'Lewis Palmer' *77*
  longifolia 12
  'Roy Davidson' *74*
Pyrethrum see *Tanecetum*
Pyrus salicifolia 'Pendula' *77*, *83*, 83

Ranunculus 129
  gramineus 129
Rhododendron 20–2, 36, 101–2
  'Amethyst' *20*
  azalea 'Knaphill' 20, *24*
  'Loders White' *21*
  'Morgenrote' *14*
  yakushimanum hybrid *102*
Ribes sanguineum 27
Robinia pseudoacacia 'Frisia' *83*, 83
rock plants 22–3
Rodgersia 129
  pinnata 74
  podophylla 15
Romneya 129
Rosa 25, 31, 102–3
  'Felicia' *103*
  moyesii 'Geranium' *42*, *102*
Roscoea 129–30
Rosmarinus officinalis 103
Rubus 103
  cockburnianus 'Golden Vale' *103*
Rudbeckia 130
  fulgida
   deamii 47
   sullivantii 'Goldsturm' *10*, *48*,
    49, *50*, *55*, *76*
  'Goldquelle' 50, *130*

Salix 83, 103–4
  alba 'Sericea' *83*
  integra 104

Salvia 104, 130
  nemerosa x *superba 130*
  officinalis 104
  × *sylvestris* 'Blauhügel' *76*
Sambucus 104
  racemosa 'Plumosa Aurea' *104*
Sanguisorba 130
Santolina 104
Scabiosa 63, 130
  caucasica
   'Blue Seal' *53*
   'Clive Greaves' *76*
  graminifolia 75
Scolopendrium see *Asplenium*
Sedum 130–1, 141
  'Autumn Joy' ('Herbstfreude') *54*,
   75
Sempervivum 70, 141
  arachnoideum 'Laggeri' *141*
Senecio 'Sunshine' 104
shade, planting associations 74
shrubs 36, 62, 84–107
  flowering periods 19, 27–32, 56–7
Sidalcea 131
  candida 'Elsie Heugh' *131*
Sisyrinchium 131
Solidago 36, 57, 131
  'Queenie' *131*
Sorbus 83
  koehneana 57
Spartium junceum 43, 104
Spiraea 61, 105
  japonica 'Golden Princess' *104*
spring 6, 14–25
Stachys 131
Stipa 138
  calamagrotis 73
  gigantea 10, *51*, *55*, *76*, *138*
  tenuissima 54, *65*, *70*
Stokesia laevis 131
structure, small gardens 60–1
sun, planting associations 75
Symphytum 131–2
  grandiflorum 'Hidcote Blue' *23*
Syringa 105
  vulgaris
   'Miss Kim' *105*
   'Sensation' *36*, *43*

Tamarix 106
Tanecetum 132
Tellima grandiflora 132
Thalictrum 132
  flavum 132
Thermopsis 132
Thuja orientalis
  'Aurea Nana' *29*
  'Golden Sceptre' *77*

Thymus 141
Tiarella 132
  polyphiyla 'Moorgrün' *132*
Tradescantia 132
trees 13, 29–32, 61, 81–3
  see also conifers
Tricyrtis 132–3
Trifolium repens 'Purpurascens' 67
Trillium 133
  erectum 17
  grandiflorum 17, *133*
  ovatum 61
Trollius 133
  europaeus 'Superbus' *133*
Tropaeolum 31
  speciosum 30, 133

Verbascum 133–4
  'Helen Johnson' *133*
Verbena 134
  'Homestead Purple' *37*
Veronica 134, 141
  armena 42
  peduncularis 'Georgia Blue' *134*
Viburnum 27, 106–7
  × *burkwoodii* 106
  plicatum
   'Cascade' *12*
   'Mariesii' *20*
Viola 134
  'Boughton Blue' *60*
  'Columbine' *134*
Vitis 31

water 44, 48–9
Weigela 107
  'Praecox Variegata' *62*, *106*
Wisteria 31, *107*, 107
  sinensis 7, 66, 67
witchhazel see *Hamamelis*

Yucca 134
  gloriosa 'Variegata' *75*

Zantedeschia 134